The music of
CHARLES WOOD
— a critical study

Ian Copley

Thames Publishing
London

The first edition of this book, published with financial assistance from the Wood family and the Council of Gonville and Caius College, Cambridge, appeared in 1978 and quickly sold out. This second edition is a facsimile of the first and has been published with financial assistance from Armagh District Council, the Arts Council for Northern Ireland, and the Cultural Traditions Group. It is being published to coincide with the 1994 Charles Wood Summer School being held in Armagh.

In the period between the first and second editions, Wood's anthems and canticle settings continue to be sung in cathedrals and churches, and on recordings. The major initiative in this latter field has been the appearance in 1993 of an ASV CD (DCA 854) which is almost entirely devoted to Wood's *St Mark Passion*. Geoffrey Webber directs the choir of Wood's old college, Gonville and Caius, with Richard Hill as the organist.

Ian Copley, author of this book, died in 1988.

ISBN 0 905210 07 7

In memorium
J Meredith Tatton

Contents

Charles Wood

Preface

It is many years since I first heard that lovely tune which Charles Wood put to de la Mare's *The trees in England*, and almost as long since, as a choir member, I first sang in his *O Thou the Central Orb*. My interest in his life and music stems directly from these two experiences.

Wood died in 1926, but apart from scattered references in contemporary musical memoirs, and some more detailed discussions of his church music in specialist volumes, neither his life nor his music has been thought of sufficient significance to merit a book devoted to them.

The centenary of his birth, in 1966, was made the occasion for a commemorative article of mine in the *Musical Times*, involving me in a consideration of his music as a whole. These investigations confirmed me in my belief that Wood's music was both undervalued and unfairly neglected. Hence this study, which seeks to do belated justice to a composer of total integrity who was a pioneer in much that he undertook.

My thanks are due to the following for a wide variety of help: Canon F J Bartlett, L Blake Esq, the late Sir Arthur Bliss, Miss N Byrn, J Cousins Esq, L Dakers Esq, R Graves Esq, the late Dr P S Hadley, Dr Herbert Howells, D Marblacey Jones Esq, C D Kenyon Esq, Dr G Knight, L Lambe Esq, G Laycock Esq, Mrs D M Middleton, W O Minay Esq, H Nelson Esq, G Palmer Esq, M Pope Esq, The Performing Rights Society, The Provincial Registrar of the See of Armagh, S Race Esq, B G H Renshaw Esq, The Editor of the *RCM Union Magazine*, The Royal School of Church Music, Revd Dr Erik Routley, Mrs L Rust, H Rutland Esq, Revd Dr R L Shields, the late Dr Heathcote Statham, E Tatton Esq, P A Tranchell Esq, Sir Michael Tippett, Miss I M Wood, Miss C E S Wood.

To the following libraries, their librarians and staff, I am indebted for much valuable assistance: The British Library, the Reference Library of the Royal College of Music, the Library of Gonville and Caius College, Cambridge, the Cambridge University Library, the Pendlebury Music Library, Cambridge, the Library of Reading University.

I am also most grateful to the following publishers for information or the loan of material: Messrs Ascherberg, Hopwood & Crewe (formerly the Year Book Press, latterly Chappell & Co Ltd), Boosey & Hawkes Ltd, British & Continental Music Agencies Ltd, The Faith Press, Galliard Ltd (now Stainer & Bell Ltd), Keith Prowse Ltd, Novello.

Finally to the late J Meredith Tatton Esq and to Max Ray Esq and E M S Wood Esq I owe more, both individually and collectively, for all they have done to further this study than I could ever repay.

Ian Copley
August 1977

CHAPTER 1

A brief biographical sketch

Wood is a not uncommon name in the county of Yorkshire, and bearers of that name who happen to be musicians are likewise not unknown. Arthur Wood (1875-1953), for instance, was a notable composer of light orchestral music, and Haydn Wood (1882-1959)[1], of whom Percy Scholes wrote 'His more serious compositions are little heard; his more trivial have a large vogue'[2], was born in Slaithwaite near Huddersfield[3]. There was also a Joseph Wood (1826-1884), whose father had been a chapel chorister in Halifax, who founded the principal music shop in Huddersfield — a business that still flourishes — and who was referred to in a directory published in 1881 as a 'Professor of Music'[4].

According to the census of 1841 there were domiciled in the village of Shepley, near Huddersfield, no less than nine families named Wood. Whether any of them were musical we do not know, but in one of them in particular some sort of musical activity certainly erupted. In the street called 'Village Top', one William Wood — evidently born in 1796 and who followed the occupation of a weaver — lived with his wife, Amelia, and their five children. The fourth child and third son, Charles, born on the 16th of April 1833, was to be, if not exactly of an adventurous disposition, at least prepared to pluck up his Yorkshire roots and settle himself elsewhere. Where and how he acquired a musical education and sufficient experience as a choralist to procure him a cathedral lay-clerkship is as yet undiscovered, but acquire it he did, for in 1853, at the age of 20, he settled in Armagh, in Ulster, as a tenor in the choir of St Patrick's Cathedral.

In this year, 1853, the Protestant Episcopal Church of Ireland, as by law then established, was centred on the two primal sees of Armagh and Dublin. In its primal cathedrals the musical organisation mirrored that of the English cathedrals, except that in Armagh, at any rate, the tradition was 'that the organist (and formerly the choristers) should be chosen from English musicians unless, as has occasionally happened, an Irish musician of outstanding ability was available for the post'[5]. When Charles Wood senior entered into his duties the organist was Robert Turle (1804-1877), younger brother of the more celebrated James Turle (1802-1882), organist of Westminster Abbey.

The young lay-clerk certainly prospered in his new environment, for on April 7, 1858, just before his 25th birthday, he married, as it were, into the cathedral. His wife, Jemima (née Taylor), who was not quite 18 at the time of her marriage, came of a long line of ecclesiastical administrators. The office of Diocesan Registrar had been held in her family for generations, and in due course her husband, Charles, succeeded her uncle in the post. In effect this made him Private Secretary to the Archbishop and a person of consequence.

The young couple occupied an 18th-century house, No 11, Vicar's Hill, directly opposite the cathedral, and in characteristic Victorian fashion proceeded to raise a considerable family in which Charles, the fifth child and third son, was born on June 15, 1866:

William George (1859-1895)
Emily Mary (1860-1877)
Robert Riddall (1862-1904)
Frances Elizabeth (1864-1911)
CHARLES (1866-1926)
Edith Susanna (1868-1931)
Walter Berry (1870-1932)
Frederick Charles (1872-1918)
Herbert Henry (1874-1945)
Florence Amelia (14.3.1877-3.11.1877)
Amy Maude Louisa (1879-1932)
Edmund Arthur (9.9.1880-15.9.1880)
Henry Evelyn (1882-1962), and
Ethel Georgina (1885-1962).

It was a musical household. All the boys sang with their father in the cathedral choir, and although only the first and third sons trained as professional musicians, the youngest son, H E Wood, who became a banker, was a talented violinist and singer. The father, Charles Wood senior, died on May 23, 1893.

The career of Charles's elder brother may perhaps be touched on at this point, for, in a sense, it anticipated several aspects of his own. William G Wood was educated in the Cathedral Choir School and studied under Turle. In 1872, when he was 13, Turle was succeeded as organist by a native-born son of Armagh, Thomas Osborne Marks (1845-1916), who had been his pupil and assistant[6]. The following year William, in turn, became Marks's assistant, and held this post until 1877. He then entered the Royal Academy of Music, won the Lucas prize for composition (1882), and settled in London as a professional musician. He became a Professor of Organ and Theory at the Academy, and from 1886 until his death in 1895 was also Organist and Director of Music at Highgate School. He was well-known, apparently, as a recitalist — playing the organ at the first concert ever to be given in the newly completed Queen's Hall. He was, too, a considerable composer. He had had an anthem *O Praise the Lord* published by Novello when he was 17, and five songs and an Evening Service were brought out while he was still a student at the RAM. His subsequent compositions included an operetta, *The bride of Cambus* (1883), three Evening Services, a concert overture, and much organ music (Fantasia and Fugue in C minor, a Sonata in D minor, three Canons, etc). The authors of *British Musical Biography* (James D Brown and Stephen S Stratton), writing in 1897, suggested that through his compositions 'he will be long remembered'. Alas, their confidence was misplaced.

Charles followed in his elder brother's footsteps. Little is known of his early years, but at eight years old or thereabouts he joined the choir and began serious education at the Cathedral Choir School. The school no longer exists and its records have been dispersed, but certain memorials remain: school prizes (including a sumptuously-bound leather volume 'for best answering in Scripture and Catechism — Dec. 1882', and the works of Longfellow with a preface by W M Rossetti commending Walt Whitman), and the legend that his prefectorial chair, engraved 'Charles Wood', was long a hallowed relic.

His success in winning the 'First Class prize in books (£3), and the Junior Grade silver medal for music in the Intermediate Examinations' was duly recorded in the columns of the *Armagh Guardian* — a paper that chronicled his achievements over the years on the principle of local boy makes good[7]. He would have daily processed from the music room in the school to the cathedral, there to sing his stint of Sullivan, Goss, Ouseley, Tours, Garrett, Smart and Hopkins among the Victorians, with occasional glances back to the 18th-century world of Nares, Battishill, Arnold and Cooke, and, even rarer, from the early 18th century, Travers and Greene[8], all accompanied on the organ that had been rebuilt in the year of his birth — 'though not for that reason', as he commented to a pupil in later years.

When he was 14, in 1880, the study of harmony and counterpoint with Dr Marks had begun, in addition to practical work on the piano and organ. He said in later life that he found he couldn't get very far on the violin but managed well enough on the viola to take part in a *Messiah* performance under Marks, and once, according to a newspaper report, to play the 'cello in the same work.

Thus the young Charles grew up; his life bounded musically by the cathedral, the Armagh Philharmonic, and music-making in the family circle. There was, especially, the example and influence of brother William to encourage him in trying his hand at composing, and all around him the charm of the Ulster countryside, the select pleasures of a cathedral city and, in his ears, the lilt of the Ulster speech.

In 1882, when Wood was nearly 16, the then Prince of Wales launched the scheme that resulted next year in the transformation of the old National

Training School for Music into the Royal College of Music[9]. Money was found for 50 foundation scholarships — several of which included maintenance — and the task of sifting the applications of the 1,588 hopeful persons who sent in their names as potential candidates began.

One of these applicants, No 411, was Charles Wood, now nearly 17. We learn from the RCM records that he was examined in Belfast on March 29, 1883, and then in London on April 20. When the results were announced he found himself elected to the Morley Open Scholarship in Composition (with maintenance), and life would never be the same again.

He had good reason to remember that day, as Stanford recorded[10]: 'It was a most dramatic and moving occasion. The examiners sat round a large horseshoe table in the Council Room of the Albert Hall . . . When the names of the successful fifty were decided upon, they were ushered in to the room in a body. By some misunderstanding outside, as I afterwards ascertained, they were one and all under the impression that they were those who had failed. When Grove told them that they were the scholars, this motley crowd of boys and girls of every walk in life from the mill and the mine up, gave simultaneously what I can only call a colossal gulp. The effect of it was so touching that Madame Goldschmidt's face collapsed into her pocket handkerchief and most of us had a curious lump in our throats'.

So on May 7, just a month before his 17th birthday, Wood entered the RCM, and an association began that was to last without interruption for the rest of his life. His principal study on entry was, of course, composition with Parry and Stanford, and as second studies the French horn with Thomas Mann and the piano with Cliffe and Faning. There were also harmony and counterpoint classes with Bridge, a choral class also conducted by Faning, and, in his second year and subsequently, the College Orchestra (Holmes and Stanford). There were to be changes in this regimen. Latterly he became almost exclusively Stanford's pupil for composition and he transferred to Franklin Taylor for piano. It is not recorded whether he was ever Parratt's pupil for organ, though it is not unlikely, since he certainly studied the organ as a co-second instrument later in his college career.

Among the group of students who began their studies with Wood that May was another composition scholar, Sidney Peine Waddington (1869-1953), who was to become his lifelong friend[11]. Waddington's reminiscences, as contributed to the RCM magazine, the *Caian*, and the *Dictionary of National Biography*, give us the earliest living portrait of Wood as a person: 'In May, 1883, there arrived at a house in Pembroke Road, Earls Court, eight male scholars of the newly opened Royal College of Music. Among them was a fair, tidy-looking youth, not quite seventeen years of age, named Charles Wood. His appearance was undistinguished: a slight figure, a face with no striking feature, an unobtrusive, though neat, style of dress.

'The eight scholars settled down, some to work, some not to work. It soon

9

became evident that Charles Wood was a very wonderful fellow. His knowledge, even then, was amazing. He could do any kind of counterpoint with the greatest ease. Fugues, Madrigals (he wrote a beautiful one when he was only 17), complicated exercises in eight parts for Double Choir, gave him no trouble at all. He did them with as little apparent effort as one uses in writing a postcard to order coals. And he worked steadily, regularly, intelligently.

'He took great pains with his composition. A hatred of bad workmanship and flippancy of style, which remained with him and grew upon him all his life, caused him to beware of a tremendous natural facility, which, though it would early have enabled him to write reams of plausible and effective music, would, he felt, only have expressed the surface of his thoughts. One could hear him pounding away at the pianoforte, trying to get the perfect shape of an elusive subject. He always said there was no use in going on with a work till the subject was good. Later in life he rarely used the pianoforte for purposes of composition, but in those days he played, or sang, or did both together, day after day till he got his subject right. After that he seemed to go on with more ease, but always with the same scrupulous striving after the best he could do. But he was always troubled by the noises around him. With him in the house were two pianists, two violinists, two singers and another composer. They could all hear each other working. The result was pandemonium. After staying a year in Pembroke Road he was moved to North End Road, West Kensington, where, however, similar conditions prevailed. He was moved again to a house in Aynhoe Road, Brook Green, where he spent the rest of his student life alone and in peace. It should be said that maintenance scholars were, at that time, put into certain appointed boarding houses. His removal to Aynhoe Road was a favour provided to meet his special case . . .

'He was a delightful person to live with in those student days. Beneath his almost commonplace exterior he had an instinctive sociability and a riotous sense of humour. His humour took the form of persistent and sometimes wild punning, but he also had an eye for the comic in everything around him. When he saw, or said, anything that amused him, his face became one large fascinating grin, compelling co-operation. He liked a joke better than anything in the world. He sometimes had an inexplicable spasm of quiet chuckling. Some thought, something he had seen or heard, had seized him, and he had to have his laugh out. He could not say why, or if he tried to explain, his explanations often failed to reveal anything perceptibly funny. But one laughed with him all the same — the look in his eyes, his own obvious enjoyment, were irresistible . . .

'Musical jokes also had a great attraction for him. He would sit at the pianoforte and make a rhymed advertisement for So-and-So's Anchor Brand Cotton to fit the tune of the "Death of Nelson"; or improvise a mock

10

sentimental ballad to "It was a summer's evening, Old Kaspar's work was done", or a canon to the words of "Old Mother Hubbard", or a grandiose choral entry in imitation of the theme of "When other lips" — a most impressive achievement in burlesque. He liked to play tricks with popular tunes. He made an extraordinarily comic ending to the "British Grenadiers" by expanding the last line to about five times its right length. All these things, done in fun, were really only an illustration of the amazing power he had of seeing the possibilities latent in musical material. His imagination worked with singular quickness in that way. Once he had got a subject, either his own or another's, he could try all sorts of ways of testing it — little bits to be taken out of it, little offshoots, little rhythmic variations'[12].

Wood prospered at the RCM and became very much a star pupil. Waddington went on to comment on his work with Stanford[13]: 'It was Stanford's privilege to teach him. It must have been a difficult if congenial task; for Wood, even in those early days, had astonishing facility and solid knowledge. However, Stanford taught him much in the way of how to construct and how to write for instruments, though he could add nothing to his intuitive feeling for vocal style. This must have been the result of his early association with Armagh Cathedral. On the whole, Stanford taught him with tact and ability — not attempting to interfere with a taste marvellously just and impeccable, but content to let him expand in his own way'.

It tended to be Wood's MS compositions that were given an airing outside the college, and the list of his surviving works that can be dated to his period of study at the RCM is impressive[14].

Although he was principally Stanford's pupil, his association with Parry had demonstrable consequences in the evolution of Wood's style, for the choral writing of Parry (at its most massive) had an influence on him as more than one mature work indicates. But Sir George Grove, the first Director of the College, was a more considerable personal mentor, especially in his student years. The foundation scholar owed much to the founding Director: friendship, professional encouragement, the opening of cultural doors (Wood cherished for the rest of his life a copy of Palgrave's *Golden Treasury* that Grove gave him), and, on occasion, helpful advice. Grove for his part made Wood something of a confidant, and would unburden himself, sometimes in a surprisingly uninhibited fashion, as to what was 'on his mind'. He also made use of Wood's encyclopaedic knowledge of Beethoven in particular and classical music in general — a fact which he duly acknowledged in his monumental *Beethoven and his Nine Symphonies*[15].

When Alexandra House (a hostel for women students) was opened in 1887, a *Song of Welcome* especially composed by the Morley Scholar in Composition was duly performed. (It turned out to be a Victorian

11

recrudescence of the Restoration Court Ode — at least in intention — to judge from the fulsomeness of the words, see p. 42).

By 1887, Wood had held his scholarship for four years — it had already been renewed once from Easter '86 to '87 — and the question of 'what next' had to be considered. A letter from Grove gives a clue to the eventual solution (October 15, '87):

> . . . The Executive Committee have extended your Scholarship and are going to get the permission of the Council to make it a *travelling* scholarship to enable you to go abroad. But now comes the enclosed from Stanford. Do you think that there is any chance of your being able to squeeze through the 'Little Go' at Selwyn?

So Wood entered Selwyn College, Cambridge, his connection with the RCM being retained through regular journeys to London for lessons with Stanford. He duly passed his 'Little Go', having previously earned Grove's commendation (letter to Wood dated May 1, '88):

> . . . Dr Stanford sent me a report on the last term which is just what I wanted . . . Your Master's report which came three or four days ago is most satisfactory. He thinks that you have every prospect of passing your first exam in June and this he attributes to your 'steady work'. He also gives an excellent account of your conduct and social position. For all this I thank you very much.

All this had been made possible by an exceptional gesture on the part of the College authorities, who extended his scholarship (as a non-resident student) until September 1889, when he finally ceased to be *in statu pupillari* at the RCM. He had taken the ARCM diploma that Easter — the first of a series of academic hurdles to be faced over the next few years.

The Cambridge which greeted him in 1888 had been revivified musically by Stanford, who had been elected Professor (non-resident) in 1887 and who was coming to the end of a distinguished Cambridge career as organist of Trinity (1873-92). There were others significant in their respective ways: G M Garrett (1834-97) of John's — University Lecturer in Harmony and Counterpoint, whom Wood was to succeed; A H Mann (1850-1927) of King's, who had raised the reputation of that College Choir to unprecedented heights; and Sedley Taylor (1834-1920), physicist and Handelian controversialist. The Cambridge University Music Society was the leading musical organisation, but there was then, as now, much sporadic musical activity based on individual colleges and undergraduate groups.

A feature of Cambridge life with important musical connotations and a particular subsequent significance for Wood was the performance of Greek plays started by Stanford in 1882 — the *Ajax* with Macfarren's music —

12

followed the succeeding year by the *Birds*, for which play Parry composed the score[16].

Into this world Wood plunged, and for the next 38 years he was to be a central figure in it. He did not remain long at Selwyn (five terms only) for in 1889 he migrated to an older foundation, Gonville and Caius, which had elected him to an organ scholarship. Though he remained a member of the teaching staff of Selwyn to the end of his life, it was to Gonville and Caius that he gave his abiding love. Through the years there was to be a stream of compositions associated with it: grace anthems, commemoration anthems, and works for the Music Society.

Meanwhile Grove kept his eye on him. The idea was mooted that Wood should write a rudiments primer for use at the RCM[17], and indeed it existed at one time in draft form, though the project never materialised in terms of a printed book. Grove was also intent on getting Wood back on the RCM staff, as the following extract from an undated letter indicates:

> I am glad that you agree to my proposal about your giving lessons here — Mr Glehn told me he thought that he had 2 hours for you. So I shall see what I have to work upon . . . I wanted to ask you a question bearing on your teaching here. There are several pupils . . . for whom 'composition' is a mistake, they have no gift or attraction in that direction . . .

Thus it was that in this same year, 1889, he was formally appointed 'Lecturer', and subsequently 'Professor' of Harmony and Counterpoint, at the College — another connection that he maintained until his death.

During this year he further augmented his income (by £30 per annum), and doubtless also his musical experience, by becoming Bandmaster of the University Volunteers — vide the illustration reproduced on p. 95. In after-years he remembered with delight the attempt — by a travelling circus — to hire the band's services to play it in triumphant procession from the station round the town to the circus field. He composed a *Quick March* while at a volunteer camp in 1896 (see p. 120) before giving up the appointment in 1897.

In 1890 the fruits of his Cambridge studies began to materialise — he graduated BA and MusB, and his first large-scale choral work, the *Ode to the West Wind*, appeared (see p. 43). In 1891 the College translated him from Organ Scholar to Organist. He proceeded to his MA in 1894 and in the same year, on October 9, his College elected him to a fellowship. (This was largely due, so *The Times* obituary informs us, to the far-sightedness of the Revd E S Roberts (1847-1912))[18]. This was the first occasion on which a Cambridge college had ever elected a fellow in music — even Stanford was never so honoured.

Wood was throughout his life a continual participant in composition competitions[19], and in this same year it was his setting of Swinburne's *Ode*

13

to Music that was selected in an open competition for performance under his direction on April 12, in celebration of the opening of the new buildings of the RCM (see p. 46). The year ended with his very successful contribution to the *Iphigenia in Tauris* — the Greek play of that year, and the awarding of the MusDoc degree. A Cambridge man who was present at the presentation ceremony was moved to write to *The Times* thus:

Sir,

It may perhaps interest your readers to hear of the high compliment paid to Mr Charles Wood on receiving his degree of MusDoc in the Senate-House on Thursday last, Dec. 6, the day immediately following the last performance of the *Iphigenia in Tauris*, for which Dr Wood had composed the music. As soon as Dr Wood had risen from his knees before the Vice-Chancellor, after the conferring of the degree, the chorus, assembled in the gallery of the Senate-House, sang with great expression and feeling the whole of the 'final chorus', commencing λγ επ ςντγχια, and making one slight alteration in the Greek, namely

$$γδγ γε γδγ$$

βιογου μαογξχοις
Και οη λη γοις σγεανοϑν×ς

to express their hearty wishes for Dr Wood's success in his future musical career.

It should be added that this expression of good feeling was not confined to the chorus, but met with the hearty approval of the highest University authorities —

'And even the ranks of proctors
'Could scarce forbear to cheer'.

Yours truly, etc.,

In 1895 Wood was associated with the formation of an undergraduate club in his own college that was to have considerable subsequent influence, the 'Scales' Club. He was invited to be its first president, and although his attendance at its early meetings was spasmodic he always played his appropriate party-piece (Schumann, Brahms and the like) and took his turn in hospitality — a feature of the meetings.

An obituary note by Sir W B Hardy, a fellow Caian and Wood's close friend for 40 years, comments as follows on Wood's influence on the musical life of the college[20]:

His capacity for friendship helped him to raise college music to a level far beyond that which it had reached hitherto. I think the claim may rightly be made that, with the exception of King's, Caius was soon ahead of every other college.

Perhaps the greatest service he rendered in this direction lay in his fostering care of the Scales Club . . . It was founded to set a standard of knowledge, of taste and of performance, and the method was as follows: some composer was chosen — say Schubert — and each member had to come to the next meeting prepared to perform something of his. Members were in this way accustomed to performing before a critical audience, and the effect upon the standard of musical attainment in the college was marvellous. Charles Wood gave of his best to the Scales. His scholarship and his genius alike were at its service. He was never ponderous, never a pedagogue, always the least consciously a musician of those present, and his sly humour was unfailing.'

He was instrumental in forming a college orchestra in 1896, when such undergraduate organisations were not common.

On January 9, 1894, a young Irish girl had entered the RCM to study piano and singing as her principal subjects, with organ, harmony and counterpoint, and even composition, as co-second studies. Her name was Charlotte Georgina Wills-Sandford, and her father (deceased) had been a Captain in the Scots Greys. Her home, Castlerea House, Co. Roscommon, indicated 'Anglo-Irish' ancestry.

Whether she was ever Wood's pupil is not known for certain, but it is not unlikely that she was, for in 1897 they became engaged, as a letter from Grove to Wood indicates (October 5, 1897):

My dear old C,
    I was very glad to get your nice letter this morning and to hear all your news in which I see only one *lacuna*, viz the lady's name. You give her a splendid character, and you have my best wishes for your success and happiness.
    Alas you will never see me at your new home. I am getting old and too fat, and the best I can hope for is to be talked about with the old affection.

In the same year Wood became the University Lecturer in Harmony and Counterpoint in succession to Garrett of St. John's College. Stanford, who was little seen in Cambridge after 1892, remained in a very real sense the non-resident Professor. As Professor E J Dent observed in his introduction to the posthumous publication of Wood's string quartets[21]: ' . . . he contributed more than anyone else to the development of musical studies in the University. Stanford, during the long tenure of his Professorship, did not reside in Cambridge, and although he exercised a valuable directing influence on musical education there, the real burden of teaching fell upon Charles Wood. As a teacher of composition he was surpassed only by Stanford himself, as a teacher of counterpoint and fugue he was unequalled.'

Wood also joined the recently formed Associated Board as an examiner. With a reasonable income assured, he could now, at the age of 31, contemplate marriage, and on March 17, 1898 (St Patrick's Day) his wedding to Charlotte Georgina duly took place.

19th-century Cambridge, like 19th-century Oxford, was fairly lavish in the provision of large and incommodious houses appropriate for the accommodation of married dons and their considerable households. Wood now moved into such a house, 17 Cranmer Road — a cul-de-sac nearly opposite Selwyn College, and this was to be his home for the rest of his life.

There was a study with a piano almost obliterated by piles of music, printed and manuscript, to which so many young undergraduates made their way for coaching. During the vacations he would sit there apparently absorbed in playing endless games of patience; but he would suddenly resort to the piano, sometimes after a stroll in the garden wherein grew the chestnut tree planted by Wood himself in honour of the birth of his eldest son, Patrick, in February 1899, and in which he was to be photographed (see pp. 92/3).

His life from now on was to follow a very regular pattern: teaching, examining, and composing when time permitted, with the occasional piece of reluctant conducting (generally a festival performance of one of his own works). There was an interesting interlude in 1901-2, when he went on an Associated Board examining trip to Australia and stayed with the Governor General, Hallam Tennyson, an honour not generally accorded to the Board's emissaries[22].

He had an aversion to staying overnight in London (he could not stand the noise of Hansom cabs on the cobbled streets) and on his RCM days would still return to Cambridge after a hard day's teaching. This devotion to domesticity was reflected in his reluctance to dine in College more than the once a week after choir practice.

Another son and three daughters, were in turn added to the family circle. There were, too, the usual domestics characteristic of a university household in the Edwardian era, and although his wife had a small private income, it was still something of a struggle to make both ends meet.

In 1904 Wood was made an honorary Ll.D. in the University of Leeds — he had been associated with the Leeds Festival since Stanford had become its conductor — but greater honours seemed to be eluding him. Not that he sought worldly distinction; with the passage of years, natural modesty was crystallising into an almost invincible shyness.

The war stirred him into the composition of a number of ephemerae, but life continued much as usual except that the disappearance of most of the male undergraduates from Cambridge resulted in the composition of at least one extended work for female voices (see p. 52).

In 1918 he suffered the loss of his elder son, killed on active service in Italy with the Royal Air Force. A pupil recalled the occasion[23]: 'One morning during the First World War, when I arrived at the College for my weekly harmony lesson, I was called into the office. Dr Wood, I was told, had received news . . . that his son had been killed at the front. Nevertheless, he had come down from Cambridge as usual to give his lessons and I was to go and have mine and not mention the subject to him. I went upstairs and walked into his room. He was sitting there at the table and looked up as I came in without greeting me. I tried to wish him 'Good morning' but the words wouldn't come out. I sat down and put my work on the table. He took it and looked at it. After a time he uttered some unintelligible words and I mumbled something in reply. Then we sat there, each staring at the table in silence. At last he sat upright and took out his watch and polished it with his handkerchief, an automatic, habitual gesture. I got up and we looked at one another; and then I went out, still without saying a word.

'The memory of that morning holds for me all the horror of the First World War. And all the frustration of Charles Wood as a man and as an artist comes back to me when I think of it'.

The immediate post-war period saw changes that affected Wood. The ebullient and dynamic Sir Hugh Allen had succeeded Parry as Director of the RCM, and Wood found himself almost an elder statesman overnight. R. Vaughan Williams, who had been his pupil, was now his colleague. Changes were taking place in the general musical ethos that did not commend themselves to him — but there were compensations. His two delightful Dickensian chamber operas had received performances at the newly-opened Parry Theatre at the RCM in 1922 and 23 respectively, and the success of the St Mark Passion, which was first given in King's Chapel on Good Friday 1922, set a coping stone on all that he had done over the years for the cause of church music.

In 1923 a long period of overwork and over-travel, finally culminating in a bout of influenza, laid him very low, and from this time onwards his health began to deteriorate. Stanford, too, had been an ailing man for some years and on March 29, 1924, he died. The University of Cambridge, reacting promptly, decided that his successor should be resident, have more considerable teaching responsibilities, and enjoy an increased stipend of £500 a year instead of the previous £250. Wood was appointed — he had, after all, been doing most of the professorial work for years — and his friends organised a dinner in congratulation that caused him weeks of apprehension as to his speech. The appointment provided that he might spend a proportion of term-time out of Cambridge and so allow him to continue his work at the RCM.

At once the musical world woke up to his eminence. He was elected President of the Musical Association (now the Royal Musical Association) on November 4, 1924; the University of Oxford presented him with an honorary MusDoc; and the Associated Board of the Royal Schools of Music tardily elected him a member. His speech of reply on this occasion should have been worth hearing[24].

But there was little real occasion for delight in all this since there could

17

be no doubt that he was a sick man. He struggled against ill health and pain; but the thrice-weekly journey to London became more and more of a burden, and though he carried on as well as he might with his teaching, his flame was burning low.

He held the Cambridge Professorship for two years only, for in June 1926 he had to enter a Cambridge nursing-home for an operation. Cancer had been diagnosed. While he was at the nursing home a quartet of men from King's College Choir came and sang to him from manuscript his previously unheard setting of Byron's *There be none of Beauty's daughters*. He was very deeply touched. A pupil who visited him there recorded his memories[25]: 'When I entered his room it was obvious that he was very ill. We talked for a few minutes about Cambridge and local affairs, and I saw that he was tired and in discomfort.

'Before taking leave of him I held his hand, which was cold and thin, for a moment. "Thank you for coming, my dear boy", he said, and I left his room with tears in my eyes, and humility in my heart, knowing that I was leaving a great man for the last time.' He died shortly afterwards, on the 12th of July. There was a funeral service in Caius Chapel and his body was finally buried in the St Giles cemetery on the Huntington Road.

So much for the outward facts of Wood's life, uneventful and undramatic though it was; but the importance and influence of a musician is not necessarily a reflection of a colourful existence. His pupil Margaret Hayes Nosek observed[26]: 'Charles Wood did not shine like a sun on the international scene. He was one of those steadfast true musicians of whom England has produced so many to her glory, who shed their inner light on those around them.'

What manner of man was he? Physically he was small in stature, with a large head and small feet. He wore a moustache and was thought by one pupil at least to have a slight resemblance in appearance to Richard Strauss. When walking he always carried a walking stick or an umbrella but held it in both hands behind his back giving him a thoughtful abstracted manner that was very characteristic. He was dapper and inconspicuous in his dress and had a certain personal fastidiousness[27]. His voice retained little of his Ulster speech except a fondness for using the word *dance* with a short 'a'. There were certain eccentricities of speech lovingly recorded by his pupils: 'peetle' instead of 'people', and 'tadle' instead of 'table'.

He had on occasion a pretty wit, with a fondness for elaborate puns. When the question of which examiners should be sent to Ireland during a time of civil commotion was mooted, 'Shinn and Faning' was Wood's suggestion. A particularly dull organ extemporisation was stigmatised as a 'Saharaband'. He once observed to a pupil that he thought it odd that Handel should have given the part of Solomon, of all people, to a castrato.

Once at dinner in his College Hall, when someone was animadverting against the folly of the University in appointing a lecturer in Russian who had never been to Russia, Wood whispered to the speaker: 'Keep your voice down, you are sitting next to a Doctor of Divinity who has never been to Heaven.'

He had his eccentricities of manner. When directing a male-voice choir he would push his spectacles up to the top of his head because, he asserted, he could hear better that way, and after directing the Sunday morning service in Caius Chapel he would return to Cranmer Road to take a lengthy bath, during which he would read the short stories of O Henry[28], an author who, like Mark Twain, greatly appealed to him.

Some of his personal likes and dislikes were also characteristic. He once told a pupil that his favourite sound was the open fifth between the two lowest strings of a 'cello, and on another occasion he observed to the same pupil that there was something rather indecent about the sound of a contralto voice[29].

So much for superficial anecdote. A close view of the mature man is provided by S P Waddington[30]:

He became a great teacher, and continued to influence others rather than let himself be influenced — not through any stupid, conscious fixity of thought or purpose, but because his nature was essentially simple and fundamental. He saw what he saw. If others saw differently the fact left him unmoved. His mind, though artistically sensitive and imaginative, was essentially practical. Philosophies, speculations, metaphysics, religious or political discussions bored him. He seemed to think them not worthwhile — a waste of time and energy, a departure from the true business of life, which was to look at life around you and make it profitable. This trait was very noticeable in him. He once went to Italy. He knew little about painting, and not much about architecture. Therefore, it never occurred to him to rhapsodise over the beauties of Botticelli's colouring or the wonderful lines of Giotto's Tower. Even the mountains and lakes hardly moved him to comment. They were there, and they were beautiful, and that was enough. But the antics of a lizard in a river-bed, the curl of an Italian's moustache, the thousand quaint characteristics in the people which he, with his eye for the comic, could see where another could see nothing, the oysters and wine at Baia, with Mount Avernus in the background, and the thought that this was Horace's country; the effect of a red parasol on the floor of the Coliseum on a brilliant day; the persistency of the beggars; such things as these filled him with delight. It was the same when he was travelling in England. He never read in a train. Looking through the carriage window, he never seemed to tire of what he saw — something unusual in the attitude of a cow or a sheep, a corn-field that was not quite what a corn-field generally is; none but himself could tell what it was that kept his absorbed attention. All this was of a piece with one of his most curious and, at times, most disconcerting qualities. He had a habit of seeing something that you yourself did not see, and it was generally of vital

19

importance. You might, for instance, think that you had so worded a syllabus so that it was beyond misconstruing. He would be sure to find some word or expression that was quite ambiguous. Or, in a piece of music, he would find out fatal defects where you had seen none. He did this without thought. It was a part of that natural sagacity, which made him one of the finest teachers, and which gave him, in his own work, such a sureness of touch.

. . . (In his maturity) his knowledge, remarkable in youth, had grown into something positively uncanny. He was a sort of Appeal Court. 'If you want to know anything, ask Wood', became a kind of slogan. Ought there to be a mordent over the third note of the 67th bar of the 49th Fugue of Bach? Or was it a shake? Wood would know. Did Beethoven ever have mumps? Wood would be sure to know that, and also when he caught it and how long it lasted. Did Barbados ever export potatoes? Had the population of the Caucasus grown since the last census? Any quaint item of knowledge was more than likely to be in his possession. Everybody consulted him — Grove, Parry, Sir Hugh Allan, Composers, Conductors, Performers, Secretaries, everybody. His loss is like losing the only existing copy of a book of reference.

. . . He had a great memory for fun. He probably knew by heart everything that the great comic characters of Dickens ever said. Mrs Gamp, Pecksniff, Pickwick, lived inside him, as it were — they had become incorporate with him. If he could find a fellow Dickens enthusiast, he would be almost ecstatically happy in merely playing a game of quotation-capping for as long as you liked. This side of his nature — his love of mirth, difficult to define in all its vitality and abandonment — was a factor of the greatest importance in arriving at an appreciation of his character. He could never be gloomy for long, even when illness began to weigh him down. It was well that it was so. His later days would have been dreary indeed but for this grace of humour.

. . . Though he was reticent in the making of new acquaintances, Wood clung to his old friends, and in the intimacy of friendship one felt for him an affection beyond the power of verbal expression. He had no meanness in him, no arrogance — he hated arrogance, self-satisfaction, ostentation above everything. He would, as it were, throw himself upon you, confident in your esteem and in your liking for him. He fell in with you, never doubted you, never sought to get an advantage over you — never thought of it. In the simplicity of his nature he was like a child. There was, in fact, something almost pathetically moving about his regard for children and animals: something of the child in him, something unspoilt, unsophisticated. His knowledge, his wisdom, his ability were never thrust upon you. He was just a dear friend, to whom you could tell your difficulties, sure of his sympathy. Naturally he compelled affection. He would do anything for you, and he showed a touching gratitude for any little thing you could do for him. In his talk he liked to share memories with you, and he was full of interesting anecdotes about people he had known. Books were his joy, but the consciously emotional, or deliberately rhetorical, or blatantly assertive style of book gave him no pleasure. He loved Dickens, Boswell, Mrs Gaskell's *Cranford*, some of the Elizabethan poets, Wordsworth, Coleridge and almost everything, even of a lower order, that was comic. In music, he thought Beethoven at his best the greatest of all composers, though at his worst he was worse than anybody. Handel was high in his affection. Bach he admired and venerated without loving him. He thought Haydn a greater man than Mozart because he was always 'up to something' — always trying to extend his own powers. Schumann, in comparison with other great composers, he did not much care for. For Schubert he had the warmest regard, and said that his 'C' Major Symphony was still the finest Symphony since Beethoven. Brahms he thought magnificent at his best, but given to dryness at times. He liked the Wagner of *The Walküre* and the first two acts of *Siegfried* better than the later Wagner. Contemporary experimentalists he frankly did not care for. Their idioms grated on him. He could not think or feel like that, but he could tell the difference between what was good and what was bad even in styles that were strange and unsympathetic to him.

His gentleness and evenness of temper have constantly been noted by the pupils and friends who have written about him in after-years. For instance, Sir W B Hardy, again in the *Caian*[31]: 'My friendship with Charles Wood, and I can claim it was an intimate one, extending over nearly forty years and ranging from standing room in the gallery at a performance of the *Meistersingers*, through the whole "gamut" of college life, to some months spent in the cramped space of a five-ton yacht, and in all that long period I can recall no single instance of ill temper. Some fantastic quip always saved the situation. His temper was indeed quick but his sense of humour even quicker.'

A man so reticent and unostentatious would be the last person to parade his beliefs, and one might wonder to what extent Wood's copious output of church music, for instance, was something forced on him — an exercise in technique. E J Dent would have it that Wood was cynically detached from his work in this field (thus according with his own severely rational vein)[32]: 'Charles Wood is remembered now almost entirely as a composer of church music. This does not do him justice, for he really wanted to write for the concert-room and the stage, and his anthems and services were of quite subsidiary interest to him. He told me himself that his only interest in them was the working-out of some ingenious contrapuntal device such as a canon by augmentation or inversion.'

Against Dent's view of the matter may be set a solitary comment he once let fall to his younger son: 'I don't go to the Chapel just to play the organ', and his intimate friendships with G R Woodward and, in his later years, with Eric Milner-White, then Dean of King's, scarcely suggest the image of an unbeliever who served the church in solely professional terms.

The main purpose of this study is to consider Wood as a composer, but his influence as a teacher cannot be ignored. The list of his pupils, both at Cambridge and the RCM is impressive (see Appendix 1).

Mention might also be made of Wood's one significant private pupil, Sir Thomas Beecham, who would travel from Oxford to Bletchley (as a halfway house) for a lesson — Wood similarly journeying from Cambridge. Beecham recorded in *A Mingled Chime*[33]: 'With Charles Wood I worked steadily and industriously for over two years, submitting to him every imaginable kind of exercise, fugues, choral pieces accompanied and unaccompanied, orchestral fragments, one grand opera [*Marmion*] (of which I myself wrote the libretto), and another in a lighter vein.'

Elsewhere in the same book (p. 72), Beecham recorded Wood's opinion that orchestration could be taught only by a master hand. Charles Reid, Beecham's biographer, noted that Tudor vocal music was another topic Beecham studied in depth under Wood's aegis. Beecham's comment on Wood was made many years later to Wood's pupil, J Meredith Tatton: 'A nice fellow, Charlie . . . I liked him.' Beecham's part in performing Wood's orchestral works is discussed on pp. 119/20.

I have already quoted E J Dent's general comment on Wood as a teacher. In another place he amplified this view: 'As a teacher of composition he seemed at first dry and uninspiring, because he paid little or no attention to "poetic content" or what the pupil thought was self-expression; he concentrated solely on craftsmanship, which after all is the only thing a master can teach. On this he was ruthlessly severe, and insisted always in the perpetual practice of strict counterpoint.' This professional approach was a wholesome corrective to the sort of dilettante attitude which could flourish among undergraduates, as Vaughan Williams observed[34]:

I do not think he had the gift of inspiring enthusiasm or of leading to the higher planes of musical thought. Indeed, he was rather prone to laugh at artistic ideals, and would lead one to suppose that composing music was a trick anyone might learn if he took the trouble. But for the craft of composition he was unrivalled and he managed to teach me enough to pull me through my Mus Bac.

In his later years he evidently gave up teaching the old-fashioned sort of strict counterpoint to which Dent (who had lessons from Wood in 1895) referred above. Tatton's memories of Wood's teaching methods are explicit[35]: 'He taught on orthodox, classical lines, but he had too much imagination to be merely academic or narrow. From the very beginning, his emphasis was all on the practical side. He taught modal counterpoint and harmony, beginning with Josquin Des Pres, Palestrina and the early hymn writers of the Reformation, especially Goudimel, the great Frenchman who died in 1572, but not forgetting the great Elizabethan English school. For harmonic work he would give us, say, the tune of one of these hymns and ask us to harmonise it as Goudimel or Bach or Brahms would have done it. He would correct it for us individually, and then discuss the original with us all, thus giving us a true object lesson in the style we were trying to master. This system he would continue throughout his teaching, always drawing our lessons and examples from the masterpieces of the great composers, never merely from text-books. We had, indeed, no text-books at all with him. He used to poke gentle fun at the old-fashioned, purely academic type of teaching which had formerly been the vogue.'

The reminiscences of two other Cambridge pupils add detail to the picture of Wood as a teacher [36]: 'He was very fond of demonstrating the use of the modes and their various applications, and his lectures were always full of interest and enlivened by his references to "old so and so", or a story to cap the reference. He was very strict in that the set lesson in counterpoint should be written according to his instructions, but in free composition he relaxed a little, and allowed one to do the best that one could. He taught that in a young person's effort all composition must be derivative: he used to say that when one had mastered the technique of writing what one wanted to write then derivation might recede and one's own musical thoughts and ideas might become more individual. He was the shyest man I have ever know. In the first year of our association he would, when talking to me, always keep his eyes fixed on my waistcoat. It was another year before he could raise them to mine.'

Finally this most lovingly observed account by Dr Herbert Howells will serve to round off this discussion of Wood as a teacher[37]:

Even when a man has had the luck to have studied with Stanford, Parratt, Walford Davies, and less 'officially' with Parry, Holst and Vaughan Williams, he could still find it possible to rate Charles Wood the most completely-equipped teacher in his experience. On the day of my entering the RCM as 'the new Composition Scholar', in 1912, Sir Hubert Parry greeted me with what he bluntly called 'supremely good news'. He told me he had arranged my going to Wood 'for Counterpoint'. So it was.

For the next five years, at least once a week, I sat at the feet of the remarkably un-remarkable Irish expatriate — ('the man from Cambridge' as one fellow once called him, with idiot incompleteness). For five years his concentrated gaze was upon my attempted Inventions, Fugues, Groundbasses, Motets. But not more than twice a term did the humour-laden, kindly, quizzical eyes seek mine in praise or blame. The quiet voice — already and long since stripped of its Irish inflexions and overtones — would be telling me how Bach or Palestrina, Haydn or Mozart, even (in mock reverence) Albrechtsberger or Frederick Gore-Ouseley, would have dealt with this or that technical problem that was struggling for solution in the work lying hopefully on the table.

As a teacher, Charles Wood was as gentle as any man could be in the presence of his pupils — gentle alike to the bunglers and the brilliant. He did not make extortionate demands upon us. Because he asked little some of us made it a principle never to go empty-handed to his lessons — I adopted that principle, and honoured it for three years — until the day came when I had nothing ready for the afternoon lesson. They used to say he could do a setting of the Magnificat at high speed. For my part I could COPY with like swiftness. On that destitute morning I copied a six-page and six-part setting of Raleigh's 'Even such is time'. I had taken the work to him three years earlier — in my first term. My swift copying was done to preserve the principle of unbroken productivity. Blandly and without qualms I presented it. For four pages he murmured approval. On the fifth his pencil began making slow circles round one line. Then — with gaze averted — he said, 'Do you remember the trouble that bit gave us three years ago?'

I learned that day an abiding characteristic of the man — mastery of the art of painless rebuke. And another fact: his incredible memory.

Like another 'Cambridge man' — the poet Gray — he never raised his voice. Over a mishandled task he would go straight to the heart of its solution. There was no palaver: instead, the authority in his explanation of how this or that composer would have dealt with the problem. A gross fault, a slipshod technical gambit, wasted means, economy ruined by prodigality, even stylistic unfitness, failed to sharpen rebuke. But a sly humour was at all times active, probing deeply but keenly.

The spate of obituaries and reminiscences that I have read unite in their account of Wood's shyness, his lack of personal conceit, his hatred of the limelight and of personal publicity. These are not the qualities that make for great renown in the ruthless competitiveness of the musical world, and the world is apt to ignore those who possess them. This book is written in the double conviction that Wood has been unjustly overlooked, or taken for granted, or simply forgotten as a composer, and that as a person, even if he were not great as the world counts greatness, he nevertheless deserves a more considered memoir than has as yet been accorded him.

NOTES

1. A distant family connection.
2. *Oxford Companion to Music*, article on Haydn Wood.
3. It is possible that Haydn Wood may have been Charles Wood's pupil at the RCM.
4. A term used for general musical practitioners, especially in working-class districts during the 19th century. See: *Reminiscences of Henry Coward* (London, Curwen, 1919).
5. Seaver, George, *John Allen Fitzgerald Gregg — Archbishop* (London, Faith Press, and Dublin, Allen Figgis, 1963), p 303.
6. A Doctor of Music, he was organist of Armagh Cathedral for 42 years, and composed several services and hymn tunes.
7. Marks's son, later the Ven Archdeacon Marks, subsequently recorded: 'In the early days of the Intermediate one of the subjects was Theory of Music. My father sent Wood and my cousin, Dr J C Marks, for the examination. When my cousin came home my father asked: "How did you do?", my cousin replied: "I did very well, but don't think Charlie Wood did much, for he left the hall in less than half-an-hour." When the results were published, Wood's name came out first in Ireland with full marks and the medal.' (From an article in the *Ulster Gazette and Armagh Standard*, Thursday, July 3, 1947).

8. Service lists were published regularly in the *Armagh Guardian* before it ceased publication in 1883.

9. Alas, it did not at the same time metamorphose the old NTS building, now the home of the Royal College of Organists, which Sir Hubert Parry stigmatised as 'about the worst building ever constructed for any purpose'. It remained the College home until the present building was completed in 1894.

10. Greene, Harry Plunket, *Charles Villiers Stanford* (London, Edward Arnold, 1935), pp 90-91.

11. See Grove (4th edition), Vol 9, p 84, also the 'Musical Autobiography' contributed by RVW to the study *Vaughan Williams* by Hubert Foss (London, Harrap, 1950), p 36.

12. RCM Magazine, Vol 22, No 3, Midsummer Term (1926), pp 71-77. Waddington was Wood's musical executor.

13. *The Caian*, Vol 34, No 3, Michaelmas Term, 1926, p 157.

14. See p 28.

15. See Copley, IA, 'An unusual glimpse of Sir George Grove', *RCM Magazine*, Vol 65, No 2, Summer Term, 1969, pp 7-9.

16. The tradition of presenting Greek plays (in Greek) with musical scores by contemporary composers began with the *Agamemnon of Aeschylus* with a score by Walter Parratt, in Oxford in 1880. Subsequent productions included: *The Ajax of Sophocles* (Cambridge, 1882), Macfarren; *The Birds of Aristophanes* (Cambridge, 1883), Parry; *The Eumenides of Aeschylus* (Cambridge, 1885), Stanford; *The Alcestis of Euripides* (Oxford, 1887); C H Lloyd, *The Oedipus Tyrannus of Sophocles* (Cambridge, 1887), Stanford, etc.

17. Two subsequent text-books on harmony and counterpoint were announced by a publisher in a series under Stanford's editorship, but never appeared.

18. Revd Ernest Stewart Roberts (1847-1912) was a distinguished scholar and university administrator who became both Master of Caius and Vice-Chancellor of the University. From 1886-97 he was an Officer in the University Volunteers, during the period of Wood's Bandmastership.

19. He is known to have taken part in no less than nine, of which he won six.

20. *The Caian*, Vol 34, No 3, Michaelmas Term, 1926, pp 156-162 and Vol 34, No 3, Lent Term, 1927, pp 162-165.

21. *Eight String Quartets* by Charles Wood, MusDoc (OUP, London, 1929).

22. Wood had been associated distantly with the Tennyson family from the time in 1892 when he was approached by Hallam Tennyson, at Parry's instigation, to correct the arrangements of some melodic settings made by Lady Tennyson of her husband's lyrics, that had been produced by a Madame Natalie Janotha.

23. Nosek, Margaret Hayes, 'Wood: A personal memoir', *Musical Times*, June 1966, Vol 107, No 1480, p 492.

24. He observed that 'The Board's premises were exiguous' — a barbed pun.

25. Personal reminiscence communicated to the author by C Derek Kenyon, Esq.

26. Nosek: Op.cit. (note 23 above).

27. He would never begin a meal without first wiping his table cutlery on his table napkin. With regard to his height, on one occasion he was rehearsing an orchestra in the confined space of an orchestral pit when one of the professionals asked him if he could sit up higher. He replied that he couldn't, as he was standing already.

28. Another favourite author.

29. Personal information communicated to the author by J Meredith Tatton, a former pupil of Wood's.

30. *RCM Magazine*, Vol 22, No 3, p 74.

31. See note 19, above.

32. In a contribution to a Festival Booklet put out at the time of the Armagh 'Wood' Festival, in 1947.

33. Beecham, Sir Thomas, *A Mingled Chime* (Hutchinson, London, 1944), pp 57-58.
34. Vaughan-Williams, *Op.cit.* (note 10 above).
35. In a personal communication to the author.
36. C Derek Kenyon, in a personal communication, and Eric Warr in the Armagh Festival Booklet cited above.
37. Extract from an essay included in *English Church Music, 1966*, a collection of essays published by the Royal School of Church Music, 1966.

CHAPTER 2

The development of Wood's musical style

Of the 19th century it may be said that, in general, it was a period during which most composers, irrespective of their nationality, shared a common harmonic *lingua franca*. This did not, of course, preclude the use of the common harmonic vocabulary in a highly personal fashion, but among the lesser men harmonic individuality was rare, except where the influence of nationalism modified a composer's use of the international language.

In the late 18th/early 19th century, English composers had tended to express themselves in terms of a harmonic style that imitated continental practice — the syntax of J C Bach as amplified by Mozart or Haydn (*cf* Linley, Storace, Attwood and, on occasion, S Wesley) — though they had always the older Handelian style to fall back on when appropriate. With the next generation the dominant continental influences were Mendelssohn (*cf* Sterndale Bennett) and, to a lesser extent, Spohr (with, latterly, the luscious Gounod idiom a potent drug for composers of church music). Parry and Stanford — the next generation on again — were certainly, consciously or unconsciously, in revolt against this harmonic tradition, but for them, as some would have it, it was a case of substituting Brahms (*cf* Parry's song *A Lover's Garland*, or Stanford's Piano Trio in E flat major, Op. 35) for Mendelssohn.

Alongside these European adhesions there nevertheless survived fitfully an older tradition — that of writing contrapuntally for unaccompanied voices — a tradition, however modified in terms of the harmonic language involved, that had its roots in the 16th century[1].

So much for the background in which Wood grew up. We have no precise details of the course of theoretical studies that the young student followed with his mentor, Dr Marks, but it may be reasonably inferred that harmony was taught on the 'figured bass' system, and that counterpoint was the old fashioned 'strict' variety involving semibreve 'canti fermi' and the 'five species'[2]. Of more importance would have been his own delvings into live music, especially the works of Beethoven, giving him the peculiar insight into that composer's mind that so amazed his contemporaries at the RCM and so delighted Grove.

To judge from the surviving works pre-dating his RCM days[3], Beethoven and Schubert seem to have been his first instrumental exemplars, and some early pieces for unaccompanied voices written while he was Stanford's pupil similarly show his awareness of that tradition of unaccompanied vocal writing discussed above. At the College, Wood was an industrious student and since in those days he was generally meticulous in dating each work — indeed in the case of the instrumental works each separate movement — we can tabulate such fruits of his industry as survive with some exactness:

1 Allegro for string quartet (1883)
21 solo songs (1884-1888)
Variations and Fugue on a Theme of Beethoven, for piano (1884)
2 movements of a 'cello sonata (1884)
1 complete string quartet (1885)
A Piano Concerto (1885-1886)
6 Anthems/motets (1885-1889)
1 Violin Sonata (1886)
A 'Ceremonial Ode', for chorus, organ and harp (1887)
6 two-part songs (1888)
2 part-songs for male voices (1888)
2 madrigals for mixed voices (1888)
A 'Quodlibet' for string quartet (1888)
3 large-scale cantatas, for chorus and orchestra (1888-1889)
A Septet for string quartet, clarinet, bassoon and horn (1889)
A Concert Overture for orchestra (1889)

Undated manuscripts of what are obviously student works include a setting of the 23rd Psalm for chorus and small orchestra, an unfinished violin sonata, three separate movements for string quartet, four separate movements for piano trio, and an Adagio for violin and piano that may well be the sketch for the slow movement of a violin concerto.

As S P Waddington put it[4]:

To Stanford came Wood as a pupil, an unassuming youth not quite seventeen years of age. He at once made his mark. In an epoch of attenuated technique, false sentiment, deliberate showiness, he appeared as one who, by instinct, had kept to the straight classical line, thorough, sincere, correct; undeveloped, of course, but already, perhaps through his training at Armagh Cathedral, possessing a knowledge of counterpoint and a sense of vocal style beyond his teacher's power to improve. Stanford taught him how to expand his instrumental style; how to make use of the more modern harmonies which Brahms and, in another school, Wagner were developing; how to manage musical forms: but wisely left him alone, for the most part, to achieve his own manner of expression . . . Greater perhaps than the influence of Wood's teachers — though he could have had no more skilful and appreciative guide than Stanford — was that of his environment. He had, even then, an astonishing, self-acquired knowledge of classical composers, but Brahms, Dvořák, Wagner, and probably most of Schumann were unknown to him. At the College he had access to their works and could hear them played. Not only

28

that, did he himself write a song, or a violin sonata, or a string quartet, he could quite easily get it performed 'con amore' by his fellow students.

What did all this add up to in musical terms? Wood's style at this time had a certain harmonic austerity, great contrapuntal strength, and a considerable technical mastery in handling the larger instrumental forms. Reference has been made to the influence on him of the music of Parry. To be specific he was influenced more especially by the massive choral style displayed in such works as the *De Profundis* or *Blest pair of Sirens* — though he never followed Parry in eschewing the delights of a sensuous orchestral palette (see the discussion of the unpublished cantata, *Spring's Summons*, p. 37).

It was a style more personal than the almost exclusively teutonic idiom affected by his contemporary Arthur Somervell (1863-1936), who had completed his musical training in Germany, or by, say, Dame Ethel Smyth (1858-1944), who was wholly German-trained. But if one studies Wood's first large-scale works — *Music* — *an Ode* (1890), the music to the *Ion* (1890) or the *Iphigenia in Tauris* (1894) — one is reminded, nevertheless, of the sort of music the followers of Brahms (Max Bruch, for example) were writing at this time.

Wood was by birth an Ulsterman, and folk-music was an integral part of the musical life of the Ireland of his youth, but apart from the one example of the use of an Irish air as the subject for a set of variations for violin and piano written when he was still a schoolboy, folk-song as such played no part in Wood's work during his student days or immediately afterwards; but in the late 1890s he began a collaboration with A P Graves (1846-1931) — following in Stanford's footsteps — in producing a volume of *Irish Folk Songs* (London, Boosey & Hawkes, 1897) (see p. 111), and from this time onwards a number of Wood's instrumental works are given a decided individuality through their use of thematic material that reflects the characteristic contours and rhythms of Irish folk-melody, or, more rarely, from the thematic use of actual folk material. Even in so unlikely a setting as a piece of church music this folk-song influence is sometimes to be noted, as, for example, in the *Magnificat in C minor* (1899) (*see Example 1, overleaf*).

If the orchestral *Symphonic Variations on 'Patrick Sarsfield'* (1907) (see pp. 120-122) is the most extended work involving a folk-song, the later string quartets show the folk-song influence in its most subtle form (*see Examples 2 to 5, overleaf*).

However much Wood was attracted by the possibilities opened up through the use of folk-material in composition, he never allowed the folk-song influence to permeate the totality of an instrumental work in the way that Vaughan Williams or Butterworth did — yet the amalgam of his 'classical' style and his folk-song proclivities is extraordinarily successful. As Professor

Example 1

Magnificat in C minor (1900) bars 20 - 24

Example 2

Quartet in A minor (1912), last movement bars 1 - 12

Patrick Hadley observed[5]: '(Wood) combined a rare knowledge of classical music with that of the music of his own country . . . . His settings of Irish tunes are to my mind far and away the most accomplished examples I know of in the realm of setting of traditional melodies of whatever country. He used the harmony that his classical training had taught him, and yet by some indefinable genius he succeeded in reconciling this with these tunes which would often be far removed in character from those of the classical epoch. Thus he would adorn and catch the spirit of these tunes in a way which has eluded time and again those setters who have theories and fads about modes, or what not; and incidentally there were few as learned as he in the matter of modes.'

Example 3

Quartet in E♭ (Harrogate 1912) last movement ( ) bars 10 - 14
(Allegro molto)

Example 4

Quartet in G minor (1916-17) 1st movement bars 6 - 11*

* Left by the composer without expression marks

Example 5

Quartet in F (1915-16) last movement bars 1 - 4
Allegro un poco vivace

* Irish folk-tune

This superb technique did not come by chance. In 1904 Wood was a founding member and vice-president of the Irish Folk-song Society, and he obviously delved deeply into the various collections of Irish melodies (Bunting, Petrie, Joyce, Forde, Pigot, Galwey, Costello, Feis Coil, etc.), for after his death among his sketches were found well over a hundred examples of folk-melodies (both songs and dances) simply harmonised for four voices, or for instrumental ensembles in short score, or with independent accompaniments as for violin and piano or voice and piano. It is possible that had he lived Wood might have experimented further in terms of a total integration of the folk-song element in the instrumental tissue. E J Dent, in discussing the late single movement for string quartet in G minor, noted that[6]: 'It is Irish in its material, and more noticeable than the Irish melody of the themes is the persistently Irish character of the harmony, with its emphasis on modal scales and avoidance of the conventional dominant cadence.'

To most of Britain's Victorian composers the modes were of little more than academic interest at most. S S Wesley once wrote to a pupil: 'Your question about modes pained me: I thought I had made a better musician and Protestant of you.' Stanford, however, saw their relevance — hence his taking lessons with W S Rockstro in modal counterpoint as a preparation for the composition of certain choruses in his oratorio *Eden* (Birmingham, 1891), and thereafter modal counterpoint became for him an effective prophylactic against an over-fondness for chromatic writing on the part of his pupils[7]. Wood, who had passed through Stanford's hands before these developments, was at one time rather sceptical concerning them[8]: 'He was scornful of Stanford's interest in modes, though he knew all about them' — thus Dent, remembering his first lessons with Wood in 1895; but when Wood, who had always been interested in the church music of the 16th and 17th centuries, became an intimate friend of an enthusiast for modality in terms of living music, his own work as a composer of church music was to be radically modified on occasion as the interest was now channelled into practical activity.

The enthusiast was the Revd G R Woodward (1848-1934), scholar, linguist, hymnologist, liturgiologist, amateur 'cellist, enthusiastic member of the Plainsong and Medieval Music Society, and the self-described fervent disciple of the Revd Dr J M Neale. They met in 1892 or 3, when Wood was still the organ scholar at Caius. Woodward had just published his first volume of carols[9], as he recalled in a letter to Wood[10]: 'Again I am more than ever grateful for your assistance and skill in harmonising my work; ever since the day, when as an undergraduate (in Gonville Court) you kindly pointed out some errors in my first venture, and said that, if I ever printed any more, you would run through the proof sheets and see that they were correct.'

The two friends entered into a musical collaboration that continued uninterrupted until Wood's death, resulting in the publication of both volumes of *The Cowley Carol Book*, *The Cambridge Carol Book* and *An Italian Carol Book*, and the hymn book *Songs of Syon*. Harvey Grace made an interesting reference to this in his *Musical Times* obituary[11]:

Wood's knowledge of old music of all sorts was encylopaedic and he had the all-too-rare gift of seeing the human where so many learned folk see only the quaint and archaic. The writer will not easily forget passing an evening with him and his close friend and collaborator . . . Dr G R Woodward — when some delightful hours were spent in exploring the collected works of Schütz and other pre-Bach worthies. It was, perhaps, only in such a combination of intimate surroundings and congenial pursuits that one saw Wood at his best, and realised the rare blend of humour, earnestness and sympathy that lay behind the shy front he showed to the public.

As a consequence of his own predilections and the association with Woodward, there are to be found among his church music, settings of the canticles to the appropriate plainsong tones:

Example 6

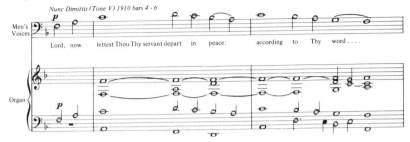

anthems and services based on 16th- and 17th-century metrical psalm-tunes:

Example 7

together with anthems and services the individual melodic lines of which, in the words of Dr David Lumsden[12], show 'the influence of plainsong and Renaissance polyphony .... Wood keeps his harmony and dissonance treatment deliberately austere and depends for his effect on tessitura, chord-spacing contrast of solo and full sections, and sensitivity to the meaning and accentuation of the words':

Example 8

Short Communion service in the Phrygian mode. Final Amen to Gloria

Further, Wood's interest in metrical psalm-tunes prompted that series of *Psalm-Tune Preludes* for organ which was to be so significant a contribution to the repertoire of English organ music (see p. 66 *et seq.*).

Thus, if one examines Wood's output as a whole — which is the intention of this study — there are to be found three elements which may be particularised as the 'classical', the 'folk', and the 'ecclesiastical'. The latter two never wholly superseded the former, and Wood never made any attempt to amalgamate them into any all-embracing personal style — in the way wherein his pupil Vaughan Williams, for example, so triumphantly succeeded. It was sufficient for him that each element was to hand when circumstances made its use appropriate. In some ways his most personal music was the most traditional in terms of its syntax, as for instance his Whitman settings, or the anthem *Expectans Expectavi*:

Example 9

Expectans Expectavi (1919) bars 12 - 22

when his inner emotional life was, as it were, momentarily exposed. Suffice

34

it to say that whichever element was uppermost, his powers of expression within it were completely adequate for the full realisation of his artistic purpose.

NOTES

1. For example:
   Maurice Greene (1695-1755), *Lord, how long wilt thou be angry* (5 voices).
   T Linley (1756-1778), *Let me careless and unthoughtful lying* (5 voices).
   S Wesley (1766-1837), *O sing unto my roundelaie* (5 voices), also the three big motets *In exitu Israel* (double choir), *Exaltate Deo* (5 voices), and *Dixit Dominus* (double choir). The various pseudo-madrigalian compositions of R L Pearsall (1795-1856), as, for instance, *Sing we and chaunt it* (4-voice and double choir versions) or *O ye Roses* (5 voices).
   T A Walmisley (1814-1856), *Sweete floweres ye were too faire* (5 voices).
2. Macfarren's treatises on harmony and counterpoint would have been likely text-books, the former appeared in 1860 and the latter in 1870. Goss's *Harmony and Thorough-bass*, which first appeared in 1833 and ran, according to 'Grove', to 13 editions, was another likely text-book. The English edition of *Albrechtsberger* that Novello's had brought out in the 1850s was another possibility, as were Ouseley's various text-books (*Harmony*, 1868; *Counterpoint, Canon and Fugue*, 1869; *Form and General Composition*, 1875). At all events, they gave Wood that intense suspicion of text-books that marked his own teaching.
3. Wood's surviving works which predate his entry to the RCM include:
   a piano sonata in G (27.7.82)
   a fugue for piano (1.9.82)
   two movements of a violin sonata (3.10.82)
   a set of variations for violin and piano on the Irish Air *The Meeting of the Waters* (18.10.82)
   a large-scale anthem, SATB and organ, *Be Thou exalted Lord* (14.11.82)
   and — most important, significant and mature, the 1st movement of a string quartet in A minor (*Andante-Allegro con brio*) (3.4.83).
4. Waddington, S P — biographical article in the *Dictionary of National Biography, 1922-30*, London, OUP, 1937.
5. Hadley, Professor Patrick — appreciation article, dated June 13, 1947, contributed (p 5) to the festival booklet issued in connection with the Charles Wood Festival held in Armagh, June 1947.
6. Dent, Professor E J — introduction to the collected edition of Wood's String Quartets (score), London, OUP, 1929.
7. He urged them to attend Westminster Cathedral, where under Sir Richard Terry a wonderful repertoire of 16th-century music was to be heard: 'All of Palestrina for tuppence' (the price of a 'bus fare from South Kensington to Westminster).
8. Dent, Professor E J — on p 4 of the Armagh festival booklet cited above.
9. Woodward, Revd G R — *Carols for Christmastide*, Series One, London, Pickering & Chatto, 1892.
10. Letter dated July 23, 1923, written from 48, West Hill, Highgate Village, N.6.
11. Grace, Harvey — obituary, *Musical Times*, August 1, 1926, Vol 67, No 1002, pp 696-697.
12. Lumsden, Dr David — 'Notes on the Sanctus and Benedictus (from the Short Communion Service in the Phrygian Mode)' contributed to *The Treasury of English Church Music* edited by Gerald H Knight and William L Reed, Vol 5 (1900-1965), London, Blandford Press, 1965, p 202.

CHAPTER 3

The cantatas

For the young British composer in the second half of the 19th century fortune might come from the publication of a successful 'royalty ballad', but the first step on the road to fame was usually a cantata commission. The romantic cantata had a surprising vogue during the 19th and early 20th centuries. On the continent such cantatas, 'based on idealised medieval, oriental, or supernatural themes, and represented by a long line of works such as Marschner's *Klänge aus Osten*, Mendelssohn's *Die erste Walpurgisnacht*, Félicien David's *Le Désert*, and Gade's *Comala* . . . remained in favour throughout the nineteenth century.'[1] In form they varied from miniature oratorios, through the 'choral suite', to settings that were wholly through-composed in structure. None of the great 19th-century British festivals — Leeds, Birmingham, the Three Choirs, or Norwich, for example — was complete without its quota of them, usually specially commissioned, and these works formed the staple fare of the smaller choral societies, who either could not run to the expense of oratorios or were lacking in appropriate numbers or technique. How many cantatas were written between the years 1850-1920, even in Britain alone, is a matter for speculation, but some idea can be gleaned from a study of the rather melancholy pages to be found at the back of old Novello editions, whereon the current repertoire of cantatas as published by that firm at the time was advertised[2]. It will be noted that favourite subjects exploited the picturesque, the dramatic and the exotic (or indeed all three combined in a narrative or ballad text), or alternatively the 'uplifting' or 'sacred'.

Wood's first effort in this direction was a setting of words taken from the 23rd Psalm for four-part chorus and a small orchestra of somewhat unusual constitution (2 B-flat clarinets, 2 E-flat horns, and strings). The manuscript is undated, but the handwriting leads one to believe that the work was written when Wood was either a schoolboy at Armagh or a young student at the RCM. He did not set the whole Psalm, but taking verses 1 and 3, with a recapitulation of verse 1, made of it an asymmetrical ternary structure. There is a graceful Mendelssohnian atmosphere about its pastorale 6/8, and as far as technique is concerned, though there is overmuch of word repetition, the young composer handled his chorus and orchestra with considerable assurance. It is possible that he showed the work to Stanford, for there are occasional pencil alterations — particularly in the instrumental parts — that do not appear to be in Wood's handwriting.

On August 20, 1885, Wood completed (and dated) the full score of a more extensive cantata, *Spring's Summons* (words by A P Graves[3]), set for tenor, baritone and soprano soli, chorus and orchestra (2 flutes, 2 oboes, 2 clarinets (A), 2 bassoons, 2 horns (D), 2 trumpets (D), timpani (D & A) and strings — also a harp part, that was added some years later). For a 19-year-old it is a remarkably mature piece of work, a romantic evocation of spring — full of a youthful poetry of expression quite unlike anything he wrote subsequently. It begins (*molto adagio*) with a horn call — shades of Weber —

Example 10

and after some answering introductory material, the tenor soloist proclaims 'Spring's Summons', which is, in effect, 'Wake-up!' (D major, 3/4. *L'istesso tempo*). The tempo then changes to *allegro* and first the orchestra and then the soloist and chorus plunge into a vocal scherzo wherein the world of nature is adjured to respond to the call (*see Example 11, overleaf*).

This movement builds up to a well-judged climax at the words: '. . . while the faithful robins sing "Cruel winter turns to spring".'

A short *Adagio* recitative (D minor, 4/8), followed by a solo for the baritone (G minor, C, *Allegro moderato*), directs the summons to mankind itself at large, the soprano in her turn elaborates the message, and a brief *adagio* coda completes the section, which is linked to a chorus for women's voices (SSAA) (A flat minor, 9/8, *Andante quasi allegretto*), preceded by an extensive orchestral prelude. The summons is now beamed at the children (*see Example 12, on page 39*).

The final movement of the cantata is concerned with exhorting the artist, the musician, and the poet, respectively, to respond to the call: the first is the subject of a short soprano solo (G major, 6/8, *Andante con moto*), the second of an even shorter recitative (C minor, 4/8, *Molto adagio*), but the third, a lengthy 'choral march' (D major, C, *Allegro moderato*) — rather four-square to begin with (one is reminded of Parry's 'ethical' cantatas) — expands into a quietly spacious coda (*molto adagio*). Although not marked *niente* — the term subsequently so beloved of Vaughan Williams — the *ppp* ending has a similar effect.

Spring's Summons was obviously performed at the RCM: the score has 'pencilled in' rehearsal numbers, and a set of MS parts has survived. It was

Example 11

subsequently revived — possibly at Cambridge, when a harp was available — but Wood apparently made no attempt to publish it. The best things in the cantata are the choral scherzo, and the chorus for women's voices, both of which might still bear performance. The orchestration throughout is assured and inventive — reminiscent somewhat of Dvořák — and the choral writing, which is comparatively easy, is grateful to the voices and effective in sound. Wood must have learned much from composing it, and Stanford's pride in his pupil would have been given a justifiable boost.

His next large-scale choral venture was a massive setting of passages from the 104th Psalm (Book of Common Prayer version) for solo quartet, baritone solo, chorus and orchestra. The full-score is dated 'London, February 7, 1887', and the orchestration demands 2 flutes, 2 oboes, 2 clarinets (B-flat), 2 bassoons, 4 horns (2 in D, 2 in C), 2 trumpets (C), 3 trombones, organ and

Example 12

Bars 16 - 20 of letter N

strings — an agglomerate of orchestral resources nicely adapted to securing a considerable volume of sound, especially when matched by an appropriately massive body of choralists. The opening chorus (v. 1-6) has a Parry-like beginning (with the overture to the *Meistersinger* hovering in the background):

Example 13

Bars 1 - 5

and leads directly into a contrasting movement wherein the rather obscure phenomena of v. 7 and 8 are graphically delineated in terms of a complex accompanied vocal fugue (F minor, 6/8, *Allegro*). V. 10-13 are set as an accompanied quartet (A-flat major, 9/8, *Andante*) with a more limpid lyricism underlining the aqueous element — 'He sendeth the springs unto the rivers . . .'

39

The third movement begins mysteriously enough (F major, C, *Adagio ma non troppo*) but the tempo soon quickens:

Example 14

and Wood plunges into graphic description:

Example 15

40

or:

Example 16

Bars 33 - 37

leading into a baritone solo (v. 24-30) (*see Example 17, overleaf*) which evokes the 'great ships' and, with the aid of the lower strings, 'that leviathan'. Then follows a pleasant lyrical interlude for the soloist to the words 'These wait all upon Thee' (D major, 3/4, *Allegro vivace*).

After a further interlude for the orchestra, the chorus enters firmly with the affirmation 'The glorious majesty of the Lord endureth', (C major, C, *Con brio*) and eventually settles down to a vast accompanied choral fugue 'I will sing unto the Lord'. Wood piles climax on climax with all the technical resources at his command (his awareness of 'Lord our creator' from Mendelssohn's *Elijah*, or 'Lord thou art worthy' from Brahms's *German*

Example 17

Bars 1 - 6
Adagio

O Lord how ma - ni-fold __ are Thy works

Requiem is manifest) and the work ends in a triumphal blaze of sound.

There is less of poetry and more of power in this setting as compared with *Spring's Summons*, and an examination of the manuscript sources leaves one with a considerable respect for their composer's technique and his ability to tackle a lengthy text with a due and appropriate regard to its overall structure.

When, on March 14, 1887, the new RCM hostel for women students was formally opened by the then Princess Alexandra, *The Times* duly reported: 'After the National Anthem had been sung the choir sang a hymn to the Princess of Wales, specially composed for the occasion by Mr Charles Wood, Morley Scholar at the RCM.' Scored somewhat oddly for chorus (SATB), harp, and organ (plus a solo violin in the middle movement), the *Song of Welcome* achieved the dignity of print, presumably at the expense of Sir Francis Cook, Bart, who had given the building and who suggested (and probably wrote) the words.

As a *pièce d'occasion* it is no better, and no worse, than dozens of other similar examples, though the use of a solo violin, harp, and organ — the latter reticent and continuo-like — shows an individual touch. The rest is the sort of thing that any one of Parry's young men could be relied upon to turn out by the yard. Wnat, in any case, could the young composer make of words such as:

Hail, gracious Princess! who has willed to be
The guardian genius of our dwelling here:
Dear to all English hearts, exceedingly
Yet have we special cause to hold thee dear,
Hail Princess! whom we cherish and revere.

Wood's next cantata, dating from 1889, was also his Cambridge MusB exercise, and consisted of verses from Psalms 28 and 88 set for soprano solo, chorus, strings and organ. However expertly such exercises may be written, they are rarely remarkable for their emotional content, but *Unto Thee will I cry, O Lord* is an exception. The opening chorus (C minor, C, *Adagio ma non troppo*) has a short but passionate introduction for strings, followed by a series of short quasi-fugal passages for the voices, with a restrained organ part. There is a delightfully naive touch in a unison/octave passage when the voices 'descend to the pit', and a telling fortissimo climax in D flat major, with the sopranos on a top A flat for 'unto Thee will I cry'.

Then follows an expressive soprano solo (A flat major, 3/4, *Andante sostenuto*) to the words 'O Lord God of my salvation', which is distinguished by a subtle contrast between the suave cantabile of the soloist and the restlessness of the string figuration.

The third movement, 'O save my people' (C minor, 6/8, *Con moto*), is a double canon (S T — A B) at the octave, and exemplifies Wood's capacity for using contrapuntal ingenuities for expressive ends.

The cantata concludes with a long chorus for all available resources (E flat major, C, *Allegro*) in the form of an introduction and fugue for five voices (SSATB), the latter in a swinging triple time (C major) to the words 'Alleluia, Amen'.

There is no evidence that this exercise was ever heard — either publicly or privately — during Wood's life-time, but an enterprising choral society might well consider it for possible performance. It is real music and foreshadows many of the characteristics of Wood's later church style.

In 1889, Wood began the composition of what was to be the first of his large-scale works to achieve publication — a setting of Shelley's *Ode to the West Wind* for tenor solo, chorus, and orchestra (2 flutes, 2 oboes, 2 clarinets (B flat), 2 bassoons, 4 horns (F), 2 trumpets (F), 3 trombones, tuba, timpani, harp, and strings). There is a reference to it in a letter from Grove to Wood that can be dated to that year[4]: '. . . I suppose Shelley's "West Wind" is better for music than the "Cloud" — there's more . . . and motion about it . . .'. There are two other references of interest in Grove's letters, one written just after Grove had received the vocal score[5]: 'I have no time but I must fire off a word to thank you for the puff of West Wind you have sent me in the very teeth of nature . . . . How I wish I could play the West Wind — but I am going to the Taylors tomorrow and I shall make him play it — I am well prepared to love it already', and one after the first performance (at an unspecified concert) in 1890[6]: 'I was sorry not to see you again but I had to go before the end of Rinaldo. I like your Ode extremely and feel tremendously proud of it. I was surprised (?) at the scoring. It's lovely. I hope to hear it again and make better acquaintance with it very soon.'

In structure it is through-composed, and is divided into five sections following the stanza structure of the poem. Brief quotations from the openings of the various stanzas will serve to indicate the general style and quality of the writing:

43

Verse 1 (B flat minor, 3/4, *Poco adagio*)

Example 18

Bars 47 - 52

Verse 2 (G minor, 6/8, *Allegro agitato*)

Example 19

Page 7 of vocal score, bars 9 - 12

(see also the remaining three verses, Examples 20-22, opposite).

An early review[7] complained of Wagnerian influence, but Brahms — the Brahms of the *Song of Destiny* or *Rinaldo* — is a much more obvious progenitor. Wood's technical assurance again is masterly, his orchestration vivid, his harmonic palette apposite to its task and his command of structure superb. Why then did not the *Ode to the West Wind* become part of the repertoire? The answer is to be found in a certain melodic aridity that characterises the work — Wood failed to react to his text in terms of vivid and memorable melodic phraseology. In its own day it was probably too modern in its general idiom to be grateful to the committees controlling the provincial festivals, and I doubt whether there is sufficient life left in it for

Verse 3 (G minor, 6/8, *Tranquillo*)

Example 20

Verse 4 (D major, 3/4, *Poco adagio*)

Example 21

Verse 5 (B flat major, C, *Allegro moderato*)

Example 22

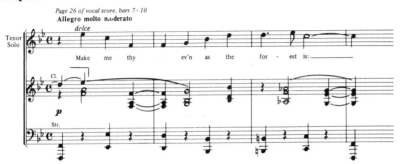

it to be worth reviving now. Nevertheless, for the young man of 23 who composed it, it promised great things.

On May 2, 1894, the Prince of Wales opened the present buildings of the Royal College of Music and one at least of Grove's dreams had thus become a reality. Among the delights of the inaugural concert, Grove had included the first performance of *Music — an Ode*, the prize-winning setting of a poem written for the occasion by Swinburne (whose muse, coddled by the uxorious domesticity of Watts Dunton's 'The Pines' at Putney, still took ready wing in the provision of such pieces).

The performance was conducted by the composer, Wood, who had earned this right by producing the prize-winning setting in competition with his fellow collegians[8]. It was his practical acumen as much as his musical superiority that gained him the prize, as Waddington observed[9]: 'Wood won the competition because he thought of what material he would have at his disposal. The College chorus was rich in female voices and poor in male voices. There were excellent violinists in the orchestra. Wood, therefore, wrote most of his Ode for female chorus and was careful to write a violin solo in the score . . . .'

Music — an Ode, set for soprano solo, chorus and orchestra (2 flutes, 2 oboes, 2 clarinets (B flat), 2 bassoons, 4 horns (E flat), 2 trumpets (E flat), 3 trombones, timpani, harp and strings, including solo violin; (MS full-score dated Cambridge, February 1893) is an admissible occasional piece. When it was revived at the RCM in 1933, *The Times* referred to it as [10] 'a beautiful piece of music in the serene style of 40 years ago . . .', and it made a similar impression when it was performed at the 900th anniversary celebrations of the founding of Westminster Abbey in 1966.

The poem itself falls into three sections, and Wood's setting duly mirrors the structure. The opening chorus for women's voices (SSAA) (E flat major, 3/4, *Allegro ma non troppo*) makes an impressive sound, and the middle movement, for soprano solo with an obligato for solo violin (G major, C, *Andante tranquillo*) provides a honeyed contrast:

Example 23

46

It is deftly dovetailed into a recapitulation of the *pomposo* opening which leads into the finale for the soloist with, this time, the full chorus SATB plus *divisis*. For once the vocal writing, which is throughout rather more homophonic than usual, does not culminate in a fugue — indeed the work ends with a quasi-chorale utterance that is extremely impressive:

Example 24

There is an increased emphasis on the sheer sensuous nature of sound in this work and, within the limits of the 'Max Bruch' style to which reference has already been made, a greater individuality of utterance. One feels that for a St Cecilia's Day concert it would make an admirable item.

Although Wood's MusB exercise had virtues beyond those required for its academic purpose, the same cannot be said of his MusD exercise presented in October 1894. He chose as his text *The White Island* (or 'Place of the Blessed') by Herrick, and his setting dutifully followed the prescribed formula — a long, Beethovenian overture for orchestra alone, an intricately counterpointed chorus for double-choir and orchestra, a long movement including accompanied canons for an SATB solo quartet, and finally an enormous accompanied fugue that spreads over page after page and involves very much word repetition. The orchestration would appear to be both economical and effective, and the usual competence in the technical aspects of word-setting can almost be taken for granted; indeed, almost all the tricks of the trade are exemplified. But that is all, and there is no reason why MusD exercise No 23 should not remain undisturbed on the appropriate shelf of the Cambridge University Library.

Wood's next choral work — now that, in a sense, his student days were finally behind him — was a setting of Milton's ode *On Time*, for chorus and orchestra (2 flutes, 2 oboes, 2 clarinets (A), 2 bassoons, 2 horns (E), 2 trumpets (E), 3 trombones, tuba, timpani, organ and strings). It was given its first performance on May 13, 1898, by the CUMS, and was published in vocal-score format the same year. Wood found something very congenial in Milton's words — indeed he seems to have found, with Parry, that the Miltonic style echoed something within his own musical nature. Certainly one feels that there is something in common between *On Time* and, say, *Blest Pair of Sirens*.

The introduction and opening is cunningly constructed over a ground bass, motifs from which act as unifying agents subsequently in the through-composed setting:

Example 25

There is an impassioned climax at the words 'Joy shall overtake us as a flood' (C minor, 3/4, *Allegro moderato*), and the final fugal section is both concentrated, intricately wrought, and fine in effect. There is altogether a sweeping imagination evident in this work, and Wood's control over his material was never more evident.

As has been noted above, the edition of Longfellow which Wood won as a school-prize had a preface by William Michael Rossetti commending the poetry of Walt Whitman, and there is no doubt that Whitman's verse struck a responsive chord in Wood himself, resulting in a number of settings more highly charged with personal emotion than he normally permitted himself elsewhere. Whitman's poetry has been a seminal influence on English composers in general from the time of Stanford's *Elegiac Ode* (1894) to Bliss's *Morning Heroes* (1930)[11], and Wood's Whitman settings are an important link in the chain of works produced as a consequence.

In 1901, Stanford succeeded Sullivan as conductor of the Leeds Festival, and on November 1 of that year Wood's setting of the *Dirge for two Veterans* (bass solo[12], chorus and orchestra) was given its first performance at a Festival concert, conducted — we may guess, reluctantly — by the composer. The work evidently made a considerable impression and it has been revived more often than any other of Wood's large-scale works — at least until Vaughan Williams's *Dona Nobis Pacem* (which contains, *inter alia*, a setting of the same words), superseded it in public estimation. Wood's setting would certainly bear revival — indeed, it should be revived — for as a commemorative or valedictory work it parallels Elgar's *For the Fallen*.

In structure it is a funeral march, episodic in form and cumulative in intensity. The opening sets the mood:

Example 26

The bass soloist intensifies it (*see Example 27, overleaf*), and the closing pages, which return to a softened version of the mood of the opening, are as lovely as anything comparable that the period produced (*see Example 28, overleaf*).

The scoring (2 flutes, 2 oboes, 2 clarinets (B flat), 2 bassoons, 4 horns (E flat), 2 trumpets (C), 3 trombones, tuba, timpani, side drum, bass drum, harp and strings), is, again, resourceful and appropriate. The whole work, by its reticence and real, if controlled, passion, gives a hint as to what Wood could have achieved had he that commanding egotism and ambition that might have carved out a more significant place for himself in the general creative life of the time.

Wood's next venture into the cantata field was undertaken at the instigation of a very remarkable friend of his, the Revd Canon T P Pemberton (1833-1921) sometime Fellow of Trinity College, Cambridge, and

Example 27

Example 28

a gifted amateur musician who, in the remote fastness of the North Riding of Yorkshire had organised a series of festivals wherein 'choral and orchestral works of the first importance have been given, and in which artists of the front rank [Joachim and Leonard Borwick are mentioned] take part.'[13]

At the 1902 'Hovingham' Festival, on August 8, *The Song of the Tempest* was given its first performance, and it would appear that the Festival chorus, drawn largely from the local villages, must have learned their part in record time since the score is dated Cambridge, July 14, 1902, barely a month previously. The text is taken from 'The Pirate' by Sir Walter Scott, and the through-composed setting duly mirrors the text, stanza by stanza. It was scored for flutes 1 & 2 (+ piccolo), 2 oboes, 2 clarinets (B flat), 2 bassoons, 4 horns (F), 2 trumpets (C), 3 trombones, harp, timpani, bass drum and strings.

In his discussion of the choral music of Sir George Dyson, Eric Blom wrote[14]: 'He is astonishingly accomplished: one feels that no technical feat would be beyond him, and in setting words . . . he invariably finds the right tone-picture to illustrate any passage. But he does, one cannot help feeling, illustrate rather than imaginatively illuminate,' and his remarks apply very much to this particular work. It is a well-made composition with everything done that a superb technique could do to bring the poem to life — but only, perhaps, in the last stanza, with its exquisite *pianissimo* ending, does the setting get off the ground, and one stanza's worth of real inspiration was not enough to give the work a place in the repertoire.

The success of the *Dirge for two Veterans* prompted a further commission for the next Leeds Festival, in 1904, and on the evening of October 7 *A Ballad of Dundee* was given its first performance, again conducted by the composer, with Plunket Greene as soloist[15]. The artistic progenitors of *A Ballad of Dundee* would have been Stanford's *Revenge* (1886), and the *Voyage of Maeldune* (1889). It follows a similar through-composed pattern, that divides itself into four sections — following the text by W E Aytoun (1813-65). This setting (scored for the same instruments as *Song of the Tempest*, plus a tuba and a third timp.) is again of the picturesque sort, perhaps showing more of the folk-song influence in certain of its melodic aspects:

Example 29

Pages 1 & 2 of vocal score, bars 23 - 31

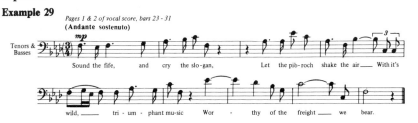

51

Again one is aware of Wood's superb technique in the craft of writing for chorus and orchestra; but Blom's statement, as applied to *The Song of the Tempest*, applies equally to the *Ballad of Dundee*. Although it seems to have been given a cordial reception at its first performance, and although it had been brought out by Breitkopf and Härtel with a German translation of the text, I know of only one subsequent performance (by Stanford at the RCM in 1913). From this time on Wood wrote no more festival cantatas.

The reasons for this can only be a matter for conjecture. It may be that the fact that his last two cantatas had each achieved little more than a *succèss d'estime* put paid to further commissions; on the other hand, it can be inferred that Wood was, from a temperamental point of view, inclining more and more to the relative intimacies of church music, chamber music and ensemble pieces for small groups as his main outlet for self expression. At any rate, he published only one more secular work, *Eden Spirits*, for women's voices and piano.

This setting of the poem by Elizabeth Barrett Browning (taken from *Drama of Exile*) was brought out in 1915 — and, as has been noted above (p. 16), it owes its inception to the fact that the exigenies of war had taken most of the young men away from Cambridge.

The musical tradition associated with cantatas for women's voices was for such works to be of a gracefully insipid character (eg, Macfarren's *Songs in a Cornfield*). The music of *Eden Spirits* is certainly graceful in the sense that it is both effective and gratefully written for the voices (two parts, sometimes blossoming into three, and then four), but it is not insipid. The piano writing, too, has a masterful economy of notes and a remarkable clarity of texture, reminiscent of Fauré. Not for nothing had Wood been writing a stream of two- and three-part songs over the years. Experience reinforced judgment as to what was effective. I suspect that Elizabeth Barrett Browning's text would be too bathetic to commend itself to contemporary performers or audiences, and this would be a pity, for there is some lovely music in the setting that deserves better than oblivion.

Wood's two final works of cantata dimensions, the *Mass in F* and the *St Mark Passion*, were intended for performance in a liturgical setting and hence can be better discussed in the context of his church music (see p. 141). Fragmentary sketches remain of two other works for women's voices — one cannot say whether the projected accompaniment was intended for orchestra or piano: *Songs in a Cornfield* (Christina Rossetti), and a canonic fragment (SSAA) to what appears to be metaphysical 17th-century words. Likewise there is the opening — in sketch form — of a work for chorus and orchestra, *By the North Sea*, which one may suspect was a war-time inspiration. A setting of *The Ballad of Agincourt* ('Fair stood the wind for France') for male voices (TTBB) and piano has disappeared[16].

Wood's cantatas have, perhaps, worn less well than any other branch of his output. They were written in too restrained an idiom to achieve an easy popularity in their own time, and they are, nevertheless, too representative of their own time to be easily acceptable in ours — for they have not receded sufficiently into the past to have acquired that patina of antiquity which makes the minor works of the 18th century, for example, currently acceptable. Yet among them is one masterpiece, *The Dirge*, one important *pièce d'occasion, Music — an Ode*; and of the others, *On Time* would certainly merit resuscitation. Time brings its rewards, and it only remains for enterprising conductors to investigate and judge for themselves.

NOTES

1. Horton, John: Chapter VIII (The Choral Works), p 283 of *Schumann, a Symposium* (ed Gerald Abraham). London, OUP, 1952.
2. My copy of Stanford's *Revenge*, for example, lists over 100 works by some 70 composers.
3. Wood was to collaborate personally with A P Graves (1846-1931), the father of Robert Graves the novelist and poet, but there is no evidence that they had even met at this time. The poem, *Spring's summons* was published in 1873 in *Songs of Killarney* (London, Bradbury, Agnew & Co, pp 113-123), and had, incidentally, been Graves's own first publication.
4. Written from 'Lower Sydenham, SE, Sunday, Sept 15', (1889).
5. Same address, 'Thursday night'.
6. Same address, 'June 11' (1890).
7. *Musical Times*, Vol 31, No 568, June 1890, p 364.
8. Grove wrote to him from the RCM on March 8, 1894: 'I hope that you will not be otherwise than pleased at my asking you to conduct your Ode at the performance at the opening of the new building. This will necessitate your rehearsing both the voices and orchestra, to which I think you will find no difficulty on the part of Prof Stanford or Mr W Parratt'.
9. Waddington, SP, in the article cited in note 12 at p 25 above.
10. *The Times*, May 10, 1933, p 10.
11. Butcher, AV: 'Walt Whitman and the English Composer', in *Music and Letters*, Vol 28, No 2, April 1947, pp 154-167.
12. According to the late J Meredith Tatton, *The Dirge* was also performed in a version for baritone solo and piano, at the Oxford and Cambridge Musical Club in London. The MS of this version has disappeared.
13. *Musical Times*, Vol 39, No 666, August 1898, p 541.
14. Blom, Eric: *Music in England* (London, Penguin Books, 1942), p 205.
15. It shared a programme with Stanford's *Songs of the Sea*.
16. A pupil of Wood's, who took part in a late performance of the latter work, assured me that it was not among his more significant achievements.

CHAPTER 4

Chamber music and solo instrumental music

After its full flood in the 17th-century the stream of chamber music produced by British composers had, by the end of the 18th-century, become a trickle, and there were few signs in the first half of the 19th-century that this situation was likely to alter. Isolated composers did indeed dabble in it as a medium for composition, and some of their music has been revived in our own day — for instance, the sonatas of James Hook (1746-1827), or the string quartets of Samuel Wesley (1757-1834) — but generally speaking few works of any importance were produced[1].

With the advent of Parry and Stanford the situation changed. The former was prolific of chamber music in his younger days[2], and the latter poured out a succession of works, significant at least in their own day, throughout his creative life[3]. It must be admitted that the chamber music of both composers shows the teutonic influence on their styles at its maximum, but without their example, plus the influence of the energetic and enthusiastic Walter Wilson Cobbett (1847-1937), the flowering of chamber music that coloured the output of many of the next generation of composers would hardly have taken place.

The cultivation of chamber music at the newly opened Royal College of Music formed an important part of the curriculum both for composers and performers, and as such was an activity more than ordinarily congenial to one of Wood's temperament. Indeed, his enthusiasm for chamber music as a channel for his creative activity predated his entry to the College. While still a schoolboy at Armagh he composed a violin sonata in two movements (dated respectively August 10 and October 6, 1882), a set of variations on an Irish air, *The meeting of the waters* (October 3, 1882), also for violin and piano, and a string quartet movement which was evidently intended for his special pre-College entrance examination (see p. 27).

Little need be said about the first two items. The violin sonata has a Schubertian diffuseness and, on occasion, something of a pallid Schubertian lyricism. The two movements are, respectively, an *Andante* in D minor (2/4), and a tarantella-like *finale* in D major (9/8, *Allegro vivace*). The six variations on the Irish air contrast Beethovenian solidity with Thalbergian glitter.

Of more importance is the quartet movement in A minor (dated April 3, 1883). It is a full-blown sonata first movement (4/4, *Allegro con brio*), preceded by a short *Andante* introduction, and demonstrates that Wood's own experiences as a player had given him a considerable command over the art of writing idiomatically and effectively for stringed instruments. It is noteworthy that the manuscript shows signs of a subsequent revision with the intention of condensing the texture through the excision of whole bars. Wood early realised the dangers of diffuseness and too four-square an approach to phrase structure.

Once at the College he was active in the composition of chamber music. There survives the first movement of a string quartet (A minor, 3/4, *Allegro*) dated September 1883, and three other movements, undated but, on the evidence of handwriting, contemporaneous (an *Andante*, D Major, 2/4; a *Scherzo*, A minor, 3/4, *Allegro molto*; and an *Allegro*, A major, C) that may have been meant to complete a four-movement work. Similarly there are four separate piano-trio movements (D minor, 3/4, *Allegro molto*; A major, 2/4, *Andante quasi Adagio*; D minor, 3/4, *Presto*; and D major, 3/4, *Allegro moderato*) that may likewise have been intended to form a complete whole and which, on stylistic evidence, could well have been written during the earlier part of Wood's College career.

In 1884 he wrote two movements of a 'cello sonata (G major, 3/4, *Allegro moderato*, dated July 1884; and C major, 2/4, *Andante*, dated December 6, 1884) and the single, undated, first movement of a violin sonata (G minor, 2/4, *Adagio/Allegro*) was probably composed at the same time.

There are two further important chamber works dating from his College days: a string quartet in D minor, written in 1885 and published posthumously, and a large-scale violin sonata in three movements (G minor, C, *Allegro*, dated July 18, 1886; C minor, 3/4, *Adagio*, dated June 15, 1886; and G Major, 6/8, *Presto*, dated July 18, 1886).

Finally some mention must be made of the *Quodlibet* for string quintet, dated May 18, 1888. This demonstrates admirably a precept he later gave his pupil, Harold Rutland: 'Any theme can be made to combine with any other theme, given a little coaxing', for in it, *Garryowen*, *The British Grenadiers*, *Home, sweet home*, *The National Anthem*, and *All through the night* are all combined together in ingenious counterpoint (*see Example 30, overleaf*).

Grove made reference to this work in an undated letter written to Wood from the College: 'I didn't write about the Quodlibet before because I wanted to hear it first. I had the parts written out but you know the difficulties — I am charmed with the look of it, and anticipate no end of fun in hearing it.'

The principal influence to be detected in the earlier College works is Beethoven, but latterly Brahms becomes a very decided stylistic exemplar. The young bloods of the RCM in the '80s and '90s looked to Brahms in much the same way as do their successors regard Stockhausen. This Brahms

Example 30

influence may be noted in the G major violin sonata (which was evidently prepared for posthumous publication, though never issued), for example, the opening of the slow movement:

Example 31

One is also conscious of it in the D minor quartet — together the two most considerable of Wood's student works. The quartet met with Joachim's approval when it was played to him at the RCM (July 15, 1889). Marion Scott wrote of it[4]: 'Though there is a somewhat tentative feeling about the earlier movements, it is amazing to see with what speed the composer's hand gathers strength, and with what clearness of thought the Quartet is carried through. The last movement in particular is full of Irish raciness and spirit'. E J Dent observed[5]: 'The work shows very clearly how completely he had mastered all the technical devices of classical chamber music'.

The violin sonata, too, has, as Marion Scott first noted (ibid.), 'a rather more mature technique than the Quartet, yet has an even fuller measure of that translucent, not-to-be-recaptured quality of youth.' It would be worth reviving, if only for the magnificent opening of the slow movement, reminiscent of the threnody Wood was to write for the *Dead at Clonmacnois* (see MS example 83), and the undoubted raciness of the finale.

In 1889, after Wood had ceased to be a full-time student at the College and had become a Cambridge undergraduate, he completed a septet for clarinet (B flat), bassoon, horn, violin, viola, 'cello and double bass, in four movements, (C minor, C, *Allegro moderato*, dated March 26, 1889, London; G major, 3/4, *Andante*; C minor, 3/4, *Presto (Scherzo)*; and C major, 3/4, with vigour). This work, like the G major violin sonata, was prepared for posthumous publication but never issued — which is a pity, for septets are few, and septets as cunningly wrought as Wood's even fewer. The *Scherzo*, for example, is a movement having a greater individuality than Wood had previously injected into his instrumental works. There are some interesting harmonic effects and a delightful trio:

Example 32

The finale, a set of variations on an original theme, demonstrates yet again Wood's superlative technique in variation writing.

The following year, 1890, Wood entered a competition in which the 'Wind Instrument Chamber Music Society' was offering a prize of 20 guineas for a wind quintet (flute, oboe, clarinet, horn and bassoon). Wood had long held that the sound of these instruments by themselves, heard continuously, was fatiguing to the ear; it was only when a chance remark from a fellow musician, reflecting on Wood's capacity to write for wind, piqued his *amour-propre*, that he decided to take part, with the result that he gained the Society's prize in the teeth of 30 other competitors. The score and parts of the work disappeared soon after the first performance and it was not until 1933, some years after Wood's death, that the parts were finally located and published. The work has four movements: F major, C, *Allegro con moto* (♩ = 116); D minor, 3/4, *Molto vivace* (♩ = 80); C major, 6/8, *Andante grazioso* (♪ = 100); F Major, C, *Allegro moderato* (♩ = 96).

As with the septet, it is the *Scherzo* which shows Wood becoming increasingly subject to modal influences, and which strikes one as outstanding by reason of its fleetness and the deftness with which it is constructed:

Example 33

The whole work — especially the finale, which starts off as a set of variations but changes course in mid-career — would be worth reviving.

Another posthumously published work that may well date from the same time as the quintet is the violin sonata in A major. This work is unusual for its time in that formally, and to a lesser extent stylistically, it mirrors the characteristics of the Baroque (pre-classical) sonata. The stylistic influence of, say, Handel is not, however, so complete as to render the work pure pastiche; on the other hand, it is far from being pure Wood. If it be borne in mind that Reger's *Concerto in the Old Style* (Op. 125), that recognised precursor of the neo-classical, was not written until just before the First World War, it will be seen that Wood was quite a pioneer — even by some years. The sonata consists of an *Andante* (♩ = 100; A major, 3/8) in binary form, followed by an *Adagio (quasi recit)* (F sharp minor, 4/4, modulating into A major), leading into an extended and spritely *Gigue*, also in binary form (A major, 9/8, *Allegro ma non troppo*, ♩= 116).

In the years following the composition of the wind quintet Wood appears to have cultivated the string quartet exclusively as his chosen medium for chamber music, and over the next 30 years he completed five full-length works, in addition to two single movements and other fragments[6]. None of these works was published in his lifetime, and although there were sporadic performances in Cambridge and elsewhere, few musicians could be said to have known them intimately, though those who did — such as Marion Scott and Thomas Dunhill — wrote enthusiastically of them[7].

The string quartet in E flat major (subtitled 'The Highgate') — presumably from the fact that it was written at his elder brother's home), consists of four movements: E flat major, C, *Allegro con moto*, dated April 6, 1892; A flat major, 3/4, *Molto moderato*, dated April 7, 1892; F minor, C, *Adagio ma non troppo*, dated April 8, 1892; E flat major, 3/4, *Molto animato*, dated October, 1893. It is a very Brahmsian work, as is shown, for instance, in the contours of the opening theme of the first movement:

Example 34

or in the texture of the *Molto moderato*:

Example 35

The most personal music is to be found in the slow movement, which is based on a ground and which, even allowing for the example of the Brahms fourth symphony, was not a common constructional device among young composers in the 'nineties:

Example 36

The finale has a fiery intensity and rhythmic drive surprising in so gentle a composer. The whole work is superbly written and should be a joy to the performers.

59

There was a gap of nearly 20 years between the 'Highgate' quartet and its successor, the quartet in A minor, first performed on February 12, 1912. As Dent observed in his introduction to the collected edition[5], the Brahmsian influence has disappeared and Wood is now using 'themes derived from Irish folk-song'. What Dent presumably meant was that Wood used thematic material that mirrored the characteristic scales, intervals and rhythmic patterns of Irish folk-song[8].

The first movement (A minor, 4/4, *Allegro un poco maestoso*) uses conventional sonata form in a highly individual way. The main theme of the second subject group, for example, is derived from the opening theme by augmentation of the first notes of the latter. The *Scherzo* (A major, 3/4, *Presto*) is delicious, with five-bar phrases later growing into nine-bar. After a short and expressive *Adagio* (F major, 2/4) there follows an extended *Finale*, the opening of which has already been quoted (see Example 2, p. 30). Wood introduces as a second theme in his rondo structure that most lovely of all traditional Irish melodies, associated with the words 'The lark in the clear air':

Example 37

Marion Scott described the quartet as being 'transfused with the heroic element of Irish poetry', which may, perhaps, strike one as a little grandiloquent. But certainly Wood's next quartet in E flat major, 'The Harrogate', whether intentionally or not, presents itself as a foil to it, being markedly lyrical, tender, even pathetic.

It was composed during a holiday Wood took with his wife at the Yorkshire spa during August 1912[9], and was first performed the following year. There is a deftly written first movement (E flat major, 4/4, *Allegro con moto*), with a development involving fugal treatment, and a *Scherzo* (C major, 3/4, *Prestissimo*) which exploits the humorous possibilities inherent in a melody founded on a scale of whole tones alternating with the ordinary diatonic scale:

Example 38

Ernest Walker's description of it[10] is both felicitous and apposite: ' . . . a wonderfully buoyant and piquant little movement with an impressively tranquil coda that, somehow or other, is thoroughly in keeping'.

The slow movement (F minor, 4/4, *Allegro con moto*) consists of a set of variations on a broad tune, having, as Dunhill observed (*op. cit.*), the characteristics of a 'Coione' or lament. In this elegiac mood one feels that Wood is at his most personal and expressive. The *Finale* (E flat major, 2/4, *Allegro molto*) is a high-spirited 'reel' somewhat in the style of a *moto perpetuo* (see Example 3, p. 31).

The indefatigable William Cobbett, who subsidised the issue of a 'Chamber Music Supplement' to be given away with copies of *The Music Student* in the years immediately before and during the First World War, was also pertinacious in organising chamber music competitions for composers and performers. In May 1914 he announced a competition with a prize of £50 for a string quartet, the violin parts of which were to be of equal importance (each 'one of two' — a 'conversation quartet'). Wood evidently contemplated entering the competition, for he commenced writing his string quartet in F major at this time, although he was unable to submit it for adjudication because it was not completed until three months after the closing date for submission of entries[11]. The quartet was given its first performance in October 1915[12]. It is, in a sense, a slighter work than its predecessors in that it has only three movements, and the third, though delightful, is decidedly lightweight. The fact, too, that the two violin parts had to be of equal importance meant that, to quote Ernest Walker again, ' . . . not infrequently Wood is consciously (and inconveniently) going out of his way to give the two violin parts equal alternate prominence. And, perfectly satisfactory as the effect of the equal violin parts may be to the quartet of players themselves, it can hardly be so to the listeners in view of the necessary disposition of the music-stands'.

The opening, fugal, movement (F major, 4/4, *Poco adagio*) has a theme which is centred on the mediant, and as such seems scarcely to belong to F major. It is 'treated fugally by the other instruments; after further development, it returns as a more sustained melody, and again this is given to the violoncello, forming a bass to contrapuntal parts; more development ensues, the theme reappearing again in the second violin. The movement is remarkable not only for the closeness of its contrapuntal texture but for its passionate depth of feeling' (Dent, *op. cit.*). It is perhaps the subtlest quartet movement that Wood ever wrote.

The *Intermezzo* (D minor, 2/4, *Allegretto*), which follows, is charming, and the *Finale*, though lightweight, as has been noted, is one of the most delightfully lilting *Rondos* in the whole corpus of chamber music. It is based on a 'folk-tune' which I have identified as *The Devil in Dublin*, (Joyce[13], No 301, p 141), which has an infectious dancing quality and which Wood treated with 'consummate deftness', to quote again from Marion Scott:

Example 39

The manuscript of the D major quartet is undated, but the work may well have been composed during the years 1915/16 or later. There is no quartet of Wood's that can surpass it in the superbly polished workmanship that went into its construction. One notes again an opening theme in its first movement (D major, 3/4, *Allegro con moto*) that tends to avoid the tonic:

Example 40

The *Scherzo* (E minor, 2/4, *Allegro vivace*), which partakes — in places — of the nature of a reel, is capricious and witty, and the slow movement (F sharp major, 3/4, *Adagio*) is another of those sets of variations that Wood used as a vehicle for his most intimate and personal utterances. Ernest Walker — no mean judge — considered the last page-and-a-half of this movement to be the pinnacle of Wood's achievement as a composer of chamber music. The *Finale* (D major, 4/4, *Allegro molto*), which is spirited and cumulative in its rhythmic excitement, rounds off the work fittingly.

In addition to the orthodox quartets, Wood also composed a set of *Variations on an Irish Folk-song*, for string quartet. It is believed to have been written in 1917, and was first performed in Cambridge on June 8, 1925. The gap is significant of the way in which Wood failed to 'push' his own works. The 16 variations exemplify yet again Wood's wide-ranging mastery of variation technique. The theme itself is not of any extraordinary beauty or interest. What is significant is what he made of it. As to why it was left as an isolated movement, one can only assume that if, as is possible, the work began life as the intended slow movement of a quartet, it soon grew too large to be stylistically appropriate in that context, (cf Beethoven's *Andante Favori in F major*).

The collected edition of the quartets also includes a single first movement in G minor — the most modal movement in the whole *corpus* — and among Wood's posthumous papers has been found another version of this same movement, but without the introductory chords of the published version. One can only speculate as to what the rest of the quartet may have amounted to. Other fragmentary movements surviving in full score include a theme and five variations (the theme being in two parts, alternating between the Dorian mode on D and D major — there are similar bifurcations in the variations); a feathery *Scherzo* in B flat major, with a double time signature, 3/4 2/4; and the opening section (six pages of full score) of a *Scherzo* in A minor that was almost certainly intended at one time as the second movement of the G minor quartet.

If one looks at Wood's chamber music as a whole, one is immediately struck by the fact that it is all true chamber music in every sense of the word. As Marian Scott observed (*op. cit.*): 'He obviously prefers purity of effect to mere mass of sound; he gives each instrument thoroughly suitable and congenial passages; he has a ready and unobtrusive command of counterpoint; and he can THINK in terms of the string quartet.'

Ernest Walker's summing up (*op. cit.*) cannot be bettered: 'Wood's music may, perhaps, not particularly stir the young blood of today — to strive and cry aloud was not in his modest nature, and harmonically he was indeed less adventurous than a good many of his contemporaries. But his mind was firmly fixed on the solid things which, all said and done, are the things which chiefly matter in art — for genius as well as talent. In all these pages we shall not find one scamped bar; all through, finely cultured musician-ship is doing its sincere best. And such best is worth a good deal.'

Wood's compositions for solo instruments and piano (other than the sonatas discussed above) are, with two exceptions, based on traditional Irish folk-songs or dances. The odd-men-out are an undated *Adagio* for violin and piano (G major, 4/4), sometimes referred to as a 'Cavatina', which may possibly be the sketch for the slow movement of a violin concerto, and which uses Wood's 'Max Bruch' style at its most passionate, and an unfinished *Rondel (?)* for violin and piano (F major, 2/4), which is much more folk-song like in its melodic idiom.

In 1923, Wood published two pieces for violin and piano: a *Jig* (F major, 6/8, *Allegro vivace*) founded on three traditional dances, two of which I have been able to identify — (Joyce, p 401, No 829, Air *Bang up*, Pigot collection; and Joyce, p 402, No 831, *Tumble the jug*, Pigot collection), and a *Planxty*[14] (D minor, 3/4, *Allegro moderato*) founded on two melodies — a *Planxty by Carolan* (the famous Irish harpist) (Joyce, p 287, No 536) and *Sir Harry M'Dermot Roe* (Joyce, p 287, No 537).

In 1927, Wood's executors brought out two more 'Irish Dances', also for violin and piano. The first (G major, 6/8, *Moderato*) is founded on two airs, the identities of which have so far eluded research, and the second (A minor, 2/4, *Allegro moderato*) founded on two song-airs: *The dew on the grass* (Joyce, p 112, No 231) and the *Sho-ho lullaby* (Joyce, p 57, No 112).

Wood also left behind him the fair copy MS of a similar violin and piano arrangement based on two Irish hornpipes (G major, 2/4), *The Silvermines* (Joyce, p 16, No 27) and *Ardlamon* (Joyce, p 22, No 39), and sketches of three similar arrangements which are capable of complete reconstruction[15]. There is, further, a delightful sketch arrangement of *The Tullach Reel* (Feis Coil collection No 15) for 'cello and piano (A minor, 4/4).

These arrangements have much in common with the solo-voice folk-song arrangements. There is the same appositeness of accompaniment, the same effective choice and, in this case, contrast of melody, and the same unerring use of a simple though subtle harmonic palette. As recreative pieces for string players they will stand comparison with many of the popular gems currently in vogue, and they certainly deserve to be better known.

Wood's piano music is inconsiderable in bulk and dates from his earlier years. One of his first surviving works is a piano sonata in G major written while he was still at Armagh (the MS is dated July 27, 1882). Like the early violin sonata discussed above, it has a Schubertian diffuseness, especially in the first and last of its four movements. The slow movement (E flat major, 3/4, *Adagio cantabile*) shows how early Wood interested himself in variation-writing, and the fact that the next movement (the *Scherzo*) is in E minor can be interpreted as representing either audacity or indifference with regard to key relationships between movements.

By the time he was 16, Wood's counterpoint studies with Dr Marks had progressed to the point where he could throw off a respectable academic fugue — as, for instance, the piano fugue in A minor (MS dated September 1, 1882), replete with all the requisite fugal devices. His next piano work, however, a set of *Variations and Fugue on a theme of Beethoven*, written two years later (MS dated July 1884) shows greater individuality and general technical mastery. The influence of Beethoven (and, it may be added,

Brahms) is now paramount and Wood's ability to handle a large-scale structure (ten variations plus an extended fugue) with a cumulative increase in intensity is noteworthy. The variations show Wood in an uncompromisingly serious mood (as befitted a young student in an English musical world founded, pianistically speaking, largely on trivialities), and we may perhaps regret that he followed this line no further.

Wood's only published opus for the piano — one can use that term since, in common with a few other of his earliest published works, it was graced with an opus number, 6 — was his *Four Characteristic Pieces in Canon*, published in 1893 (the first was dated October 6, 1892, and the remainder June 1893, Cambridge). These pieces, all based on canons at the octave, owe something to the example of Schumann, but more to the style of Parry (one is reminded of the latter's *Shulbrede Tunes*), and are remarkable for their ingenuity and for the amount of musicality they are able to display despite it.

The opening of the first piece will serve as an example:

Example 41

Although Wood's piano music is of little importance in his total output the same cannot be said of his organ music. In the main, Victorian organ compositions, when original, had tended to be the work of organists providing fodder for their own recitals, or voluntaries for liturgical employment, and were written for the Victorian organ, which was moving towards the pseudo-orchestral in its tonal resources. The gradual replacement of tracker actions by pneumatic actions had made possible an ease of performance — particularly with regard to *legato* chord- and octave-playing, quick changes of registration, and the like — that brought about a revolution in the general approach to writing for the instrument.

As an organist Wood had certainly come under the influence of Sir Walter Parratt (1841-1924) during his student days at the RCM, and the Parratt school of organ playing, 'founded on accurate part-playing, clean phrasing and simple registration'[16], provided the background for Wood's own organ compositions when, in due course, he turned to this field of writing.

The influence of the Bach revival caused English organ composers to explore the possibilities of producing works akin in style and ethos to

Bach's Chorale Preludes but based on hymn or psalm tunes in the native repertory. Wood was to be active in this field and alongside his masters, Parry (who was not primarily an organist), and Stanford (who, though for many years an organist was, as a composer, prolific in all fields of musical endeavour), took the lead in writing works for the instrument of more serious import than the general run of similar works produced by their organist contemporaries.

Wood's first published organ composition appeared in 1908 as No 23 in a series of organ compositions brought out under Stanford's general editorship. This work, *Variations and Fugue on Winchester Old* (the metrical psalm-tune commonly sung to *While Shepherds watched their flocks by night*), consists of nine variations with a link movement joining them to an elaborate chorale fugue. They are mainly 'classical' variations — in the sense that the structure and harmonic implications of the tune provide the framework binding them together, and the first five variations are severely though unobtrusively canonic in texture. For example, variation two is a double canon:

Example 42

Variations six to eight, which are more relaxed in idiom, have perhaps the lovelier music — as, for example, in the use of the parallel-sixths formula in variation seven (*see Example 43, opposite*).

The final fugue is an exhilarating affair, with lively movement in the manual parts contrasting with the solidity of the psalm tune as a *cantus firmus* on the pedals.

Number 24 in the same series, also published in 1908, was Wood's *Three Preludes founded on Melodies from the Genevan Psalter* (presumably the French-Genevan Psalter of 1551)[17]. Wood's interest in, and indeed devotion to, the psalm tunes and chorale melodies of the 16th and 17th centuries, and his wide use of them in both vocal and instrumental works, is almost unique among British composers. In utilising psalm tunes as a basis for

Example 43

chorale preludes Wood was, of course, taking a calculated risk that they might not be much performed since the melodies were, with a few exceptions, little known to the generality of organists. He seems to have taken note of the various ways of treating a chorale melody used by Bach in the *Orgelbüchlein*, by Brahms in the late chorale preludes, and generally by Karg Elert and Reger among the more recent Germans; but an examination of his psalm-tune preludes, taken as a whole, leaves one impressed by the considerable variety and originality of treatments employed.

The first prelude on the tune for Psalm XII, *Exaudi Domine* (Frost p 395, quoting Zahn no 900; D minor, 6/8, *Poco allegretto*) uses the first four notes of the *cantus firmus* as a figure which is developed with great skill and economy (S A B):

Example 44

The psalm tune itself appears in long notes as the tenor. The prelude exhibits that tender austerity characteristic of so much of Wood's organ music.

The second prelude, on the tune for *The Song of Simeon* (*Nunc Dimittis*; Frost pp 208-9, A major, 2/4, *Andante sostenuto*) opens with two preludial bars; then, over a lovely semi-quaver figure, rather like the accompaniment figure in Somervell's *Shepherd's Cradle Song*, the psalm tune is presented in canon at the octave. The prelude is rounded off with a four-bar coda that mirrors the opening. There is both tenderness and subdued power in this prelude.

The third prelude of the set is founded on the tune for Psalm CXXIV (*Nisi quia Dominus*), that same tune (Frost, pp 169-70) commonly sung nowadays to the words 'Turn back, O man, forswear thy foolish ways'. It presents the tune, in the outer parts, as a canon at the fourth below (D major, 2/2, *Allegro con brio*), with a leaping 'joy' motif between them:

Example 45

The whole is rounded off by an extended ten-bar coda founded on the first line of the tune with the 'joy' motif in the bass.

Four years later, in 1912, Wood followed up the three preludes by bringing out, under Stanford's editorship, *Sixteen Preludes for the Organ* (founded on Melodies from the English and Scottish Psalters), in two volumes. These preludes differ from the three earlier psalm-tune preludes in that they are based solely on the tunes themselves, rather than the tunes in the context of the particular psalms with which they were associated (a wise precaution since the association of a tune with a particular psalm is by no means universal or inviolate).

The first set opens with a very dramatic prelude on *St Mary's* (Frost, p 407; D minor, 4/4, *Adagio*). After some introductory matter derived from the tune, the tune itself is heard complete on the swell (without pedals), harmonized with agonised appoggiaturas in the inner parts. Then follows a brief interlude based on the first line of the tune in diminution. The full tune is then repeated, this time on the pedals in octaves. A closely-packed development section heralds a return to the mood of the opening, and the work ends *ppp* on a D major chord.

The second prelude, on the proper tune to the *Old LXXVIIth Psalm* (Frost, pp 127-8; E flat major, 3/4, *Poco allegretto*), presents the psalm tune in triple time on the pedals, with a descant counter melody above a rather angular rising quaver figure on the manuals. It is a subdued and forbidding work, though not without an austere dignity.

The third prelude of the set is a trio movement based upon *Martyrs' Tune* (Frost, pp 257-8; C minor, 4/4, *Adagio*) in which the psalm tune, in the treble, is given in a highly decorated form:

Example 46

becoming

Example 47

The fourth is a most interesting treatment of *Cheshire Tune* (Frost, p 203; F minor, 2/4, *Andante con moto*) in which an opening section of 29 bars (manuals only), based on the first line of the tune in diminution, is followed by the whole tune in the tenor in octaves, with the opening melody now in the treble and bass, set as an invertible canon. The whole effect is one of elemental strength.

York Tune (otherwise *The Stilt*, vide Frost, p 256; D flat major, 4/4, *Adagio*) is one of the most attractive of the preludes, alternating a diminution of the tune's opening with some development of individual motifs cemented with some very personal harmonic progressions which anticipate *Expectans Expectavi*. The complete psalm tune, as such, does not appear.

Newtown Tune (Frost, p 267; F major, 4/4, *Allegretto*) is treated with the first two lines presented as a *cantus firmus* in the treble, having imitative parts in diminution of the opening notes below. The first two lines are then heard again in the pedals, with the imitative parts above. The same procedure is then followed with the last two lines of the tune, the whole being rounded off by a short coda over a tonic pedal.

A similar structural sequence is followed in the rather melancholy prelude on *Southwell* (Frost, p 106; A minor, 4/4, *Adagio*) except that this time each single line of the tune is heard alternating in the treble and bass. The accompanying grief-laden counterpoints are not derived directly from the *cantus firmus*.

The first book of the preludes is rounded off by a jubilant setting of the proper tune for Psalm CXIII (Frost, p 158; F major, 2/2, *Allegro vivace*) when, under a thematically derived quaver counterpoint, the psalm tune is presented in canon at the octave between the 'mene' and bass.

The second volume opens with a spacious and rather stern setting of the tune associated with the *Old CXXXVIth Psalm* (Frost, p 188; D minor, 2/2, *Allegro maestoso*) in which the odd-numbered lines, presented in simple four-part harmony, and the even-numbered lines, in octaves in the treble, are supported by throbbing triplets. There is a climactic coda in the tonic major.

The second prelude, on the *Lincoln Tune* (Frost, p 283; G major, 4/4, *Allegretto*) has the plain tune in the bass (8 pedal) with an independent texture — suggestive of bells — with a two-against-three-cross-rhythm on the choir and swell (the whole being written in invertible counterpoint). It is by far the most joyous prelude in the book.

The third prelude is based on the proper tune to *Psalm CXXXVI* (Frost, p 189; A flat major, 4/4, *Adagio*) and is constructed as a close canon at the octave between the treble (thickened out with chords) and the bass (pedals), with a throbbing triplet 'mene'. It is an austere setting with few in the way of ingratiating qualities.

It is followed by a lilting pastoral movement (G major 9/8, *Allegretto pastorale*) based on the tune written by Henry Carey (1685-1745) for Addison's paraphrase of the twenty-third psalm ('The Lord my pasture shall prepare') known to our hymn-books as 'Carey's' or 'Surrey' (*see Example 48, opposite*).

The prelude on the *Old CIVth Psalm Tune* (Frost, p 152; A minor, 9/4, *Molto maestoso*) uses motifs drawn from the tune and filled out with fistfuls of chords on the manuals, with the psalm tune itself in a decorated form on the pedals. Again there is an atmosphere of elemental strength about the setting.

The prelude on the *Old XXVth Psalm* (Frost, p 88; E major, 4/4, *Andante sostenuto*) has more of an airy lightness and a rather Brahms-like

Example 48

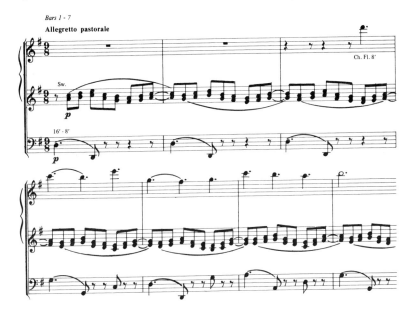

Bars 1 - 7

Allegretto pastorale

texture in its four-part harmony. The psalm tune itself is presented between chains of parallel sixths in the right hand, with a staccato pedal below, the whole being preluded and postluded by matter for manuals alone deriving directly from the tune.

The seventh prelude is headed *Nunc Dimittis (from Sternhold and Hopkins)* (Frost, p 83; D flat major, 3/4, *Adagio ma non troppo*) and makes use of a canon at the fifth below in the right hand over a rhythmic figure in the left, both over the psalm tune itself on the pedals. One is reminded of a river winding its way inexorably towards the sea.

The second volume is rounded off by a prelude on the *Old CXXXII Psalm Tune* (Frost, p 182; A major, 3/4, *Allegro*) which is avowedly pastiche Bach, the manuals having typical Bachian figuration (derived none-the-less from the tune) while the unadorned psalm tune itself — in triple time — is heard on the pedals. Again, it is a highly exhilarating affair and concludes the sequence as with a joyful dance.

When one considers these 19 psalm-tune preludes as a whole, one is struck by the variety of treatments involved — indeed no two tunes are elaborated in exactly the same way. Not for nothing did Vaughan Williams comment that in teaching the craft of composition Wood was unrivalled. It is the combination of this technical virtuosity coupled with the display of

71

disciplined musicality in the matter composed that makes the preludes so important, both as works of art in their own right and as landmarks in the history of English organ music.

In 1915, Wood published some teaching pieces for organ — *Bourrées I & II* (G minor, *L'istesso tempo*) and a *Gigue* (G minor, 6/8, *Molto allegro*) — and in 1928 his executors brought out an *Allemande* (G minor, C, *Allegro moderato*), a *Courante* (G minor, 3/4, *Allegro molto*) and a *Sarabande* (G minor, 3/4, *Andante*), the whole being intended to make up a *Suite in the Ancient Style*. They are all bogus baroque suite dances in binary form, cleanly written for two manuals and pedals, and were probably intended as introductory material to prepare a student for the trio sonatas of J S Bach.

Among Wood's posthumous papers was found the incomplete fair-copy manuscript of a set of organ variations on an original theme — 17 bars long and having the unusual phrase structure 5 + 5 + 4 + 3 (D major, 2/4, *Andante*). The first three variations, based in classical fashion on the structure of the theme, are complete, and the fourth is half-finished (a rough sketch which has also survived shows the openings of two further variations). One feels that this work might have developed into something substantial and is left wondering why the composer abandoned it.

On October 7, 1918, Sir Hubert Parry died, and a few years later there was published *A little Organ Book in memory of Sir Hubert Parry*, which bore the following foreword: 'At Sir Hubert Parry's funeral in St Paul's Cathedral on October 16, 1918, a few of his friends made a small wreath of melodies which were woven together and played. The pieces in this Book have been written and given by these friends and a few besides, as a rather larger wreath, in memory of him.' Wood was among the twelve composers who contributed to it[18], and his piece, an *Andante* (D major, 2/4), turns out to be based on the theme from the abandoned variations — indeed its first 17 bars are note-for-note the same. Such, however, is Wood's craftsmanship that one would not suspect that the continuation — a gentle meditation on the theme — was a subsequent development.

In 1933, seven years after Wood's death, his *Prelude and Fugue in G minor* was published, and prompted an enthusiastic review from Harvey Grace, writing in the *Musical Times*[19]: 'Usually one regards posthumous publications with a certain degree of misgiving, too often justified by results. Charles Wood's *Prelude and Fugue in G minor . . .* is a notable exception. It is, perhaps, the finest of Wood's organ works, containing all the science that we look for, plus an unexpected degree of real passion in its final pages. In many respects, too, it is original. The *Prelude* is elegiac in character (suggestive of an Irish Lament) — an *Adagio* with a middle section of a more cheerful character. The fugue is in alternating bars of two-four and three-four — in other words in five-four time — and its subject at once foreshadows interesting harmonic results, the C sharp of the opening phrase being noted as D flat in the second phrase and used in the minor ninth of F major. The fugue is a double one, but the composer spares us the usual lengthy excursions by combining the two subjects after a brief exposition of the second. Up to this point the music has been of the normal, rather severe type we expect from Wood, but there follow half a dozen pages highly dramatic in character, though there are present also some ingenious stretti. A solo Tuba is needed here, though the work is playable on an ordinary three manual.'

Little more need be said except to note that the final *stretto maestrale*, in which the subject is combined with itself both in augmentation and diminution, is a wonderful example of the art that conceals art.

Finally it may be mentioned that among a pile of Wood's rough MSS were found two organ fugues — one on a chorale — that are typical in their economy and polish of the work of a musician to whom good counterpoint was second nature.

A few of Wood's organ works are in the general repertory, but his other instrumental pieces have been largely forgotten. It is high time that they were revived. There is so much good music here — music that ought to be heard again. After the earthquake and the fire, the still small voice has its own consoling virtues.

NOTES

1. Among the early and mid-Victorians, Sterndale Bennett (1816-75) wrote a string quartet in G minor (1831), a sextet for piano and strings in F sharp minor (1835) and a piano trio in A minor (1839); George Macfarren (1813-87) 'made a valiant attempt to break into the field of the string quartet (the precedents were Bishop's quartet in C minor, of 1816, and examples by Barnett, Walmisley and Ouseley) by composing six works of this order. Apart from the first in G minor, they were, however, undistinguished and rapidly passed into limbo' (see Young, Dr Percy M, *A History of British Music*; London, Benn, 1967, p 454); and Cipriani Potter (1792-1871), who produced, *inter alia*, a sextet for piano, flute, clarinet, viola, 'cello and bass, and a horn sonata.
2. String quartet No 1 in G minor, 1867; No 2 in C minor, 1868; Nonet for Wind instruments, 1877; Piano trio in E minor, 1878; Fantasy sonata in B minor for violin and piano, 1878; Piano quartet in A flat major, 1879; String quartet No 3 in G major, 1878-80; 'Cello sonata in A major, 1883; String quintet in E flat major, 1884; Piano trio in B minor, 1884; Piano trio in G major, 1884-90.
3. 'Cello sonata in A major (Op 9); Violin sonata in D major (Op 11); Piano quartet in F major (Op 15), 1882; Piano quintet in D minor (Op 25), 1886; Piano trio No 1 in E flat major (Op 35), 1889; String quartet No 1 in G major (Op 44), 1887; String quartet No 2 in A minor (Op 45), 1887; String quartet No 3 in D major (Op 64), 1897; Piano trio No 2 in C minor (Op 73), 1899; 'Cello sonata No 2 in D minor (Op 39), 1893; String quintet No 1 in F major (Op 85), 1903; String quintet No 2 in C minor (Op 86); Serenade-Nonet for strings/wind (Op 95); String quartet No 4 in G minor (Op 99); String quartet No 5 in B flat major (Op 104), 1908; String quartet No 6 in A minor (Op 122); Clarinet sonata (or

viola) (Op 129); Piano quartet (Op 133); Piano trio No 3 in A major (Op 158), 1918; String quartet No 7 in C major (Op 166); String quartet No 8 in E minor (Op 167).

4. Scott, Marion M, 'The Chamber Music of Charles Wood', in 'Chamber Music — a Supplement to *The Music Student*,' No 18, January 1916, pp 42-44.
5. Dent, Prof Edward J, Introduction to *Charles Wood — 8 String Quartets* (London, OUP, 1929).
6. There is a mass of miscellaneous sketches, of string quartet fragments and of folk-tunes arranged for string quartet in short score.
7. *Vide* Scott, Marion M, *op cit*, and Dunhill, Thomas F., article in *Cobbett's Cyclopedic Survey of Chamber Music* edited by Walter Wilson Cobbett, 1st edition, London, OUP, 1922.
8. When the collected edition of Wood's quartets was published in 1929, this statement stirred up considerable controversy concerning the morality of basing instrumental works on unacknowledged folk-material, and whether there was more musical virtue in folk-influenced as opposed to Brahms-influenced thematic material. See Walker, Ernest, 'Charles Wood's String Quartet', *Monthly Musical Record*, Vol 59, No 708, December 2, 1929, pp 1-2, and Hull, Robin: 'Charles Wood, Quartet in D'. *The Listener*, Vol 17, No 418, January 13, 1937, p 96.
9. The first holiday for some years without their children. Wood was very insistent on the necessity for a composer of 'keeping his hand in', and is said to have composed this quartet especially with this purpose in mind.
10. Walker, *op.cit.*
11. The first prize was awarded to Frank Bridge. The Cobbett medal, for services to chamber music, was awarded to Wood posthumously in 1932.
12. Marion Scott gives this date — the published score says 1916.
13. Joyce, P W, *Old Irish Folk Music and Songs*, London: Longmans, Green & Co, Dublin: Hodges, Figgis & Co, 1909.
14. Planxty — 'A harp tune of a sportive and animated character, moving in triplets. It is not intended for, or often adaptable to, words, and is slower in pace than a jig' (Stainer and Barrett). The planxty used does not conform very closely to this definition.
15. The first is founded on two reels, *The nine points of knavery* (Joyce No 447, p 251) and a *Clare Reel* (Hoffman edition of Petrie, No 81). The second is founded on three melodies which have been identified as *The Hornless Cow* (Hoffman edition of Petrie, No 112), a *Hop-jig* (Hoffman edition of Petrie No 16), and *Black Bush* (Hoffman edition of Petrie, No 126). The third is based on two melodies, the first of which has been identified as *The Violet* (Joyce, no 708, p 354).
16. See the article on Parratt in Grove (5th edition), Vol 6, p 560.
17. Wood seems to have followed the versions of the psalm tunes quoted in Zahn. In this study I shall quote the versions given in Frost, Dr Maurice, *English and Scottish Psalm and Hymn Tunes, c 1543-1677*, London, SPCK and OUP, 1953.
18. The other composers who contributed included Stanford, Herbert Brewer, Allan Gray, Charles Macpherson, Ivor Atkins, Frank Bridge, Harold Darke, Walter Alcock, Thalben Ball, Henry Ley and Walford Davies.
19. *The Musical Times*, Vol 75, No 1095, May 1934, p 418.

CHAPTER 5

The stage works

E J Dent once related that Wood had confided in him his regret that he had not been able to centre his musical output on works for the concert room and the stage[1]. Whether this represented a permanent conviction, or merely a temporary feeling of dissatisfaction with his composing lot, we do not know; but there is little doubt that had he been born in another time or country, Wood could have been a considerable composer of operas, *cf* Saint-Saens. He lacked that necessary assertiveness of temperament, that ingrained pertinacity or, indeed, pugnacity, in the furthering of his own artistic interests, that would have enabled him to gain an operatic hearing in Victorian or Edwardian England (*cf* Stanford himself or Dame Ethel Smyth).

Despite the example of his elder brother, whose operetta *The Bride of Cambus* appeared in 1883, Wood does not seem to have attempted any music for the stage until 1890, when the commission came his way to provide the music for the Cambridge Greek play of that year, the *Ion* of Euripides. It is possible that Stanford, who sat on the organizing committee, in company with several other distinguished Cambridge men — including Professor Jebb (the president), Oscar Browning, and M R James — may have been instrumental in putting Wood's name forward. Certainly he associated himself in a very practical way with the production as 'trainer of the Chorus' and, we learn from the *Times* review, as conductor.

The prestige of these University Greek plays, both in Oxford and Cambridge, in the 1880s and '90s was considerable. They were the subject of long and thoughtful notices by the august music and dramatic critics of the serious London papers, and special matinée performances were given for the convenience of London-based audiences. What proportion of these audiences (whether London or provincial) were familiar enough with classical Greek to follow the action without the adventitious aid of a translation may be a matter for speculation, but, as his sketch-books show, there is no doubt that Wood himself was sufficient of a Grecian to set the language directly and with precision.

Wood's music for the *Ion* (his Op 4), which received its first performance on November 19, 1890, survives in the form of a printed vocal-score and a large MS full-score and set of parts[2]. Two practical considerations affected the writing: the size of the orchestral pit at the theatre, and the absence of female voices in the chorus. Wood's theatre orchestra consisted of 1 flute, 1 oboe, 2 clarinets (A), 1 bassoon, 2 horns (E), 1 trumpet (E), timpani (E and B), and strings, and his skill in handling it attracted the attention of the contemporary reviewers.

The disposition of the music was as follows:

ACT 1

1   Prelude (E major, 3/4, *Moderato con moto*)
2   Entry music for Ion (A major, 3/4, *Andante sostenuto*)
3   Solo (Ion) and Chorus (A major, 3/4, *Andante sostenuto*)
4   Melodrama 1 (E major, 3/4, *Poco adagio*)
5   Melodrama 2 (C major, C, *Moderato*)
6   Chorus (E flat major, 3/4, *Allegro ma non troppo*)

ACT 2

7   Introduction (G major, 3/4, *Maestoso*)
8   Chorus (D minor, ₵, *Allegro agitato*)
9   Melodrama 3 (No fixed tonality, C, *Andante*)
10 Melodrama 4 (A flat major, 3/4)

PRELUDIAL SCENE TO ACT 3

11 Introduction and Chorus (F minor, C, *Allegro moderato*)
12 Entr'acte (B flat major, 6/8, *Poco allegretto*)

ACT 3

13 Introduction and Chorus (C minor, 6/8, *Allegro agitato*)
14 Melodrama and Chorus (C minor, 6/8, *Allegro agitato*)
15 Melodrama (A minor, 3/4, *Sostenuto*)
16 Chorus (C major, 3/4, *Andante pesante*)
17 Entry music for Athena (E flat major, 3/4, *Allegretto tranquillo*)
18 Final Chorus (D major, C, *Allegro moderato alla marcia*).

Although a number of these items are in fact only a few bars long, the full score itself runs to 187 pages, and the elaborate chorus sections, especially, show Wood making the most of his dramatic and musical opportunities. An extract from the original *Times* review is of interest in this connection[3]:

> The music . . . is extremely clever; most effectively scored for small orchestra, and thoroughly appropriate. The pretty solo for Ion in the opening scene, the charming close of the First Act, the suggestion for which is taken from the description of the 'Haunt of Pan' sung by the chorus, the graceful and original introduction to the Third Act, are the most successful portions of the score, but some of the short incidental passages and the final march call also for commendation. On Thursday, at the first performance, the audience did

their best to drown the music by their conversation, but enough was heard to give brilliant promise for the composer's future career.

In general Wood may be said to be employing his 'Max Bruch' style at its most effective. There is no attempt to write 'antique music', though there are occasional glimpses, as with Fauré, of modal influences — a near-phrygian cadence, for example

Example 49

a melody in the myxolydian mode,

Example 50

or the use of juxtaposed root position triads at certain pivotal points in the score, as for instance at the entry of Ion:

Example 51

Wood himself seems to have been unhappy about his music, or so we may judge from the existence of a consolatory reference in a letter to him from Grove[4]: 'I like what you say about your Greek play — I feel with you (if I may say so without presumption) in the little unimportant literary work it has been given me to do. As to being satisfied with it I never feel near that point! I was struck half an hour ago with a remark of *Leopardi* quoted by M Arnold as to great writers "who are modest in that they compare themselves, not with other men, but with that idea of the perfect which they have before their mind".'

The impression made by the *Ion* music doubtless contributed towards his being invited to write the music for the next Cambridge Greek play production, the *Iphigenia in Tauris* of 1894 (in fact the *Times* critic publicly asserted that this was so). The performance took place on November 30 and was conducted, as were the subsequent performances, by Wood himself. The use of the same theatre meant the same sized orchestral pit, so Wood used the same orchestral resources as in the *Ion*. It is unfortunate that the original full-score has disappeared and that of the original orchestral material only the instrumental parts of those movements that were utilised in the Orchestral Suite have survived. Nevertheless, sufficient remains for the quality of the orchestral writing to be assessed. For the rest of the music we must rely on the published vocal score.

The music was arranged as follows:

ACT 1
1   Prelude (D minor, 3/4, *Lento*)
2   Slow march (E major, C, *Andante sostenuto*)
3   Chorus (D minor, 3/4, *Andante*)

ACT 2
4   Introduction (B minor, C, *Molto adagio*)
5   Chorus (E minor, 4/4, *Andante sostenuto*)
6   Entr'acte (A minor, 6/8, *Poco allegretto*)

ACT 3
7   Introduction (D minor, 3/4, *Allegro con brio*)
8   Chorus (D major, 3/4, *Maestoso*)
9   Adagio (E flat major, 3/4, *Adagio*)
10   Final Chorus (B flat major, ₵, *Allegro maestoso*)

Wood's music again made a considerable impression, at least to judge from the comments made in contemporary reviews. The *Times* critic delivered himself as follows[5]:

Mr Wood's prelude is based on two subjects — a vigorous phrase in D minor of unmistakably tragic cast and a capitally contrasted theme in the relative major, a beautiful melody of happier expression; possibly the first is meant to represent the cruel office that the exiled Iphigenia is required to perform as the votary of Artemis, and the second the brighter prospects that her flight opens before her. The first is heard again in the orchestral opening of the chorus that divides the first from the second act, a finely-conceived musical description of the voyage of the two friends. In the course of the first act the only piece of incidental music is a graceful and appropriate accompaniment to the offering made by Iphigenia on behalf of the brother who she believes to be dead. A short introduction to the second act is separated by the whole of that act from the 'halcyon' chorus before referred to. This has received a musical setting that is entirely worthy of it; beginning with a sorrowful subject of ballad-like simplicity, in which a reference to the Phrygian (ecclesiastical) mode seems to be intended, the chorus is developed with very remarkable skill to a vivid anticipation of the happy home-coming that is predicted for the brother and sister. The home-sickness of the maidens who are left behind is finely conceived in the music, but the effect is weakened by the employment of a male choir. The charming orchestral pictures of the sea voyage and the dances that will greet the return of the wanderers remind the hearer not a little of some of Max Bruch's best work in the same kind, and the chorus is a work of distinct power and beauty, which must be placed higher than anything the composer has yet done. The fine hymn to Apollo, which, according to the Cambridge arrangements, divides the two scenes of the third act, is broad and dignified, and its musical interest is well sustained; and the final chorus, or epilogue, is a melodious march-measure, akin to more than one of the finales that have been heard here for the first time.

The orchestration is extremely skilful, and the composer has done his best with the resources at his command. With a band of 23 it is not possible to produce very broad effects, but Mr Wood has wisely preferred refinement to grandeur. His use of a solo violin and a solo viola in the 'Halcyon' chorus is extremely happy.

The fact that the score consists of only ten numbers — as opposed to the 18 of the *Ion* music — means that there are fewer of those tiny vignettes, a few bars only in length, that characterised the earlier score. Melodramas have been dropped altogether.

Again, as in the *Ion* music, there is no deliberate attempt to produce an 'antique' score (the sundry fragments of ancient Greek music, then recently discovered and tentatively transcribed — the *Epitaph of Seikilos*, for example — were wholly ignored). In comparison with the *Ion* music there is a greater amplitude of melody (often very Parry-like) and if one is still reminded of Max Bruch, at least Bruch had a strong predilection for classical subjects[6].

To select characteristic snippets from what is a remarkably homogeneous score is not easy, but one may note especially the Slow March (number 2) in

Act 1:

Example 52

the opening of the 'halcyon' chorus (number 5) in Act 2,

Example 53

and the broad tune of the final march (*see Example 54, opposite*).

The classics no longer occupy that dominating position in university studies that once they held, and there have been no Greek play performances either at Oxford or Cambridge since the 1920s. To perform either the *Ion* or the *Iphigenia* using the English translations made especially by Dr A W Verrall (1851-1912) would be to offer a poor substitute for the original, so the chances of hearing Wood's music revived in its proper context may be

80

Example 54

No. 10 (bars 1 - 4)

counted negligible. On the other hand, if some enterprising conductor, following in Beecham's footsteps, revived the *Iphigenia in Tauris Suite* we could well be charmed by the quality of imagination displayed in the music.

It must have been in the late 1890s or early 1900s (to judge by the musical calligraphy) that Wood began the preliminary sketches for *Pat in Fairyland*, 'A FANTASTIC OPERA in a Prologue and Three Acts by John Todhunter'. Dr John Todhunter (1839-1916), a medical man who nevertheless became Professor of English at Alexander College, Dublin, in 1870, though now generally forgotten, was a not unimportant figure in the history of the 19th-century Irish literary movements[7]. We do not know why the work was left unfinished, though one senses a division of aims as between Wood and his librettist, the former being apparently wishful to write a romantic and lyrical fantasy (to judge from the surviving music), with the latter inclining more towards a comic opera in the Gilbertian tradition. At all events the project foundered and Wood's contribution eventually found its way into the library of Gonville and Caius College, while the libretto is preserved in the library of Reading University (MS 202/4/5/1).

Of Wood's music there survives an incomplete overture (16 pages of full score plus two pages of short score sketches), almost the whole of the Prologue in two scenes (80 pages of full score) and the opening of the First Act proper (17 pages of full score). Wood's rough sketches also survive for the greater part of the second and third acts.

The plot may be briefly summarised as follows:

PROLOGUE (*Scene One*)
Setting — the grounds of Castle Rackrent, somewhere in Ireland.
Two boys, Willie and Tommy, are playing among the haycocks when their elder sister, Mary, comes to call them in for supper and bed. There is an altercation between them, but finally they agree to behave if Pat, a farm-worker, will tell them a story as he has promised. Pat enters and eventually embarks on a comic ballad about an Irish giant. He breaks off on seeing the estate agent, Mr Crawley, in the distance and asserts that Crawley, having a down on him, will soon turn him off the estate. The family assure him of their protection, but he insists that there is nothing for it but to leave this world for Fairyland, and explains how this may be done. Fairy voices are heard calling

81

and the venue changes to:

(Scene Two)

Fairyland, itself. The Lord High Chamberlain of Fairyland meets up with a set of mythical and historical characters who introduce themselves severally and at length. Eventually they join together in chorus to greet the arrival of Angus Ogue (the Fairy King). Mary, Pat and the boys awaken to find themselves in Fairyland. Angus Ogue greets the newly arrived strangers. Pat and Mary are recognised as having royal connections (they are the lost son of the King of Munster and the lost daughter of the High King of Tara, respectively), and being thus ennobled, Pat embarks on a passionate love-song. Angus Ogue interrupts with the warning that great deeds must be accomplished before Pat (now Prince Cormac) and Mary (now Princess Maurya) may be betrothed. A magic sword must be won — the boys are to be its guardians — and the Prologue ends with an impressive tableau.

ACT ONE

Setting — the Palace of the High King of all Ireland, at Tara.

The King is looking and feeling seedy, and the Queen and their three daughters (Princesses Nora, Enna and Maurya) reprove him for his unkempt appearance and ask him what is the matter. In an *Aria* he informs them that an anthropophagous giant has arrived in the land and is demanding the three Princesses as tribute. It is decided that the Court Herald shall summon a 'Champion' to come forward who is prepared to fight the giant in single combat. The Herald's first clarion call is heard (off stage) but, instead of a champion, three dwarfs (emissaries of the giant) enter with a formal demand for the Princesses to be handed over. The King sends a defiant message and is about to proclaim himself his own champion when the Herald's summons is heard again and 'Leitmotif' the squire of a Seigfried-like figure, 'Dummkopf', enters, closely followed by his master. There is much fun with a 'cap of darkness', in the midst of which a second would-be champion, a very Scottish figure, 'Prince Malcolm', enters with his attendant 'Sandy', followed shortly afterwards by the much travel-stained 'Prince Cormac'. All three offer themselves as champions and conveniently pair off, Dummkopf with Nora, Malcolm with Enna, and Cormac with Maurya. The act ends with a passionate love duet between the two latter.

ACT TWO

Setting — a wood near Tara.

The two boys are guarding the sword, buried to its hilt in a stone. Dummkopf and Malcolm enter with their attendants and fail to release it. Cormac enters, releases the sword and is girded with it. The King and Queen and all their court enter, and the King sings a comic song about the approaching confrontation. The three Princesses are ceremonially bound to adjacent trees, and the three champions agree on an order of battle. In turn Dummkopf and Malcolm are overcome by the giant. Finally Cormac vanquishes him, severing his head, and while he releases the captive Princesses, Dummkopf (who has recovered somewhat) steals the giant's head. Both Enna and Nora make

Cormac flattering proposals, much to Maurya's disgust, but Cormac remains true to her.

ACT THREE

Setting — back in the Palace of the High King of all Ireland.

Dummkopf, producing the head, demands half the kingdom as a reward. There is a general squabble which is settled by the severed head itself revealing the truth. Dummkopf exits in disgust. The giant, brought back to life again, re-enters metamorphosed into Sir John Bull, an English gentleman — he wins the regard of Nora, so with a triple betrothal all ends happily.

Readers may well recognise parallels between this farrago and later English comic opera such as Holst's *The Perfect Fool* and Vaughan Williams's *The Poisoned Kiss*; indeed, Wood's librettist, in introducing a comic pseudo-Wagnerian figure, anticipated the 'Traveller' in the former work by some years. One might wonder, conversely, whether the idea of having a severed head on the stage was suggested by Strauss's *Salome*, which appeared in 1905, and how the stage-craft for manipulating a *singing* head was to be managed.

Musically the work is a mixture. There are folk-song-like tunes, the King's lament in Act One, for instance:

Example 55

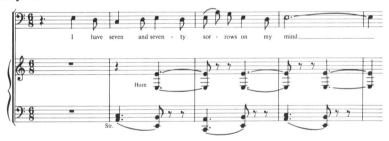

spoof Wagner for Dummkopf and his squire:

Example 56

83

The Dwarfs utter their demand to the music of the *British Grenadiers*, and the final love duet in Act One has an Italianate amplitude of passion:

Example 57

Despite the use of what may be thought of as 'set numbers' the operatic texture itself is continuous, and although there are certain character motifs appearing, appropriately, at different points in the work, the texture itself may be regarded as more Verdian than Wagnerian. There is a stylistic dichotomy as between the set numbers (which tend to be folk-song influenced) and the interconnecting recitatives, the music of which has much less individuality. The choruses are mainly homophonic and give the impression of being part-songs writ large. One suspects that Wood was influenced to some extent by the example of Stanford's opera *Shamus O'Brien* (1896), which, as a recent successful revival has demonstrated, has a very similar pedigree[8].

The critics, in noticing this recent production, have commented on the assurance and beauty of the orchestration, and there might have been a similar reaction had the unfinished Wood opera been completed and performed, for the scoring is both economical and effective[9]. Had the overture been completed it would have made a pleasing concert item outside its operatic context. It is based on material taken from the opera itself, and has something of that same compactness and vivacity that is associated with the operatic overtures of Wolf-Ferrari.

Other tunes from the Prologue worth quoting by way of indication of the musical significance of the whole are: Pat's ballad in scene one (*Example 58*), the opening of scene two (*Example 59*), and the fairies chorus from the same scene (*Example 60*).

Whatever the reason for Wood's failure to complete the work, the result was to lock up a lot of good music, for Wood never made any further use of the *Pat in Fairyland* material in any other connection.

From his youth Wood had been a Dickensian, and was, as such, a devoted student of *Pickwick*. He could quote large chunks of the book by

Example 58

Well 'twas on'st up-on a time in the good old an - cient times When the

Kings were ma - king wars___ an' the Bards were ma - king rhymes

Example 59

Str. & W.W.

heart, and to show oneself as a fellow enthusiast was to exhibit an immediate passport to his regard.

In 1920, when, as a memorial to Sir Hubert Parry, a fully-equipped opera theatre was opened at the RCM (now enjoying something of a post-war renaissance under the dynamic directorship of Sir Hugh Allen), the incentive came for Wood to turn again to operatic composition. To take a scene from *Pickwick* and turn it into a short chamber-opera was a natural step, and in December 1921 *A Scene from Pickwick* was completed. It received its first performance on June 20, 1922 (there had been a private dress-rehearsal the previous day). Conducted by Wood's friend and fellow-professor, S P Waddington, *Pickwick* shared a double bill with Vaughan Williams's *The Shepherd of the Delectable Mountains*. It was given twice on this occasion,

Example 60

and was revived on at least two other occasions during Wood's lifetime.

The libretto, which was presumably Wood's own work, is based on the first part of Chapter 18 of *Pickwick* — 'Briefly illustrative of two points — first, the Power of Hysterics, and secondly the Force of Circumstances'. Wood took particular trouble to ascertain beforehand the orchestral resources to be available, scoring the work accordingly for 1 flute, 1 oboe, 2 clarinets (B flat), 1 bassoon, 2 horns (F), 1 trumpet (C), timpani (D and A), and strings. The characters, in order of appearance, are Mr Pott (baritone), Mr Winkle (tenor), Mrs Pott (soprano), and the maid, Goodwin (mezzo-sop).

After a few bars of *A-hunting we will go*, and some portentous octaves on the strings, Mr Pott enters in a passionate rage:

86

Example 61

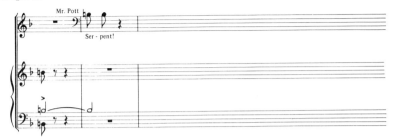

His reading from the offending article in the *Independent* is supported by the sort of chordal accompaniment that old-fashioned organists used to provide for a monotoned 'Lord's Prayer' or 'Creed'.

The 'Lines to a Brass Pott' are set to a hilarious tune, and when the great moment comes and Mrs Pott commences her hysterics, Wood's masterly use of the augmented triad in his orchestral part shows that he was not unaware of the harmonic tricks of composers of more avant-garde temperament than his own:

Example 62

Goodwin, the maid, offers loyal sympathy over a caressing semi-quaver figure in the accompaniment, and Mrs Pott recollects her early love:

Example 63

When, finally, Pott has capitulated, the four characters join in an ensemble in which counterpoint aids characterisation,

Example 64

and *A-hunting we will go* rounds off the work.

A Scene from Pickwick is a little gem. One might not have expected Wood to have so light a hand in managing the totally through-composed operatic technique. The vocal lines are spritely and full of character, the accompanying textures nicely varied, and the orchestration vivid and economical. Even with the accompaniment transferred to the monochrome piano, *Pickwick* would still make a first-rate curtain-raiser for one of those small-scale touring 'intimate' opera groups, whose performances so delight music clubs and schools in remote places.

Its success evidently prompted Wood to cast around for a successor and he turned eventually to another more-or-less self-contained Dickensian episode, the family party and conference at the Pecksniff household, described in Chapter Four of *Martin Chuzzlewit*. Again he was, apparently, his own librettist, and with the exception of the opening words — inserted to make the scene intelligible in the absence of the preceding chapters — there is hardly an alteration to Dickens's dialogue, or of the characters' actions as described by Dickens.

The work was given its first public performance in the Parry Theatre at the RCM on February 12, 1924, having received at least one private performance the previous term. It shared a double-bill with Armstrong Gibbs's *The Blue Peter*[10].

The Family Party exhibits many of the same characteristics made familiar in *A Scene from Pickwick*, though the whole work is on a larger and more elaborate scale. It is scored for 2 flutes, 1 oboe, 2 clarinets (B flat), 2 bassoons, 2 horns (F), 2 trumpets (B flat), 2 timpani (F and C) and strings. The singing characters, in order of appearance, are Merry (soprano), and Cherry (mezzo-soprano) (Pecksniff's daughters), Pecksniff (baritone), Mr Spottletoe (baritone), Ned Chuzzlewit's daughter (soprano), Anthony Chuzzlewit (baritone), Mrs Ned Chuzzlewit (contralto), George Chuzzlewit (tenor) and Nephew (baritone?). There is, in addition, a four-part chorus of relatives.

There is no overture, the curtain rises after a few introductory bars; the texture is continuous, as in *Pickwick*. Pecksniff dominates the operatic scene, just as in the book. He has a motif, an old Irish mixolydian melody (according to J Meredith Tatton, Wood's pupil), which is used to evoke his general character. Out of it all his music grows:

Example 65

When Anthony Chuzzlewit tells Pecksniff not to be a hypocrite, the appropriate motif creeps in in the form of an old chorale played on muted strings as on a bad church organ, and above it Pecksniff sings to his daughter:

Example 66

Wood makes the most of all the humorous points in Dickens's chapter, and adds a few of his own through the use of apposite quotations — as, for instance, when at the mention of 'Swans' there is a wisp of *Lohengrin* in the accompaniment, or when, at a comparison being made between a 'family party' and a 'funeral party', a snatch of the *Funeral March* from Beethoven's piano sonata Op 26 appears. The old English tune *O dear, what can the matter be?* is cleverly adapted to make the final chorus of *Gone, gone, that's what the matter is.*

Wood, composer and Dickens-lover, wrote this score *con amore* and his delight in what he was doing shines through every bar. It would certainly bear revival, for although the harmonic and melodic idiom may seem somewhat dated, the vitality of the music is unaffected by the passage of years. Above all, as with the other Dickens opera, the singers who can act have doubly rewarding roles, for character is manifest in every note of the melodic lines. Had he lived longer, Wood must have explored this vein further.

NOTES

1. See p 21.
2. Preserved in Caius Library.
3. Issue of November 28, 1890, p 11, col 1.
4. Letter written from Kensington Gore and dated September 26 (1890?).
5. Issue of December 1, 1894.
6. His choral works *Odysseus* (Op 41) and *Achilleus* (Op 50), for example.
7. He wrote the biography of 'Patrick Sarsfield' (see p 120).
8. The original version of *Shamus* had spoken dialogue. Stanford added recitatives to turn it into 'Grand Opera' (*cf Carmen*), later.
9. The opera is scored for the following orchestral resources: 2 flutes, 2 oboes, 2 clarinets (B flat), 2 bassoons, 2 horns, 2 trumpets, 2 trombones, 1 bass trombone, timpani, harp, and strings.
10. Armstrong Gibbs had been one of Wood's Cambridge pupils. See Appendix One.

11 Vicar's Hill, Armagh. The tablet over the front door reads 'The birthplace of Charles Wood, Doctor of Music 1866-1926'.

Above: Armagh Cathedral, which has a memorial tablet to Wood.
Below: 17 Cranmer Road, Cambridge, as it was in 1914. The chestnut tree grew from a chestnut planted when Wood's eldest son, Patrick, was born in 1899.

Wood in the Cranmer Road garden, 1925.

Laying the foundation stone at the new Royal College of Music building in 1890. Wood is third from the right in the second row from the front. Among others in the photo are Sir George Grove (centre, back), Sir C V Stanford (with light top hat), Sir Walter Parratt and Sir Hubert Parry (black top hats) and Sir Frederick Bridge (third from right, front row).

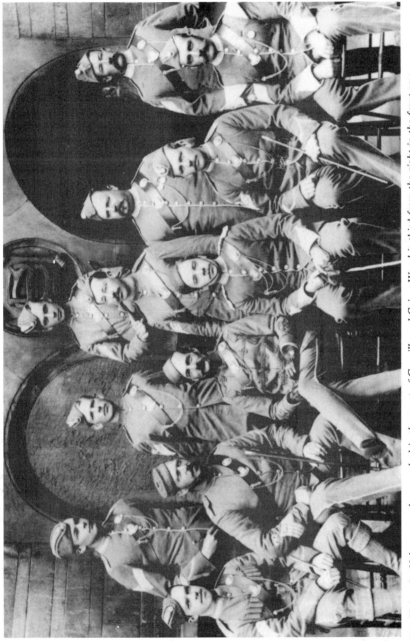

The University Volunteers, photographed in the court of Gonville and Caius. Wood is third from the right in the front row.

TO THE
BELOVED MEMORY OF
CHARLES WOOD,
COMPOSER,
PROFESSOR OF MUSIC IN
THE UNIVERSITY OF CAMBRIDGE,
PROFESSOR & FELLOW OF
THE ROYAL COLLEGE OF MUSIC,
FELLOW OF
CONVILLE & CAIUS COLLEGE,
BORN AT ARMACH, 1866,
DIED AT CAMBRIDGE, 1926.

Wood's gravestone.

CHAPTER 6
The songs

When looked at in the context of the worth of the music produced, the Victorian art-song was at its lowest ebb in 1883, the year of Wood's entry into the Royal College of Music. In terms of the volume of production, however, the composition of art-songs was a booming industry — partly as a consequence of the 'ballad concerts' which, since 1867, had existed primarily to exploit and promote them.

In general, Victorian song may be said to have been derived from one or more of three main seminal influences, with a certain amount of cross-fertilisation. The first was operatic: the Italian opera of the period of Rossini and his immediate successors — for example, *Lo, hear the gentle lark* (published 1864), composed by Sir Henry Bishop (1786-1855), complete with flute *obligato*. The second harked back to the English 'ballad opera' style of the 18th century, eg *Simon the Cellarer* (published 1847) by J L Hatton (1809-1886). The third influence, and one which was particularly important, was the solo lied and duet style of Mendelssohn (further watered down): Hatton's *To Anthea* (1867) is a characteristic example. The more sentimental French and Italian vocal Romances made another significant contribution, and after the years 1870-75, when Gounod was living in London, his stylistic example was avidly followed by those aspiring to write 'Sacred Songs'.

It must not be thought that there were no good songs written during this time, despite the very mediocre general level. An examination of the voluminous corpus of ballads written by 'Claribel' (Charlotte Alington Barnard, 1830-1869), might yield some surprises — and isolated master-pieces such as Loder's *The Brooklet* (1860?) or Sullivan's *Orpheus with his Lute* (1866) have been deservedly treasured.

The publication of Parry's first book of *English Lyrics* in 1881 had presaged better things, and the appointment of Stanford as a professor of composition at the Royal College was to have an incalculable influence on the scores of young men and women (beginning with Wood) who passed through his hands. Some of Stanford's views on the craft of song-writing were set down in his book on composition[1], and these may be supplemented by incidental references in Plunket Greene's life[2]. He emphasised the importance of real sensitivity to words, quoting Purcell as an example, and economy of notes in the accompaniment (his scathing 'You've brought me a piano concerto with voice accompaniment, study your Schubert, me boy!' must have bitten home to its recipient). Through his example, as much as his teaching, he demonstrated the importance of cultivating literary taste, and in this, of course, he was at one with the director, Grove, whose influence on the general culture of the students was, as has been noted, profound.

It is an inestimable advantage to a student composer to assess the effectiveness of what he has written through performance, and Wood had the stimulus of the presence among his fellow students of a number of vocalists able, and indeed avid, to sing his songs. Anna Russell, for example, one of the leading young singers of her time at the College, performed his songs both publicly and privately[3], and Grove offered his advice particularly over the choice of texts[4]:

> Thank you for your letter, also for the songs which I shall forward to Mr Mühlen as soon as I hear he is in Russia and can pass them through the Post Office — else they may discover some treason in the words or music. I continually sing over the melodies — alas it is all I can do — with delight.
>
> You have now fully established yourself in my mind as a writer of songs of sentiment — I would like now to see a good quick or brilliant song or two from you, such as Mendelssohn's *Reiselied* in E minor or Schubert's *Aufenhalt*. What do you think of that?

or[5]:

> I have been thinking of words for you. How would Byron's 'I wish to hear my quivering lyre' do for you? He uses very fine idiomatic English. I am afraid of your wasting your time on translations from the Danish, for translations are always 2nd rate even when done by good writers . . . I want you to write a good rattling energetic song where sentiment rather gives place to fire and brilliancy.

and[6]:

> . . . you must play me the two new songs you have written. On the other side [of this letter] there are two stanzas of W Scott's (Legend of Montrose) very delicate and pretty . . . there were 8 or 10 more and my pen fell from my hand! But these, especially the 2nd, are very sweet.

We may divide Wood's considerable output of songs into two main categories: original settings (including a number of pseudo folk-songs) and solo-voice arrangements of traditional Irish melodies. Fifty of the original songs survive, and of these only 12 were published in Wood's lifetime. Twenty of them can be firmly dated to his student days at the RCM[7], and if they show the 'classical' side of his musical personality uppermost, they also show enormous technical and musical competence. On occasion they evince a romantic ardour reminiscent of Schumann, or that quieter lyricism that stems from Brahms. Take, for example, the opening of the earliest surviving song, *O skylark, for thy wing*, words by Mrs Hemans (E major, 3/4, *Allegro*; MS dated January 7, 1884):

Example 67

Another song from the same year (1884), *Had I a cave*, poem by Robert Burns (C minor, 3/4, *Adagio*; MS dated January, 1884), had the distinction of a performance, with the accompaniment scored for orchestra, at a public concert given by the College[8], and the solitary surviving song of 1885, *The Song of Thekla* (Schiller, tr Coleridge) (C minor, C, *Non troppo allegro*; MS dated August 13, 1885) shows the 19-year-old composer revelling in the delights of picturesque pianism to point the dramatic highlights.

Wood wrote eight songs the following year and six of them eventually achieved posthumous publication. The three Tennyson settings — *The splendour falls* (E flat major, 9/8, *Andante con moto*; MS dated January, 1886), *Ask me no more* (from *The Princess*) (E flat major, 3/4, *Andante*; MS dated September 21, 1886), and *Fortune and her wheel* (from *The Marriage of Geraint*) (A major, 6/8, *Allegro*) — may well be compared with similar settings in the Somervell *Maud* cycle of 1898. They are perhaps a shade too consciously and obviously onomatopoeic in their accompaniments, but again one is struck is by the professionalism of the compositional technique displayed — especially when they are compared with the generality of songs written at that time. They remind one of the songs of Frank Bridge a generation later — for instance, his setting of *Go not happy day*.

At the mid hour of night (Thomas Moore) (F major, ₵, *Adagio*; MS dated June 8, 1886) was heard, together with a still unpublished setting of *Does the road wind uphill all the way?* (Christina Rossetti) (G flat major, C, *Andante*; MS dated June 5, 1886) at that memorable evening when a representative group of RCM scholars were summoned to perform before Queen Victoria at Windsor[9].

At the mid hour of night was perhaps the most important song that Wood had composed to date — indeed it is reputed to have been his favourite of all his songs[10]. It begins quietly enough with what was a subconscious reminiscence of Schubert's *Due bist die Ruh'*:

Example 68

but builds up to a powerful climax early in the middle section, which is followed by a long, slow return to the tranquillity of the opening (*see Example 69, opposite*).

One might well wonder what the Queen made of it. Such disciplined yet passionate outpourings were not, one feels, common in the vocal repasts that came her way. Had it been written by Duparc rather than Wood it could perhaps have stood a better chance of acknowledgement as a masterpiece in its own right.

Example 69

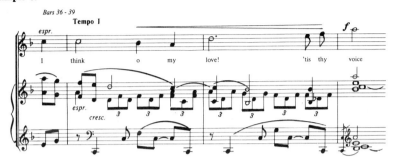

Goldthred's Song (Sir Walter Scott, from *Kenilworth*) (D minor, 3/4, *a tempo gusto*; MS dated June 26, 1886), which also was not published until 40 years after its composition, has interest in that its melodic line shows a certain folk-song influence — not of Irish folk-song, but German:

Example 70

as found occasionally in the works of Schumann and Mendelssohn (for example in the latter's *Song without Words* Op 53, No 5, subtitled *Volkslied*).

Of the six songs surviving from 1887, *The hour and the Ghost* (Christina Rossetti) (D minor, C, *Allegro agitato ma non troppo*; MS dated October 31, 1887) is notable as an example of a dialogue song with *three* protagonists: the Bride, the Bridegroom and the Ghost. It challenges the singer's powers of trinitarian characterisation (three in one and one in three), and the setting is appropriately dramatic. It was performed at an RCM concert in the November of that year and evidently puzzled at least one critic[11]. Another song, *Through the Twilight* (Alexander Grant) (C major, ₵, *Allegretto(?)*), won a competition organised by the *Musical World* and the judges (Mr Alfred Blume and Mr Goring Thomas) wrote of it:

> [We] recognise in this setting remarkable musical invention, perfect freedom from clap-trap and commonplace striving for popularity, and strict adherence to declamatory emphasis, the last being an especially important point in an English composer.

The poem Wood was given to set had itself been selected through a competition organised by the same musical journal. Wood's share of the

101

prize money (7 guineas) must have been a useful acquisition for an indigent student. An unfinished copy of the MS survives.

Two songs can definitely be dated to 1888. *The Maid of Neidpath* (Sir Walter Scott) (C major, C, *Slowly and with expression*; MS dated March 1, 1888) is another essay in the volkslied style. *They are all gone into a world of light* (Henry Vaughan) (C major, C, *Andante*; MS dated April 9, 1888) is a more innately personal utterance, though it shows Wood's awareness of Parry's song style:

Example 71

The use of a quasi-recitative in the middle section of its ternary structure was an innovation (*cf* Vaughan Williams's later use of the same device in *Silent Noon*). It moved Grove to some sombre reflections in a letter from his Sydenham home on April 11:

> I am so glad that you have set those beautiful words of Vaughan — now that dear Louise Kellett has departed it gives me an additional figure to think of as [one of] these. But oh dear, if one could really believe — not only feel, but believe — in the next world! Forgive [me] for this outburst, dear Wood, but if you had lost two daughters and half a dozen of the most intimate friends possible, you would feel the same.

Of the four songs surviving from 1890 the two Hemans settings, *The Death of Clanronald* (B minor, 3/4, *Allegro deciso*) and the *Lament of an Irish Mother* (subtitled *Keene*) (D minor, C, *Poco allegro*) show Wood expanding his stylistic range. The first, still in the *volkslied* tradition, has a Brahmsian amplitude of melody:

Example 72

The second, which has a pentatonic motif in the accompaniment,

Example 73

and a pentatonic opening to the vocal line, shows Wood allowing himself to be more and more influenced by the characteristic melodic shapes of his native Irish folk-music:

Example 74

The Windflower (F major, 3/4, *Poco allegretto*; MS dated Cambridge, 1890) was the first song of Wood's to achieve publication in his own lifetime. It is a setting of words by Sir Harold Boulton, who had conceived the idea of issuing a symposium of settings of his own verses, made 'by some of the Best and Best known (sic) British Composers'. The composers invited — or who accepted the invitation — to contribute form an interesting cross-section, and give a fair idea as to who were regarded as 'Best and Best known composers' in terms of public reputation. The list of contributors includes Barnby, Cellier, Corder, Cowen, Charles Lloyd, Mackenzie, MacCunn, Parry, Somervell, Stanford, Goring Thomas and Wood himself. Sullivan and Elgar are perhaps the two most significant absentees.

Wood's setting is neatly written, semi-strophic in form, rather Parryesque in style, and of no great distinction.

The Rover (Sir Walter Scott) (C major, 3/4, *Andante con moto*; MS dated 1890), on the other hand, has much more vitality, though some of the word-setting strikes one as surprisingly wooden — or at least unsubtle. It achieved posthumous publication.

The *Four Songs* composed in 1891 and published the following year represented a new departure in more than one sense. The choice of poets was new, and the accompaniments, while still owing something to the example of Parry in his *English Lyrics*, have become lighter and more concise, and the melodies are more subtly organised and lyrically impulsive.

An Ancient Love Song (E flat major, 9/8, *Andante tranquillo*), the first in the set, will stand comparison with the later settings of the same lyric (*In an arbour green* — anon, 16th-century) by Warlock and Moeran, for instance. Over a delightful accompaniment figure the voice joyously moves forward in a lilting 9/8:

103

Example 75

The second song in the group is a setting of Suckling's *Why so pale and wan, fond lover?* (F major, 3/4, *Allegretto*; MS dated July 22, 1891) and if it reminds one of Parry's setting, it does not suffer overmuch in the comparison. The ending is delightfully emphatic:

Example 76

The third song, *How can the tree but waste and wither away?* (Lord Vaux) (E minor, 3/4, *Andante con moto*; MS dated July 20, 1891, Cambridge) juxtaposes long vocal questioning phrases, set over a running *basso-continuo* quaver accompaniment, with dramatic answers supported by equally dramatic tremulos.

Finally, in *Ah! Robin! jolly Robin!* (a lyric attributed here to Sir Thomas Wyatt) (D major, C, *Allegretto scherzando*; MS dated July 19, 1891, Cambridge), Wood rounded off the cycle with a simple ABABA affirmation of love that ripples off the singer's tongue in a mood of unclouded joy. The *Four Songs*, which have been out of print for years, deserve revival, if only on account of the first and fourth.

It would appear from a number of nearly illegible sketches which have survived, that Wood had been dabbling in setting Whitman since his student days[12], and certainly, as has been noted above, there was

104

no poet for whose works he had a greater personal sympathy. In this same year (1891) he turned to Whitman again in earnest, and completed a setting of *Darest thou, O Soul* (D flat major, C, *Andante sostenuto*) which was eventually published posthumously. It is a deeply felt, even passionate, song, semi-strophic in form and remarkable for its use of root-position chords in the accompaniment, which gives it a certain elemental strength. The climax is powerful and quasi-orchestral in texture.

Then follows a gap so far as songs that can be precisely dated are concerned, and it was not until 1897 that Wood returned to writing original songs. Again the poet was Whitman. In *By the Bivouac's fitful flame* (from *Drum Taps*) (D flat major, 3/4, *Molto adagio*; MS dated August 30, 1897), Wood produced a finely judged and most impressive setting that anticipates many of the features of the choral *Dirge for two veterans* written four years later, *cf* the opening:

Example 77

and the music for 'which wind in procession, thoughts, O tender wandering thoughts' which parallels the 'sad procession' in the *Dirge*. The song remains in MS but was evidently sung by Plunket Greene, who gave a singer's assessment of Wood as a composer in the course of his Stanford biography[13].

The success of some of the lighter folk-song arrangements in the Graves/ Stanford collections (*Father O'Flynn*, and *Trottin' to the fair* are examples) resulted in something of a vogue for such things, and in this same year Wood joined with A P Graves (his folk-song collaborator) in writing a pseudo folk-song. *I was wishful he'd stay* (G major, 3/4, *Poco allegretto*; MS dated December 20, 1897, Cambridge) was published in 1901. It is not without charm, but Graves's words are unremittingly arch: 'Dublin' rhymes with 'Trouble in'.

From 1898 date the two solo Whitman settings that were published in his own lifetime: *O Captain! My Captain!* (B flat major, C, *Andante sostenuto*; MS dated February 28, 1898, Cambridge; it was published in 1899) and *Ethiopia saluting the Colours* (A flat major, 4/4, *Alla marcia*; MS dated February 28, 1898). The former, which has been rather overshadowed by the latter in public estimation, is a dramatic — even melodramatic — setting of a blatantly rhetorical poem on the death of Abraham Lincoln (eg, 'O heart! heart! heart! O the bleeding drops of red, where on the deck my Captain lies, fallen cold and dead'). The alternating sections *Allegro molto moderato* and *Andante sostenuto* rather give the impression of a Brahms Ballade that has taken unto itself a vocal line. When Plunket Greene sang them both at the Hovingham Festival, Stanford, who was present, wrote thus to his old pupil (letter dated July 12, 1911, from Hovingham Hall):

> My dear Charles — your Ethiopia made a sensation today and had to be sung twice over to shouts of 'encore!' Harry Greene sang it splendidly. Everyone including your humble servant was bowled over by it. But the humble servant was still more bowled over by 'Captain, O my Captain' which is *great* [underlined four times]. Long life to you and more of 'em. Yrs ever, C V Stanford.

Ethiopia saluting the colours is commonly regarded as Wood's supreme achievement as a song writer, and was indeed included among the select total of 50 songs that Gerald Moore chose to analyse in his masterly and invaluable *Singer and Accompanist*[14]. Plunket Greene, who was a great interpreter of the song, has an anecdote concerning it[15]: 'But for Stanford, *Ethiopia* might never have seen the light . . . he had hidden it away in a desk, where Stanford found it, knowing his man and burgling his rooms. Except for a slight alteration of the old woman's quasi-recitative it was the same as the present printed version. The virulent abuse on the subject of over-modesty which he received on that occasion was the making of him, but he was always a hopeless "traveller" in his own wares.'

The image of the passing regiment was again interpreted by Wood in terms of a march rhythm — a quicker march this time, echoing the tramp of marching men (*Example 78*).

The band misremembers *John Brown's body* (*Example 79*).

The march is interrupted when, at bar 41, the old woman tells her story (quasi recit) (*Example 80*).

Finally the march resumes, and the soldier narrator moves on, musing over what he has heard. The song ends quietly.

The Outlaw of Loch Lene (F sharp minor[16], 3/4, *Con fuoco*; MS dated December 17, 1898), published in 1900 'and sung by Plunket Greene', is a magnificent declamatory ballad which deserves to be far better known than it is. Its voice part has a fine freedom of phrase structure and the folk-song influence is powerfully felt in its melodic shape (*Example 81*).

The accompaniment is picturesque and inventive, if still a shade Brahmsian in texture.

From 1898 onwards Wood's production of songs slackened considerably as far as MSS than can be dated are concerned. There were two of the

Example 78

Bars 1 - 7

Example 79

Bars 32 - 34

Example 80

Bars 41 - 44

107

Example 81

Bars 8 - 14
(Con fuoco)

O ma-ny a day have I made good ale in the glen,

lighter pseudo folk-songs: *One morning in May* (E flat, 3/4, *Andante con moto*, published 1899), *The Potato Song* (D major, 6/8, *Allegretto*, published 1909) — both settings of words by A P Graves. *Tim, an Irish terrier* (W M Letts) (C minor, 6/8, *Allegro molto*) is a more extended setting, very reminiscent of Stanford's *Bold unbiddable child*. *Fineen the Rover* (C minor, 3/4, *Con brio*), a setting of words by Robert Dwyer Joyce, published in 1912, is another declamatory ballad — very much in the vein of *The Outlaw of Loch Lene* — and has a sweeping melody constructed mainly in seven-bar phrases. It was transposed upward a third from the original key when published. *Home to Glenties* (Patrick MacGill) (C minor, 2/4, *Andante up poco allegretto*), which was published in 1913, is an essay in nostalgia, and might be described as a more refined and musicianly version of the 'Galway Bay' theme.

Of the two unpublished wartime songs, *Roll up the map of Europe* (W L Hutchinson) (A major, 2/4, *Moderately fast with vigour*) was an attempt at a 'patriotic' song, and *The Munsters at Mons* (A P Graves) (F major, 2/4, *Alla marcia (Allegro)*) was a more successful 'Irish' song on a similar theme.

There remain for discussion some eleven original songs which are undated and of which seven were published posthumously. Among those which remained in MS is a particularly impressive setting of *On the Camp Hill, Hastings* (Thomas Campbell) (F sharp minor, 3/4, *Andante*) — another of those threnodies in which Wood's most personal feelings found musical expression:

Example 82

Bars 1 - 4
Andante   dolce

In the deep blue of eve, Ere the

p

By way of contrast, *Resignation* (Adelaide Proctor) (C major, 4/4, *Andante sostenuto*) is a rather deplorable 'song of uplift' appropriate to the best Pleasant Sunday Afternoon traditions.

A simple strophic setting of *Holy Thursday* (William Blake) (A minor, 4/4, *Allegretto*) has a folk-song-like melody and a studied simplicity and economy of accompaniment that reminds one of the best of Wood's unison songs. Brought out in 1931, it was the last of the solo songs to achieve publication (the remainder of the published undated songs had appeared in the posthumous *10 Songs for low voice* of 1927).

The gem of that collection is undoubtedly *The dead at Clonmacnois* (Irish of Enoch O'Gillan, translated by T W Rolleston) (E flat, 4/4, *Moderato*) — 'a meditation among the tombs' to give it a misleadingly facetious description. It is yet another of those songs in which Wood responded powerfully to the imagery of mourning, this time — and most unusually — in a major key:

Example 83

It is semi-strophic in setting, cumulative in intensity, and builds up to a considerable climax.

Stanford had set the fashion for writing song-cycles based on Anglo-Irish lyrics — eg *An Irish Idyll* (1901), *Six songs from the Glens of Antrim* (1908), *Cushendall* (1910), *A fire of turf* (1914), and *Songs of a roving Celt* (1919). Wood evidently contemplated something similar, and turned to the verses of Moira O'Neill, author of *An Irish Idyll* and *Songs from the Glens of Antrim*. The four songs: *Denny's daughter* (B flat, 3/4, *Andante*), *The sailor man* (D minor, 6/8, *Allegro moderato*), *Birds* (C major, 2/4, *Allegretto*), and *At Sea* (B flat, 3/4, *Moderato con moto*), all published in the posthumous *10 Songs*, will bear comparison with the Stanford settings, for stylistically they are almost indistinguishable. There are the same folk-song-like melodic lines, *cf*, the opening of *Sailor man*:

Example 84

Bars 9 - 13

(Allegro moderato)

Sure a ter - ri - ble time I was out o' the way, O - ver the sea, o - ver the sea.

the same economy of notes in the accompaniments, and the same feeling for atmosphere (*cf* the opening of *At sea*). An enterprising baritone might make a good thing of them.

Finally, mention should be made of the splendidly vigorous and onoma-topoeic setting of Dekker's *Song of the Cyclops* (C minor, 4/4, *Allegro con brio*), to be found in the same volume.

The history of the Irish folk-song movement is a tangled one, with musicians who knew little Erse preserving tunes without their associated words, and poets who were no musicians preserving words without reference to tunes. The whole matter is discussed authoritatively in Frank Howes' *Folk Music of Britain — and beyond* (London, Methuen, 1969, pp 238-250). Suffice it to say that this bifurcation of activity, not to mention the bilingualism exhibited in the spoken word, may be held to explain why the tradition of turning Irish folk-melodies into art-songs with English words goes back so far — at least to the collaboration between Moore and Stevenson, who issued their first volume of *Moore's Irish Melodies* in 1807.

In parallel with the practice of Robert Burns and his lesser successors, the Irish poets (writing in English) provided words for individual airs — a tradition that stretches from Sir Samuel Ferguson (1810-1886) (*The lark in the clear air*) to W B Yeats (1865-1939) (*Down by the Sally Gardens*), and Padraic Colum (1881-   ) (*She moved through the fair*). It should be noted that, of the enormous corpus of traditional Irish folk-melodies, the larger and musically superior part originally had Gaelic words, and the provision of alternative English words was regarded as a necessary preliminary to publication in performing editions.

A leading light in the provision of English words, and of the dissemination of Anglo-Irish poetry in general, was A P Graves (1846-1931) (see p. 52). Graves, whose father had been Bishop of Limerick and whose brother, C L Graves, was the editor of *Punch*, was the father of Robert Graves, the poet and novelist. He followed, like Matthew Arnold, the occupation of 'Inspector of Schools'. The *Dictionary of National Biography* says of him: 'He gained the greater part of his position in the world of letters as a poet of Irish nature and country life, and as an essayist on Irish musical and literary subjects. He was a leading figure in the recently founded London Irish Literary Society, of which he was twice president, and as an editor and anthologist performed service in the cause of under-

110

standing and appreciation of Ireland — her poets, her folk-lore, and her music. His "translations", however, both from the Irish and the Welsh, were based on other people's translations, for he had but a smattering of Gaelic and no Welsh'. He acquired a bardic title, 'Canwr Cilarne' ('Singer from Killarney') — one of the few non-Welsh-speaking literateurs ever to do so, and his name is frequently met with in musical contexts during late Victorian and Edwardian times[17].

He joined with Stanford in the production of *Songs of Old Ireland* (1882). *Songs of Erin* (1892), *Irish Songs and Ballads* (1893), and, for school use, *The National Song Book* (1907). It is likely that it was through Stanford (though Grove, who knew the Graves family, is another possibility) that Wood and Graves commenced collaboration on their own account, first of all with *Irish Folk-songs* (1897) (25 songs), and subsequently with two volumes of *Irish Country-side Songs* (1914 and, posthumously, in 1927), each containing six songs. A third volume with lyrics by P J McCall, and containing seven songs, was also issued posthumously in 1928. The first volume of a series to be called *Anglo-Irish Folk-songs*, with words 'written, edited and arranged by Padraic Gregory', containing a further six songs, was eventually brought out in 1931. There were, in addition, two separate folk-song arrangements with words by A P Graves: *Nell Flaherty's Drake* (1895) and *I mayn't or I may* (1901). A further folk-song arrangement, *The Crucifixion* (words A P Graves), survives in MS[18].

According to various lists found among Wood's papers after his death, a further 46 folk-song arrangements were either composed or contemplated, and it is known that 35 of these 46 — presumably in the form of completed MSS — were sent to a publisher and subsequently lost by the firm concerned. Of the lost 35, the sketches of 15 are extant, together with the sketches of one additional setting not recorded on any of the lists. These can be reconstructed, complete as to words, and more or less complete as to music. Similar complete sketches of four other settings on the written lists, but not sent to publishers, have also survived. There are in addition ten songs in sketch, of which only the tune has been identified (Wood rarely inserted the words in his sketches), and six sketches of folk-song settings of as yet unidentified tunes to, as yet, unknown words. So there are in total, 52 published solo settings, one complete MS setting, 20 settings complete in sketches, ten sketch settings that only require identification of the words, and six sketch settings requiring identification of both words and music. It is a considerable tally.

The lyrics, whether by Graves or the other versifiers, fall into four main categories:

(1) Traditional English words, either as originally collected, or printed 'with minor changes. It will be noted that such songs are very much

in the minority (eg, *My love wrote me a letter*, the words and tune of which originally appeared in the *Irish Folk-song Journal*, Vol 14, April 1914, p 35).

(2) Words that are either translations (or paraphrases) or are generally based on the Irish originals appropriate to the air (eg *Credhe's Lament for Cail*, published in *Irish Folk-songs*, p 103).

(3) Original modern poems deriving their subject matter from the traditional name of the air (eg *Beside the River Loune*, published in *Irish Folk-songs*, p 19).

(4) Original verses on original topics made to fit the air, but not deriving directly or indirectly from it (eg *Love at my heart*, published in *Irish Folk-songs*, p 15.)

These settings are, of course, strophic in form and sometimes quite extended in length, with considerable variety in the nature of the accompaniments to successive verses, for since the melody and key are unchanging, the only variable is the accompaniment. Wood's superb variation technique stood him in good stead when he was engaged on these arrangements.

Their quality is largely determined by the innate musical worth of the airs themselves. The earlier settings are the most Stanfordian in style, and show Wood's basically 'classical' harmonic palette adapting itself to the setting of modal tunes without difficulty or incongruity. The *Irish Folk-songs* book covers a wide range of styles, from the airy lightness of *The Cuckoo Madrigal* to the dramatic intensity (almost Schubertian) of *Credhe's Lament for Cail*, and contains some lovely music.

After their collaboration on this venture, neither Wood nor Graves made any attempt to follow it up with further similar volumes until 1912, or thereabouts (the publication of Joyce's latter book, and of the O'Neill collection, may have provided the incentive). Most of the initiative with regard to which tunes were to be used with which words seems to have come from Graves — at least, to judge from a few letters that have been preserved, eg:

Red Branch House,
Wimbledon.
Oct 12/12.

My dear Wood,

I have done that air for Harry Greene with words on 'The Wicklow Mountains' and asked him to pass them on to you, if he likes them. I have just come across these words of mine to a capital tune in Ling's Dance Music of Ireland, 'Around the World for Sport'.

They are perhaps a trifle sophisticated, but I could make them more human if you like the idea. I send you P J McCall's Book. There really are some good things in it; particularly 'The Dance of the Old Couple', 'Herself and Mysel.' and 'Old man's song', p 119. 'The Bonnie Blue Handkerchief' and 'The Piper from Blessington' are worth thinking of, too, also the 'High Caul Cap'.

This man is a friend of mine and he really has humorous stuff in him; more even than Frank Fahy. So do look through the book and see what you think. Then there is 'Cockles and Mussels' herewith; never well done, though a dear old air. I have got a version of this somewhere modified by me from what I said. I also send an absurdity from Limerick which might amuse Harry.

Yours very truly,

Alfred P Graves.

In the preface to their first volume of *Irish Countryside Songs* (dedicated to Plunket Greene) they noted that: 'The group of Irish Countryside Songs is the first instalment of a series of more than fifty, drawn from the Bunting, Petrie, Joyce, and O'Neill collections, the Irish Folk-song Journal, and the Irish Song-book — to which the first of the signatories below has written fresh, or adapted old lyrics to Irish airs, edited and arranged by the latter.'

The style of accompaniment of these later folk-song arrangements is more individual, and the harmonies more subtle, than in the earlier volume. Take, for instance, the ostinato patterns — almost Beethoven-like in *The Drinaun Dhun* (MS sketch):

Example 85

the chains of thirds in *Curly-locks* (MS sketch):

Example 86

and the drone-like ostinati in the *Sho-ho Lullaby* (surely one of the loveliest tunes in the Irish folk-song repertoire, and one of the most effective lullaby settings ever made by Wood — or by anyone else):

Example 87

'Tis the cry_ of a grey cur-lew up in the sky, that's trou-bling you.

The fashion today is for folk-songs to be sung, in general, by pseudo folk-singers aping the vocal peculiarities of the original performers, with guitar accompaniments, the procrustean rhythms of which are only equalled in banality by their harmonic crudity. [I do not myself see that to sing a song originally meant to be unaccompanied, to a crude guitar accompaniment, is to produce any more authentic a performance than could be achieved with a considered piano accompaniment — but this is a digression.]

Whether one regards Wood's folk-song arrangements as denigrations or transmutations into art-songs is really quite irrelevant. The important point is that there is here a wonderful body of songs to be explored, and certainly worth the exploring.

NOTES

1. Stanford, Sir Charles V, *Musical Composition — a short treatise for students* (London, Macmillan & Stainer and Bell, 1911), ch 8.
2. Greene, H Plunket, *Sir Charles Villiers Stanford* (London, Arnold, 1935), ch 13, p 202.
3. Later the wife of Marmaduke Barton (1865-1938), the pianist, a fellow student of Wood's and, in time, a fellow professor, who gave the first performance of Wood's Piano Concerto — vide the Grove letters — and the article in Grove, Vol 1, p 476.
4. Letter from Grove, written from Lower Sydenham, and dated September 1, (St Partridge).
5. Letter from Grove written from the RCM, and dated October 15, 1887.
6. Undated letter from Grove.
7. 3 to 1884, 1 to 1885, 8 to 1886, 6 to 1887, and 2 to 1888.
8. A surviving full orchestral score MS shows that Wood had mastered the art of balancing a solo voice against the orchestra.
9. *Vide The Times* of June 28, 1887, and the exultant account by Grove himself quoted on p 377 of Graves, C L, *The life and letters of Sir George Grove, CB* (London, Macmillan, 1903). Anna Russell, with the composer at the piano, evidently did justice to the music. *Does the road*, transposed downwards to make a contralto solo, was subsequently scored by the composer — the MS score survives.

10. Personal reminiscence of his pupil, J M Tatton.
11. *Monthly Musical Record*, issue of January 1, 1888, article headed 'Dec 1887 — Five Concerts': 'New compositions by students have also been heard. A part song "Waken lords and ladies gay" with 4 horns obligato by Mr J Smith, may be classed with Mr Wood's setting of Christina Rossetti's "The Hour and the Ghost". Both are appropriate in style, and clever, and both, alas! are wanting in ideas.'
12. An unfinished sketch of a setting of *As toilsome I wander'd Virginia's Woods* has survived.
13. Greene, *op cit*, p 252.
14. London, Methuen, 1953.
15. Greene, *op cit*, p 252.
16. The original key of the MS version was G minor.
17. He collaborated with Stanford, Parry, Mackenzie, Liza Lehmann, and Esposito.
18. A score of this song with the accompaniment arranged for string quartet has survived. It was included in at least one posthumous programme with the Mangéot Quartet.

CHAPTER 7

The orchestral music

Sooner or later Stanford's pupils tackled the orchestra. Usually they were encouraged to write a concert overture or a suite[1], and if he thought reasonably well of their efforts Stanford would tell them to copy out a set of parts, and the work would be tried out with the College Orchestra. As Stanford himself recorded[2]:

> Young composers were taught abroad upon paper and only the most finished examples of their work ever reached the point of a hearing. We went on the principle that the hearing of a composition is the best lesson the writer can get, and that the perspiration and agony from which a composer suffers when he hears the sounds of his own inexperience is the most valuable part of his training.

Stanford could, of course, be very scathing when a work failed to meet with his approval; Wood's younger namesake, Thomas Wood (1892-1950), recollected that Stanford said of *his* Concert Overture[3]: ' . . . and if they ever *did* play this, ye'd sweat till y'r shirt was a rag'.

Wood, it may be recollected, had studied the French horn as a co-second study and played it 'adequately, if not brilliantly in the College Orchestra'[4]. This meant that he learned his orchestration from the inside, as it were, and if he never became a master orchestrator as did Holst, a student trombonist in the next generation, at least he learned the art of scoring with economy and impeccable clarity. He once observed to his pupil, Beecham, that the only way to learn effective orchestration was to study directly with the masters of the art (*cf* Vaughan Williams's work with Ravel). Wood never regarded himself as a great orchestrator, though, as in every other department, he was always a meticulous craftsman — a little conservative, perhaps (he notated for natural brass almost to the end of his life), but knowing exactly what he was doing.

According to S P Waddington[5], Wood composed two overtures during his student days at College. One of these may well be a certain *Overture in D minor*, the score of which has been lost subsequent to Wood's death. There is no record of the other score. Wood's first surviving venture into the realm of orchestral music took the unexpected form of a full-scale piano concerto (*cf* Sterndale Bennett, who wrote no less than four during *his* protracted student days). Moreover, not only was the concerto written but it was actually performed, and in public at that, within a few months of its completion: Stanford must have thought very well of it! The soloist on this occasion (July 22, 1886) was Marmaduke Barton, Wood's fellow student, and the *Musical Times* said of it[6]: 'The work is of a most elaborate and ambitious order, full of cleverness, but over-luxuriant in detail.'

It consists of the usual three movements:

F major, ₵, *Allegro molto tranquillo.* d = 84 (dated December 15, 1885)

B flat major, 3/4, *Adagio*

leading into

D minor, 9/8 3/4, *Allegro ma non troppo* (dated March 16, 1886) and is scored for the following orchestra: 2 flutes, 2 oboes, 2 clarinets (B flat), 2 bassoons, 2 horns (F), 2 trumpets (F), timpani (F and C), and strings.

The first movement is constructed on orthodox classical lines, with a spacious orchestral exposition in which the main thematic material is given a deliberate airing. Chief among the procession of themes are, in the first subject group,

Example 88

and in the second,

Example 89

This spaciousness is mirrored in the second exposition, the lengthy development and recapitulation. The piano writing throughout is disciplined and generally restrained in texture, but occasionally a certain romantic passion bubbles to the surface. Wood seems to have superimposed Schumann on Beethoven in a rather uncharacteristic rhetorical juxtaposition.

The slow movement is episodic in structure, with a good deal of antiphony between the orchestra in 3/4 and a barcarolle-like piano part in 9/8, and has considerable lyrical intensity.

The finale, with its double-time signature, is rhythmically exuberant:

117

Example 90

(Bars 1 - 3)
Allegro ma non troppo

Piano

Indeed, if one compares it with, for example, the finales of the Sterndale Bennett concerti, one is struck by its virility and bite.

The chances of the concerto ever being revived must be judged remote, but for all that it is a not unimportant work, and in the slim procession of English piano concertos it has more than a purely historical significance.

Wood's next orchestral work was almost certainly a *Concerto in one movement* (F major) for organ and strings, and was evidently written in 1889 (the year he became bandmaster to the University Volunteers). There is a letter from Grove dated September 15 that makes simultaneous reference to the concerto and the bandmastership appointment. The reference to the concerto is brief but intriguing: 'I am so pleased about your Concerto — it is so good to hit [on] a new form which shall not be extravagant — tell me more about it.' Unfortunately the score and solo part have been lost (apparently by a publisher to whom it was offered posthumously) and only a set of string parts remain preserved in Caius College Library. Organ concertos are uncommon, and apart from the Handel series and the Poulenc Concerto for organ, timpani and strings, no other examples remain in the repertory, so the loss of this Wood concerto could be a real matter for regret.

In this same year, 1889, as well as writing his setting of Shelley's *Ode to the West Wind* (see p. 43 above), Wood completed a concert overture, *Much ado about nothing*, scored for 2 flutes, 2 oboes, 2 clarinets (A), 4 horns (2 in F, 2 in G), 2 trumpets (D), 2 trombones, 1 bass-trombone, 3 timpani (G, A, D), and strings. The MS score (G major, 6/8, *Allegro molto*) is dated April 1, 1889, London, and includes a number of pencilled alterations which suggests that Wood revised some details of the scoring after the experience of a performance. This overture is a mature work, in full sonata form, and is chiefly remarkable for its bounding rhythmic impetus. The first subject group is held together by a rhythmic figure which is presented on the 1st bassoon, and gradually taken up and expanded by the whole woodwind chorus:

118

Example 91

A second theme, headed *appassionato*, appears on the strings:

Example 92

A cognate melody is combined with the opening rhythmic figure (letter B) until the real main theme of the second subject group appears in the orthodox dominant:

Example 93

A further theme emerges (also combined with the opening rhythmic figure) and is worth quotation:

Example 94

The subsequent adventures of this outpouring of thematic material show Wood as being both inventive, economical and, as in the concerto, full of rhythmic panache. It is for this quality, rare on the whole in 1889, that the work might be worth reviving.

In 1894 Wood composed the incidental music for the Cambridge Greek play of that year, the *Iphigenia in Tauris*, and at some subsequent period he fashioned from the complete score an orchestral suite which Beecham was to perform on more than one occasion in the years before the First World War. The fashioning of the suite involved no additional composition but rather the amplification of the scoring by the addition of 2nd flutes, 2nd oboes, 2nd clarinets, 2nd bassoon and 2nd trumpet parts to the movements selected, namely:

(1) The Prelude to Act One.
(2) *Andante sostenuto* from Act One.
(6) Entr'acte from between Acts Two and Three.
(8) Chorus from Act Three (minus the vocal parts)
(10) Final chorus from Act Three (minus the vocal parts).

The musical content of these items has been discussed in the chapter dealing with Wood's dramatic music. The suite, as such, was never published, though a set of parts (adapted from the original orchestral parts that went with the original Cambridge stage production) were on hire from a publisher, minus, however, any score. A new score has been reconstructed from these surviving parts.

Two years later Wood demonstrated his versatility by composing a *Quick March* for the band of the University Volunteer Rifle Corps (of which, it may be recalled, he was still at this time the salaried bandmaster). The march was evidently written during the period of a spring Volunteers' Camp, for the score is dated 'Queen's Hotel, Farnborough, March 15, 1896'. The march (B flat major, 2/4) was scored for flute and piccolo (military band instruments pitched in D flat, and hence playing from a part written in A, a semi-tone below the sounding note), clarinets 1, 2 and 3 (B flat), cornets 1, 2 and 3 (B flat), saxhorns 1, 2 and 3 (E flat), baritones 1 and 2 (B flat), a euphonium (B flat), trombones 1 and 2, a bass trombone, an E-flat bass, a B-flat bass, bass drum and cymbals. Wood also added parts for bugles in B flat, playing either in unison or very simple three-part harmony. There is no trio, and the music is of no great distinction, though the incorporation of the bugle parts is evidence of Wood's ingenuity in these matters.

On January 6, 1899, Wood completed the full score of what was to be his most elaborate orchestral work, *Patrick Sarsfield — Symphonic Variations for Orchestra on an Irish Air*. He once told Dr Heathcote Statham — his sometime pupil — that he had written the work while on his summer holiday. Presumably he meant that he had sketched it out in short score — another example of 'keeping his hand in'. When the work was given its first performance is not known, but it was taken up by Beecham and performed at his concert with the New Symphony Orchestra at Queen's Hall on November 14, 1907[7], and Beecham certainly brought it out again at the Guildhall, Cambridge.

It would appear to have been the first large-scale set of orchestral variations by a British composer to be based on a folk-tune (one thinks of Delius's *Brigg Fair* [1908] and Somervell's *Normandy* variations for piano and orchestra [1911?] as later examples), and it is very likely that it was written under the kindly shadow of Parry's *Symphonic Variations*, which were composed in 1897. Elgar's *Enigma Variations*, which dated from 1898, and which did not appear until 1899, were probably too late to be much of an influence. The Parry influence was more one of overall structure than of style, for we learn that his variations were 'grouped on a plan of Parry's own ... which suggests four symphonic movements'[8], and Wood's 32 variations follow a similar basic structure.

The theme itself, a traditional Irish tune associated with the name of the 17th-century Irish Jacobite commander and patriot, is ten bars long (4 + 2 + 2 + 2), and might be described as being most exceedingly 'apt for variation' — having a spiritual kinship with a certain theme by Paganini. It is presented by the full orchestra (2 flutes and piccolo, 2 oboes, 2 clarinets in B flat, 2 bassoons, 4 horns (2 in E flat, 2 in D), 2 trumpets in E flat, 2 trombones, bass-trombone and tuba, timpani, triangle, harp, and strings:

Example 95

The 32 variations that follow, and which generally lead from one into another, divide themselves into four groups: variations 1-10, 11-16, 17-27, and 28-32. Within each group there is a general kinship of key and tempo. Variations 1-10, for example, retain the basic 4/4, G minor, while in variations 11-16, which correspond somewhat to the slow movement of a symphony, 11-13 are in E flat major or E flat minor, and the time-signature is altered to 3/4.

There is almost no limit to Wood's technical virtuosity in these variations. A favourite device is to take the same motif and present it through several variations in terms of a cumulative increase in the complexity of texture within each individual variation. See, for example, variations 17, 18 and 19:

Example 96

121

Example 97

Example 98

There is great variety of instrumental colouring, coupled with a classical clarity in scoring most untypical of the general run of orchestral music in the period. My comments are, of course, based solely on a study of the score, for the last recorded performance took place at the Royal College of Music in 1918. But certainly the *Patrick Sarsfield Variations* will bear revival, for the intellectual power and fecundity of invention displayed in them command one's profound admiration. This is no anaemic brain-child of a remote academic, but the work of a fine composer at the height of his powers.

The only other work appropriate to this chapter that can be precisely dated is well known to thousands of men and women who have never heard of Charles Wood, and it will doubtless come as a surprise to many soldier musicians to learn that the regimental march of the Royal Signals (formerly the Royal Corps of Signals) was the work of the then Professor of Music in the University of Cambridge. I quote from the *History of the Royal Signals Band*[10]:

> From the earliest days the Band had been playing the march past of the Royal Engineers, 'Wings', but in early 1926 it was decided to have a march that would be associated with the Corps only.
> The Commandant of the Signal Training Centre, Brigadier H Clementi-Smith, DSO, suggested that a prize of fifty pounds should be given to anyone composing a suitable march that was accepted by the Corps Committee.

Several good tunes were submitted, but only two of these remained before the selection board on the day of the final choice. These two were played over and over again to numerous officers and critics, and the march finally chosen was an arrangement by Dr Charles Wood.

It is a combination of two separate tunes, 'Begone Dull Care' and 'The Newcastle Air', and is now recognised as the official march past of the Royal Signals under the title 'Begone Dull Care'.

Although the military band full-score was prepared by a Kneller Hall expert from Wood's piano score (now preserved at Caius College) — it would not, presumably, have been beyond Wood's powers to have scored it himself — certainly his composition experiences as a Volunteer bandmaster, all those years before, stood him in good stead, for it is a first-rate march, as anyone who has marched to it will testify[10].

There remain, deserving of mention, three undated fragments, and two arrangements.

As far as is known Wood never completed a symphony, but as two of these fragments indicate he at least started one on more than one occasion. The first fragment (C minor, C, *Allegro ma non troppo*) runs to 15 pages of full score (2 flutes, 2 oboes, 2 clarinets (B flat), 2 bassoons, 4 horns (2 in E flat, 2 in C), 2 trumpets (C), 2 trombones, bass-trombone, 3 timpani, and strings) and consists of a complete exposition (with repeat marks) followed by 42 bars of development. The second fragment (F major, no speed indication) is scored for a similar sized orchestra to the first, the only difference being that the horns are all crooked in F and there are only two timpani. It is a more extended torso, running to 35 pages of full-score and is complete as to exposition, development and recapitulation, breaking off after 11 bars of Coda. To judge from the evidence of the handwriting, both these fragments (each, incidentally, is labelled 'I') belong to Wood's student days. Both show how deeply he had studied his Beethoven, and both would make interesting exercises in pastiche composition for a present-day student to complete.

The third fragment (D major, 3/4, no speed indication) would appear to have been written much later in Wood's career, and consists of eight pages of full-score (102 bars) for 2 flutes, 2 oboes, 2 clarinets (A), 2 bassoons, 4 horns (D), 2 trumpets (D), 2 trombones, bass-trombone, 2 timpani, and strings. In form it is reminiscent of the sort of 'Intermezzo' movement which Brahms would occasionally write in lieu of a scherzo, but the style has something of the amiable discursiveness that we associate with Dvořák. The canonic opening is infectious in its lilting warmth (*see Example 99, overleaf*).

Of the two arrangements, the first is a setting for string orchestra of *The dear Irish boy* (taken from the Feis Coil Collection, p 26, No 59). A full score has been reconstructed from Wood's original short-score MS. It is a

Example 99

simple but subtle harmonisation of a most lovely melody and could be an admirable concert item for an amateur string orchestra. The second is a set of five Schubert Valses scored for an ensemble consisting of flutes, clarinet (B flat), strings and piano (one suspects an *ad hoc* student orchestra at Caius, where a set of parts, without a score, has survived). The Valses selected have been identified as numbers 1, 2, 3 and 6 (in the order, 1, 2, 6 and 3) of the *12 Deutsche Tanze* (1817), and number 4 of the *Ländler* (1824). Again, this might make a delightful item for an amateur instrumental group.

Other than the band-parts of the Royal Signals March, which were brought out posthumously, none of Wood's orchestral works has been published, and the chances of any of them achieving publication in the near future are, it is to be feared, minimal. The chances, indeed, of any of it even being performed again may well be judged equally remote. Yet who would have forecast, even ten years ago, that a commercial recording of Parry's orchestral music (including the *Symphonic Variations*) would be issued? Certainly Wood's *Symphonic Variations* — if nothing else among his orchestral works — deserve better than the dust of oblivion, and if they are ever revived, our usual dismissal of most late nineteenth-century English orchestral music (other than Elgar's) as dull and uninspired may well be due for a timely revision.

124

NOTES

1. See the account of the training of James Friskin (1886-   ), given in Plunket Greene's biography of Stanford, pp 98-99.
2. In *Pages from an unwritten diary* (London, Arnold, 1914), p 219.
3. Wood, Thomas, *True Thomas* (London, Jonathan Cape, 1936), p 197.
4. Waddington, S P, article in the *Dictionary of National Biography*.
5. Waddington, S P, RCM obituary, p 72.
6. Review, *Musical Times*, vol 27, no 522, August 1, 1886, p 475.
7. Review, *Musical Times*, vol 48, no 778, December 1, 1907, p 809.
8. Tovey, D F, *Essays in Musical Analysis*, vol 2 (London, Oxford, 1935), p 142.
9. I am indebted to the Bandmaster, Royal Signals Band, for this information.
10. During his period of war service, the author took part in more than one church parade accompanied by its strains. He, too, was then in ignorance of the composer's name.

CHAPTER 8

The smaller secular vocal works

From his student days onwards Wood was prolific in the composition of small-scale vocal works (madrigals and part-songs for mixed or male voices, part-songs for female voices — SSAA or SSA — and accompanied three-, two-part or unison songs); and, alongside them, a stream of folk-song arrangements for similar vocal resources. In all, over 150 original works have survived, of which 108 were published in Wood's lifetime, and 26 posthumously.

S P Waddington, in his biographical sketch[1], commented on the uncanny contrapuntal facility that Wood had displayed, right from his youth, and of the ease with which he could compose, among other things, a madrigal. Wood's surviving madrigals are eight in number, of which three achieved print. One MS, *The Alienated Mistress*, was lost posthumously. *If love be dead*, an elaborate 5-part setting (SSATB) of words by Coleridge, brought out in 1886, was, apparently, Wood's first published work. *Slow, slow, fresh fount* (SSATB) to words by Ben Johnson, written in 1888 and published in 1889, was apparently composed for the annual competition for an original madrigal sponsored by the Madrigal Society, and duly gained the Molineaux Prize and Gold Medal. Grove encouraged Wood over this work, as the following extracts from his correspondence indicate[2]:

> I have just cut open the Musical Times and seen a lovely looking part-song [Wood's setting of 'How sweet the moonlight sleeps upon the bank' (Shakespeare), brought out in the issue of May 1, 1888, — in G flat] of yours which I hope to hear soon. As to the madrigal, I should like you to get the first prize with a big one (à 5, or à 6) but of course you must do as you can.

also

> I am glad that the words [of 'Slow, Slow, Fresh Fount'] commend themselves to you; to me they always seemed conceited — that is full of conceits, or unreal images — the "spring tides", the "drowning" — I never cared for them, but am glad that you do.

and

> I have already asked J Lucas [who was to publish 'Slow, Slow'] about the madrigal — and called on him today, but he is in the country. We will go through it probably on Wednesday week. God help you, dear Wood, you have been a good pupil to me — one after my own heart.

An unpublished MS companion piece for SATB, *Love, farewell*, dated April 14, 1888, a setting of words by Robert, Earl of Essex, was, similarly, intended for a competition. *Whence comes my love* (John Harrington), set for SSATB, was dated July 17, 1891, and *The complaint of a deserted lover* (Thomas Wyatt), SATB, dated July 18, 1891, which exists in two separate MSS, one signed with a composer's pseudonym, was also evidently a potential competition entry.

So, too, was an undated setting for SSATB of *Come, come you servants of proud love* (Beaumont and Fletcher). Wood's third published madrigal, *The bag of the bee* (Herrick), was brought out in 1929. His pupil J Meredith Tatton related an interesting circumstance concerning it[3]:

> I was sitting by his side having a private lesson from him. It was a very warm day, and the windows were open in his study, and there came a sudden gust of wind which blew down a piece of MS from near the ceiling — (the room, you know, was piled high with books and music almost to the ceiling wherever possible). Anyway, this half-completed MS fluttered down to where Wood was sitting, and he looked at it, saying, 'I haven't seen this for thirty years'. I remember that when Waddington and I were going through his MSS after his death, the same MS turned up again, completed by then, the recent work being, of course, in much lighter ink than the thirty-year-old beginning.

Stylistically all these works are examples of brilliant pastiche. They remind one of the madrigalian compositions of R L Pearsall (see p. 35) in that, like that composer's madrigals and ballets, they exhibit most of the characteristics of the Elizabethan madrigal, excepting that rhythmic variety, occasional harmonic audacity, and general independence of bar-line accents that are so noteworthy in the originals.

The opening of *The bag of the bee* will serve as an example of Wood's madrigal style:

Example 100

Wood wrote two admitted 'Glees'. Of them, *A song for a dance* (Francis Beaumont), for SATB and published posthumously in 1927, has a rhythmic deftness that would make it worth while reviving.

Wood's original part-songs for mixed or male voices represent his particular contribution to the continuing tradition of the English part-song. The late-Victorian or Edwardian part-song, heir to the 'Glee' of the 18th and early 19th centuries, and, deriving from the somewhat Mendelssohnian mid-Victorian part-song, had been revivified by Parry, Stanford, Elgar, Granville Bantock and Wood himself. Their songs differed from those of earlier composers (eg Hatton) and their more conservatively minded contemporaries (Barnby, for example) in that they did not restrict themselves so exclusively to purely strophic settings; their harmony was more subtle, their range of modulation more extensive, their use of counterpoint more general and their sense of atmosphere, as expressed through tessitura and chordal spacing, more acute.

Furthermore (though not invariably), these composers tended to set texts of more literary substance than had their predecessors. From the 1850s almost until the early 1950s the composition and publication of part-songs was almost a major British musical industry. They were demanded by those choirs, large and small, whose formation had been one of the significant consequences of the industrial revolution and 'Chapel evangelism'. They were required by family groups for drawing-room performance in an era of considerable domestic music-making, and they were to become part of the staple fare of the competitive festival movement. The early application of mass-production techniques to music printing, and the use of cheap labour in the music publishing and distributive trades, kept their costs low and ensured their very widest dissemination. The *gratis* composition enclosed with each issue of the *Musical Times* was, when secular, usually a part-song, and most of Wood's earlier efforts appeared in that journal.

Of Wood's original part-songs for mixed voices, 27 were published in his life-time, and nine posthumously. It is likely that certain of these last had been reconstructed and edited by his musical executor, S P Waddington, from surviving complete short-score sketches. In addition, there are three dated and two undated part-songs in full-score autograph MS, and three undated full-score MS in the handwriting of S P Waddington which may, similarly, represent editorial reconstructions. Moreover, there are six part-songs that survive in the form of apparently complete short-score rough sketches, two sketches (incomplete?) of settings of verse not so far identified, nine unfinished songs, fragments of three more, and six works known to have been lost posthumously[4]. This makes an impressive total of 70 works known to exist or to have existed.

They all have in common that same effective and painstaking workmanship that has characterised Wood's composition in other fields. There is not a scamped bar. He knew precisely what he was doing; his instinct for vocal effectiveness was extraordinarily acute, and there can be few mixed-voice choirs of whatever size that may not find some item both stimulating and rewarding, for there is great variety in the musical textures of these songs.

The most dated are the purely homophonic, where, in general, his use of a fairly conventional chordal vocabulary is too predictable to have much impact on contemporary ears. There are, of course, exceptions when one feels that Wood has responded in a more personal way to his text — the magnificent *Time* (Sir Walter Scott) of 1914:

Example 101

stands out in this connection.

In the main the more contrapuntal the approach, the better the result. There is a whole series of songs that have affinities — rhythmic and otherwise — with the breezy jovialities of Parry's *Welcome Yule* or *Love is a babble* — as, for example, the early *Blow, blow thou winter wind* (Shakespeare) (1890), *It was a lover* (Shakespeare) (1893) or *The Countryman* (Anon) (1898). There are homophonic settings that have unsuspected contrapuntal depths, like *Come sleep* (J Fletcher) (1908) with its unobtrusive canon at the octave between the soprano and tenor.

Occasionally a particular image in a poem will spark off an appropriate texture. 'Bell' sounds seem to have fascinated Wood, as, for example, in Shakespeare's *Full fathom five* (1891):

Example 102

How sweet the tuneful bells (W L Bowles) (1908), or in the unfinished *How soft the village bells* (Cowper) (undated), which might have proved an atmospheric, as well as a contrapuntal, delight:

Example 103

Wood's masterpiece in this direction is undoubtedly *I call and I call*, a setting of Herrick's lyric (1905), which will stand out in any company as a *tour de force* of onomatopoeic writing:

Example 104

In one or two songs the consequences of Wood's immersion in the music of the 16th century manifest themselves in the harmony — though not in terms of pure pastiche — as, for instance, in some fairly late Campion settings, *Awake, awake* (1914) and *Follow, follow* (1922).

Finally, one should mention the existence of a handful of part-songs which, by reason of the complete appropriateness of their means to their ends, are among Wood's finest works and miniature triumphs of the creative imagination. On such a list should certainly be included *Music, when soft voices die* (Shelley) (1908):

Example 105

and *Lullaby* (otherwise *Golden Slumbers*) (Dekker) (*Op post* in 1927):

Example 106

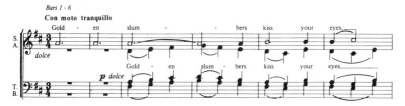

which have a magical atmosphere all their own, and rare at any time in choral music.

One work deserves mention on historical grounds. In 1899, Sir Walter Parratt, organist of St George's Chapel, Windsor, and Master of the Queen's Musick, having *The Triumphs of Oriana* in mind, invited a number of distinguished composers, poets and versifiers, to contribute to a similarly intentioned compilation, a set of *Choral Songs by various writers and composers in honour of Her Majesty, Queen Victoria.* The collection, which was duly performed at Windsor for the delectation of its widow, included part-songs by Mackenzie, Stanford, Walford Davies, Sir Frederick Bridge, Sir George Martin, Parry, A M Goodhart, Arthur Somervell, Elgar, C H Lloyd, Stainer, Parratt himself and Charles Wood, whose offering, a massive six-part work, *The century's penultimate* (MS dated July 14, 1899) to words by one A C James, must have tested the vocal technique of the choir involved.

When writing for mixed voices, Wood does not seem to have had any particular choir in mind. The opposite is true of his original works for male voices, three of which are specifically linked with named vocal groups. Several others were undoubtedly written for his own use as director of music at Caius College — so in a sense they were conceived of as being *gebrauchs-*

131

musik — a term that does not necessarily exclude works of serious artistic endeavour.

The male-voice choir in its various formats (TBB, ATBB, ATTB, TTBB) is a wonderfully sonorous and well-balanced vehicle for vocal composition. It is true that the individual vocal lines tend to be squeezed too closely together for elaborate contrapuntal writing to be either easy or effective (especially when the medium is TTBB), but as a harmonic medium it is unsurpassed, and in terms of sheer technical perfection, a good male-voice choir has the edge on most other choral mediums — almost any choral subtlety conceived by the imaginative composer can be a practical possibility.

Wood's works for TBB comprise two posthumously published settings, two MS settings, and four that survive as apparently complete short-score MS sketches. There is one MS ATBB setting. Of his ATTB settings, three were published in his lifetime and two posthumously, one remains in MS and two in short-score sketches — of these one was left apparently complete and one unfinished. The TTBB settings outnumber the rest. Three were published in his lifetime, three more posthumously, four survive in MS, two (with piano accompaniment) as incomplete full-score MSS. Two TTBB songs are known to have been lost after Wood's death.

One's critical reaction to these works, viewed *en masse*, is not dissimilar to one's reaction to the original works for mixed voices. The same technical mastery and the same instinct for what is vocally effective are apparent. The most successful works are those in which one senses that Wood had a greater personal commitment to the text — as for instance in the settings of Shelley's *When winds that move not* (1913), written for ATTB and inscribed 'To the Gentlemen of St George's Choir, Windsor', or of Byron's *There be none of beauty's daughters* (1926, brought out in 1927) and dedicated to the King's College Cambridge Quartet (ATTB)[5]:

Example 107

and, perhaps finest of all, of Whitman's *A clear midnight* (TTBB), published posthumously in 1926:

Example 108

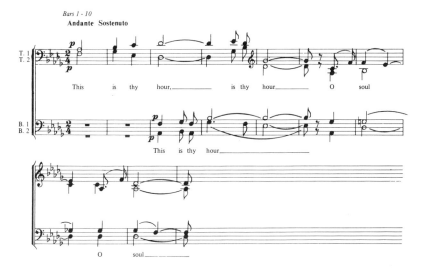

Of the three works which have a piano accompaniment, the early MS, *Fight, brothers, fight* (author unknown — tenor solo, TTBB), (August, 1888), exhibits the full-blooded intensity of a Verdi chorus[6], and the later *Sailors' song* (poem by Sidney Dobell), set for TBB and piano, has an engaging nautical liveliness that could make it worth reviving[7].

Wood's original part-songs for female voices include two for SSAA, the first of which has an optional and the second an integral piano part, and two for SSSS, one with an integral piano part and the other unaccompanied. All were published during his lifetime. There are, in addition, three songs for SSA and piano, three for SSA unaccompanied, and two for SSS, one with piano accompaniment and one with an accompaniment for two violins as an alternative to the piano. All but one were brought out in his lifetime.

The unaccompanied female-voice choir is a decidedly tricky medium to handle, in that of its nature it is somewhat top-heavy — hence, perhaps, the preponderance of settings that include a piano accompaniment. Of the works for four voices, *Cowslips for her covering* (1913) (words by Herrick, SSAA and piano), a canon in doubled thirds at the fifth below, has a rapt intensity of expression, and is another wonderful example of that art which conceals art. The words are given a wholly appropriate setting. Wood listed it as No 6 of a set of nine canons for various combinations of female voices and piano.

133

Example 109

Golden Slumbers (Dekker) (1920), a double canon 4 in 2, is another *tour de force* of contrapuntal ingenuity, and a ravishingly lovely sound as well:

Example 110

One of the more memorable three-part settings (Canon 7), *Good precepts* (1913) (Herrick), uses canon by inversion in the outer voices set against a 16th-century psalm tune as a *cantus firmus* in the middle voice, the whole supported by a gently rocking independent piano part.

Music when soft voices die (Shelley) (1915), SSA and piano, has a Schumannesque warmth in its gently undulating vocal parts (*see Example 111, opposite*).

To music bent (1921) (Campion) likewise uses a canonic structure, 3 in 1, with a piano accompaniment so designed that, as has been noted above, it can also be played on two violins.

Example 111

As for the rest, there is not one setting that does not have some peculiar musical interest, and any women's choir capable of sustaining three independent lines should find something to engage them in this part of Wood's output.

One consequence of the passing of the 1870 Education Act was the general establishment of the 'singing class' as a feature of the curriculum in the state schools, and the opening up of a large market for the sale of 'school songs'. The competitive and non-competitive festivals reacted in time to this stimulus by including classes for school choirs and the smaller-sized women's choral groups, and by the late 1920s and early 1930s the production of 'school music' items had in its turn become a flourishing industry.

Victorian school music, on the whole, presents a rather melancholy picture. The words set are usually of little literary merit, the vocal lines are, at best, Mendelssohn-and-water, and when the vocal writing is in two parts their movement is almost exclusively in parallel thirds and sixths — following the example of such minor German composers as Franz Abt (1819-1885), whose vocal duets once enjoyed a considerable popularity in this country.

The founding during the mid-1900s of two new publishing firms, each of which set out to produce a significant school-music list[8] had important consequences, in that they led the way in improving standards through insisting on a better choice of words and a higher level of musical achievement in setting them. Those moderns who despise the Edwardian or Georgian school song in its ubiquitous single-copy quarto leaflet format (Brahms-and-water or whatever), might well give pause were they to compare it with what it replaced.

Together with his masters, Stanford and Parry, and alongside a considerable number of his contemporaries, Wood contributed largely to the 'Year

Book Press' catalogue, and subsequently to a rival series initiated by another publisher. It is perhaps surprising that a man who was regarded as something of a cloistered academic should have turned so surely to this particular creative outlet. His songs are not solo-songs recast, but compositions genuinely conceived in terms of the school singing-class or choir, being smoothly and economically written within the competence of the average choral group and the moderately accomplished accompanist. Though, obviously, they are not all equally inspired, they are nevertheless worth examining as pioneer examples.

Wood published 17 original unison songs in his lifetime, and another six were brought out after his death. One survives in the form of a complete MS sketch, and one was lost posthumously. They vary in quality though not, of course, in competence, but in some cases it is the text set that limits their use with today's young children, who are apt to turn their noses up at 'There are fairies at the bottom of my garden', *et hoc genus omne*. The earliest to appear, *She will not drink the blood red wine* (Anon), which was published in 1909, might well have been a solo song; indeed, with its folk-tune like melody and rather Brahmsian accompaniment it could be worth reviving as such. *The Knight's tomb* (Coleridge), of 1918, is a characteristic Wood slow funeral march and might, similarly, be worth reviving.

Martin Ackerman, assistant organist at St George's Chapel, Windsor, and general editor of the Year Book series, had conceived the idea of issuing a volume of short settings of children's verses by Christina Rossetti. *Kookoorookoo, and other songs* (1916) contains 26 such settings, of which Wood was responsible for three[9]. Of these, *Boats sail on the rivers* is a gem:

Example 112

A sequel, *Kikirikee*, containing 34 songs, four of which were Wood's, appeared in 1925[10].

Of the rest of Wood's original unison songs, some of the best appeared

136

posthumously. *A song of the sea* (Anon) (1926) has a pleasant 18th-century atmosphere reminiscent of Dibdin, and in *The trees in England* (de la Mare) (*Op post*, 1929), Wood produced a melody of heart-easing loveliness with a haunting final phrase that will, I am sure, continue to be sung for as long as school choirs and festivals survive:

Example 113

Bars 12 - 20
(Andante)

Of all the trees in England From sea to sea a - gain, The Wil - low love - li - est stoops her boughs Be - neath the driv - ing rain.

Wood, the contrapuntalist, was naturally attracted towards the two-part song with its canonic and imitative possibilities. He published 30 such songs, and another three were brought out posthumously. In 1888, Wood had composed a set of six vocal duets — or alternatively two-part songs — for female chorus S_1 and S_2. It had been his original intention to dedicate them to Grove, who, however, advised him otherwise[10]:

> I am glad to hear it, tho' I wish there had been a 1 before the 5. [Had he sold them outright for £5?]. However, my dear, there must be a beginning for every Beethoven or Mendelssohn!
> I am very pleased at the idea of dedicating them to your humble friend — but don't you think that it would be more appropriate to dedicate them to CVS[tanford], to whom you really owe far more than to me! I am really in earnest. Please God we shall live a few years longer and there will be other opportunities.

So when they were finally published, in 1892, they bore a dedication to Stanford. On reading them through one is immediately aware of Wood's superb technique — its flexibility and economy, its melodic discipline and its harmonic ease, eg the opening of the first song, a setting of Milton's *Now the bright morning star* (*see Example 114, overleaf*).

Of Wood's subsequent two-part songs, the most significant are those of canonic construction, the more so in that their canonic writing is so unforced and unobtrusive as in many cases to be almost unnoticed. Seven of the set of nine so-designated canonic part-songs were written for two voices[11]. Of these, one might pick out No 2, *The best of rooms* (Herrick), a canon at the fifth below; No 3, *To music* (Herrick), a two-part canon by inversion; and, best of all, *The ride of the witch* (Herrick) (*see Example 115, overleaf*).

Example 114

Example 115

— a canon at the unison and a gripping and picturesque setting that has thrilled choirs and their audiences since it first appeared in 1913.

The other non-canonic two-part songs include a delicate setting of *Who is Sylvia?* (Shakespeare) (1909) — MS dated January 22, 1891 — and what must have been one of the earliest school-song settings of the 15th century, *I have twelve oxen* (1916) (Anon).

The leaflet school-song is becoming a rarity. It is no longer regarded as economic by publishers to issue new works in this format, and with all the changes that have come about in school music during the last few years, the singing-class no longer dominates the curriculum as once it did. If some enterprising researcher ever studies the leaflet school-song as a genre, he will find that Charles Wood will stand high in the hierarchy of contributors — both for the number of outright 'winners' he composed and the generally very high level of craftsmanship displayed in the remainder.

Wood made arrangements of folk or national songs for every vocal combination discussed above with the exception of SSSS, SSA and piano, and ATTB. Fifteen examples were published in his lifetime, nine posthumously, and there are in addition 13 arrangements, apparently complete, in short-score MS sketch, one unfinished MS sketch, and nine arrangements of Irish melodies, apparently for SATB, for which there are no words. Three arrangements which were accepted by publishers but never issued must be presumed lost[12].

As may be expected, there is a predominance of Irish material in this mass of work, Twenty-eight of the arrangements are based on Irish melodies. For the rest Wood seems to have drawn largely on Hullah and Chappell for both words and music. He set no recently collected English, Scots or Welsh melodies.

The arrangements vary from simple strophic settings to more complex works involving variation technique, and the song textures themselves (in the version for unaccompanied voices) from the plainly homophonic to the ingeniously contrapuntal. Their musical value is largely dependent on the musical worth of the melodies chosen for arrangement.

Wood's use of variation technique in these arrangements is of interest. He will set the first stanza of a poem using a straightforward harmonisation of the melody. Subsequent stanzas are treated as variations using a wide variety of vocal textures. In this Wood was something of an innovator[13], and the five sets of folk-song variations themselves are interesting examples of his comprehensive variation technique employed (especially in the examples for unaccompanied male or female voices) in a somewhat restricting medium.

As test-pieces for mixed-voice groups and women's choirs in competitive music festivals, a few of Wood's part-song arrangements continue to be heard, and the male-voice choirs (musically speaking ultra-conservative in their tastes) still keep a handful of his works in their creaking repertoire, but the school song — unison or two-part — is, as has been noted, no longer a fundamental class-room standby, and Wood's contributions to this field have been largely put on the shelf.

Much of the music that has been discussed in this chapter has been long out of print and little regarded, but when the Victorian or Edwardian part-song is eventually revived — perhaps after as long an entombed silence as had the madrigal — there will be some delightful surprises awaiting the revivers, and the conviction will be forced upon them that some very lovely music (Wood's among it) was wantonly allowed to die.

NOTES

1. Waddington, S P, 'The late Dr Charles Wood', *RCM Magazine*, Vol 22, No 3, Midsummer Term, 1926, p 71.
2. Letters to Wood (1) written from the RCM and dated May 1, 1888.
   (2) written from the RCM, undated.
   (3) written from Lower Sydenham, SE, and dated May 7 (or 17?)
3. In a letter to the author dated November 6, 1968.
4. See Appendix Three, p 199.
5. The members of the quartet visited Wood in the nursing home during his final illness and performed the song to him. This was the last time he ever heard his own music.
6. The piano introduction is, alas, missing in the surviving MS.
7. The work survives in the form of a set of vocal parts and a piano score that has the piano part in outline sketch only. It is possible to reconstruct a complete full score from this material, but some of the details are still matters of conjecture.
8. Stainer and Bell, established in 1907, and the 'Year Book Press', founded in 1908.
9. Contributors included Sir Walter Alcock, Sir Frederick Bridge, Sir Percy Buck, Thomas F Dunhill, C H Lloyd, Mackenzie, Parratt, A J Silver, Stanford, Sir Donald Tovey, and Wood himself.
10. The contributors this time included Sir George Dyson, C S Lang, Hubert Middleton, Hilda M Grieveson, Emily Daymond, Herbert Howells, Henry Ley, F J Read, Edgar Bainton, Dorothy Stewart, Thomas F Dunhill, Martin Ackerman, Sir W H Harris, Alan Palmer, Charles Macpherson, R T White, Basil Harwood, and Wood.
11. See catalogue of works for full details of this series.
12. See Appendix Three.
13. Rutland Boughton had written three sets of choral variations on folk-songs between the years 1905 and 1909.

CHAPTER 9
The church music

Of all of Charles Wood's considerable output of compositions, only his church music is still substantially performed. A number of his services and anthems early found their way into the music lists of the cathedrals, collegiate churches and college chapels of the Anglican communion and have held their place in the repertory ever since. A smaller number of works are part of the musical heritage of those parish churches possessing choirs capable of performing them, and they are not unknown to Free Church and Roman Catholic choirs. Not a Christmas goes by without our hearing one or other of his carol settings, and there is little doubt that until liturgical innovations make the continued performance of his works impossible, Wood's will still be an honoured name in the church music circles of the English-speaking community throughout the world.

Wood's earliest surviving church-music settings date from his student days. An anthem for SATB and organ, *Be Thou exalted, Lord* (C major, 4/4, *Allegro*) survives from the time of his studies with Dr Marks at Armagh (MS dated November 14, 1882), and he wrote more church music by way of exercises as part of his studies in counterpoint at the RCM. A canonic setting of the doxology *Praise God from whom all blessings flow*, for unaccompanied double choir (C major, 2/1, *Allegro moderato*), dated March 2, 1886, exemplifies his early contrapuntal facility, and settings of *O God of Hosts, the mighty Lord* (F major, 2/2, *Adagio*, based on the Psalm-tune *Bedford*), for unaccompanied SSAATTBB, dated Easter term, 1886, and *Through the day thy love has spared us* (F major, 2/1) for unaccompanied SATB, words by T Kelly (1769-1855), dated December 31, 1886, indicate a partiality towards using metrical psalm-tunes as thematic material that anticipates his later interest in the subject, and an early fondness for writing church music based on non-scriptural words.

Late Victorian church music (outside the works of the quadvirate of Stanford, Parry, Basil Harwood and Alan Gray), although in some sense deriving from the continuing tradition of cathedral music stretching back to the 18th-century, was stylistically influenced by Mendelssohn, Spöhr and, to some extent, Gounod. Like the late Victorian part-song and ballad, it developed by reason of the commercial application of mass-production techniques to music publication and distribution. It met a need brought about by the proliferation of parish church choirs — themselves a consequence of post-Tractarian endeavours on the part of parishes to emulate the practice of cathedrals. At its worst it was characterised by an easy theatricality of expression[1] to which the three-decker Victorian church organs contributed — a reliance on harmonic effects of a fairly predictable sort, and an insensitiviy to the texts set, as exemplified by what Tovey once referred to as the chorister's fortieth article of religion — 'As it was, it was in the beginning' — brought about by an all-embracing dependence on the four-bar phrase as a melodic norm. Similar characteristics are also to be found in the weaker Victorian hymn- and carol-tunes — static basses, predictable harmonies, flaccid rhythms and four-square melodic shapes.

This state of affairs produced its inevitable reaction. The foundation in 1888 of the Plainsong and Medieval Music Society — itself another consequence of the post-Tractarian interest in musico/liturgical matters — was symptomatic of a change of taste, at least on the part of a small minority; and the establishment of the Church Music Society in 1905 pointed to a more specific predilection towards reform. In hymnology the publication of the *Yattendon Hymnal* in 1899, the revised *Hymns Ancient and Modern* in 1904, and the *English Hymnal* in 1906 all contributed to a new outlook with regard to hymn-tunes, and in the history of the carol revival the appearance of the first *Cowley Carol Book* in 1901 was an important mile-stone.

Sir Henry Hadow, writing on the subject of church music[2], stated that there are 'three diseases from which religious music can suffer: the disease of virtuosity, which over-elaborates the technique of composition and so tends to lose sight of its meaning; the disease of theatricalism, which over-emphasises the meaning at the expense of true dignity and reverence; and the disease of sentimentalism, which enervates the meaning by relaxing it into a soft and facile prettiness, unworthy alike of the sincerity of religion and of the chastity of art'.

The church music of those composers whom Dr Erik Routley has grouped together under the general title of 'the conservative craftsmen' (Parry, Stanford, Walford Davies, Harwood, Somervell, Wood and Bairstow), who were active from the late 1880s onwards, may be said in essence to have derived from Brahms in that he was a strong basic influence on their common harmonic and textural language. On the whole these composers were well aware of the traps for the unwary that Hadow was later to formulate, and if one compares their music with that of their less progressively minded contemperaries, this is very apparent.

When Wood ended his student days he was thus able to bring what I have already called his 'Max Bruch' style to church music — a style that sometimes rose to a more personal utterance — and alongside it a very considerable facility in contrapuntal writing, derived from years of study in old-fashioned strict-counterpoint[3] which could be the basis for much 16th-

century-influenced unaccompanied polyphony. In due course other
influences made their mark: plainsong, for instance, the melodic contours
of which were to shape the part-writing of some of the later services. His
encyclopaedic knowledge of 16th- and 17th-century psalm-tunes and chorales
and their contemporary treatments — an interest that, together with a
mutual delight in plainsong, he shared with his friend G R Woodward —
was also a potent seminal force. Melodically speaking, the characteristic
intervalic relationships of Irish folk music were occasionally to manifest
themselves in the vocal lines of his services, anthems and hymn-tunes.

Wood's output of church music may conveniently be considered under
five separate headings:

>   Introits and anthems
>   Services
>   Extended liturgical choral works
>   Original and arranged hymn-tunes
>   Original and arranged carol-tunes.

Among his 'exercise' anthems happens to be the first outstanding piece of
church music of his maturity: *O Lord, rebuke me not* (G minor, 4/2, *Slow*),
for SSAATTBB, is dated August 21, 1885, and was therefore written while
Wood was still at the RCM. It is a very remarkable work for a 19-year-old
composer, being a study in the massively sonorous, with carefully contrasted
antiphonal effects as between the upper and lower voices. It has a very real
and sombre power, far removed in style and spirit from the conventional
published anthems of its period. Indeed, one would have to go right back to
S Wesley's *In exitu Israel* to find a comparable piece of choral music. It
would be worth reviving. I quote the opening:

Example 116

Wood's first published anthem, which appeared in 1890, was the first of two short but weighty miniatures. *Try me, O God* (E flat major, 3/4, *Andante con moto*), for SATB and organ, is the better known, and its successor, *I will arise* (D major, C, *Adagio*), also for SATB and organ, which appeared in 1894, is the more original. Both have their moments of pure Brahms (see, for example, the concluding bars of the organ part of *Try me, O God*) but both of them are rich in that quality of 'gravitas' which in so much of the church music of the period — and indeed of our own day — is so noticeably lacking.

Also in 1890 the first piece of Wood's church music known to have been written directly as a consequence of his work at Caius College was performed. Its full title is of interest:

'PRECAMINI FELICITATEM'

Grace Anthem composed for commemoration days of

Gonville and Caius College,

Cambridge,

by

Charles Wood, BA, MusB, Organist Scholar of the College,

and first sung at the Perse Commemoration, December, 1890.

It was published in 1892 — presumably at the behest of the College.

Precamini felicitatem (G major, C, *Allegro moderato*), for SATB unaccompanied, (MS dated December 4, 1890) is an impressive work founded on, but not slavishly following, 16th-century models. It shows that 'real feeling for the liturgy' which, as C B Phillips has observed[4], informs all Wood's church music. It is ternary in structure and concludes with an 'Amen' of a restrained loveliness that harks forward in spirit to the *Phrygian Communion Service* of 30 years later. For those with ears to hear, it should have been obvious that a new voice had appeared among church-music composers, and that the days of complacent platitude were numbered.

For a commemoration service celebrating the 550th anniversary of the foundation of Gonville and Caius College (June 22, 1898), Wood made a setting of *Heaven* by Jeremy Taylor (1613-67), which was published during the same year — again, presumably, at the behest of the College authorities. This setting, for SATB and organ (G major, 4/2, *Moderato*) must be one of the earliest of that variety of hymn-anthem which uses choral partita techniques as Dr Routley has defined them[5]: 'hymn-anthems . . . are essentially hymn-tunes set with varied organ part, varied choral treatment, descant, fa-burden, and any other composer's device that will turn three or four verses of the same tune into an attractive anthem.' The technique is applied here to an original tune of Wood's, involving his 'psalm-tune style', and dealing with a hymn stanza of some metrical complexity. The result has an impressive vocal dignity commensurate with the solemnity of the liturgical occasion that called it forth.

144

Another occasional 'college' work was a *Grace anthem for Ascension Day* (D major, 3/4, *Allegro un poco maestoso*) for unaccompanied SATB. This setting of Latin words (O Rex Gloriae, Domine virtutum qui triumphator hodie, etc), dated April 29, 1899, alternates homophony and imitation with a deceptive rhythmic simplicity that has its own subtlety of expression. It remains in MS.

Wood's next anthem is not strictly an anthem but rather a Latin Grace: 'Oculi omnium in Te sperant, Domine, et Tu das escam ilorum in tempore oportuno. Gloria Tibi Domine. Amen.' This is the official 'Grace' of the Worshipful Company of Musicians. In 1904 the Company offered a prize for an appropriate musical setting. Wood gained the prize, and his version — a canon 4 in 1 for unaccompanied SATB (A flat major, 3/2, *Rather slowly*) — is sung, by singers hired for the purpose, at all full-scale dinners of the Company. It was published in 8vo format in 1932 (Cramer Choral Library No 30). *Oculi omnium* is a magnificent example of Wood's contrapuntal skill and his sense of the art which conceals art.

Example 117

In a similar canonic vein is the anthem *I will call upon God* (D major, ¢, *Andante*) for unaccompanied male voices ATB. The two upper voices are in strict canon at the 4th above, while the lower voice is canonic, by inversion and augmentation, at the octave. The MS is dated July 16, 1905, but the work did not appear in print until 1912, when it was brought out by the newly founded Year Book Press (see pp. 135/6). Without being particularly crabbed, it lacks the sensuous beauty of sound of *Oculi omnium* and the chromaticisms appear to be intellectually planned rather than musically inevitable.

For the Caius commemoration of October 6, 1910, Wood set — as a hymn-anthem — those same words, first set by Orlando Gibbons, that Stanford was to use for the last of his *Three Motets for unaccompanied chorus*, Op 135, three years later[6]. *Glorious and powerful God* (A major, 4/2, *Maestoso*), for SATB and organ (MS dated September 18, 1910), presumably, also published at the behest of the college — is a massively

sonorous Parry-like work which again demonstrates Wood's apposite sense
of occasion, as may be seen in the final 'Amen':

Example 118

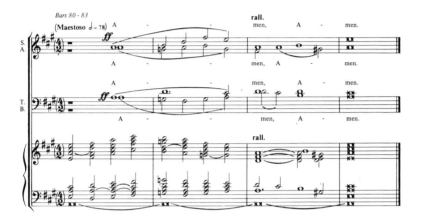

In August 1910, according to the MS, Wood made a setting of Campion's
Never weather beaten sail (D major, 4/4, *Andante*), for SATB and organ,
which was not published until 1935[7]. It is an easy, singable, effective
setting, making no stylistic effort to emulate the 16th century, and avoiding
harmonic and rhythmic commonplace by one or two deft and characteristic
touches. Apart from a few pedal notes, the organ part doubles the voices
throughout. Wood was here providing something for the ordinary parish
church choir not too far removed from the Victorian fare with which they
were familiar, but which yet had sufficient originality to commend it to
those for whom the Victorian was anathema.

Wood's next anthem (MS dated December 1913), entitled *Ascension
Hymn*, was a setting of words by his friend and collaborator A P Graves,
but he subsequently revised it to a new set of words by Eric Tatton (brother
of J M Tatton, Wood's pupil and amanuensis). In this form it was
published in 1927. *Who through the desert vale* (A flat major, 4/2,
Moderato) makes use of Wood's 'part-song' style in its vocal writing and
has a very fully written organ part. The text allowed Wood to make use of a
free ternary structure, with a middle section involving the tenors and basses
in unison. It is less austere in idiom than many of his anthems and,
paradoxically, the more dated.

According to J M Tatton[8] it had been in the year 1912, and during a

146

period of ill-health, that Wood wrote a number of large-scale works at the specific request of Martin Ackerman, then editor of the Year Book Press series, and was very hurt that they were not immediately issued as a group. Tatton believed that these works were 'the great choral works for double choir for the, I think, five(?) great festivals of the Anglican liturgical year.' The assumption is that at least some of these works were subsequently published but their precise identification is very much a matter for conjecture. Among them might have been found:

Great Lord of Lords (6-part double choir, ATB), published 1913;

Hail, gladdening Light (8-part double choir), published 1919;

Glory and honour and laud (SATB with divisi), published 1925;

'Tis the day of Resurrection (8-part double choir), offered to the YBP posthumously and published 1927;

Father all Holy (SATB with divisi), offered to the YBP posthumously and published 1929;

O King most high (8-part double choir), offered to the YBP posthumously and published 1932;

Once He came in blessing (8-part double choir), offered to the YBP posthumously and published 1935.

No dates of composition can be assigned to any of these works: even such rough sketches as survive give no indication as to when they were written. *Once He came in blessing* might, loosely, be regarded as suitable for Christmas. *Glory and honour and laud* is described on the publisher's list as an Easter anthem, but the words show it to have been intended for Palm Sunday. *'Tis the day of resurrection* is obviously intended for Easter, and *Great Lord of Lords* or *Father all Holy* would be appropriate for Trinity.

Wood's enormous skill, both in counterpoint and the management of large-scale unaccompanied choral designs, and his great sense of liturgical appropriateness in style and texture, are strongly to the fore in this series of works — which also reveal him exploring non-scriptural texts from a wide variety of sources.

Great Lord of Lords (D major, 2/2, *Maestoso*), for a double choir of male voices, is a setting of a poem by H R Bramley (1833-1917), of 'Bramley & Stainer' fame, and anticipates in some ways the choral writing of Parry's *Songs of farewell*. Wood makes of the text a long-phrased ternary structure, with a middle section carefully contrasted in terms of key and texture. Again, Wood builds out of the 'Amen' a lovely coda (*see Example 119, overleaf*).

Hail gladdening light (A major, 2/2, *Con moto*), a setting of Keble's well-known translation of a 3rd-century Greek hymn, uses a full 8-part double choir and relies much on antiphony between the two choirs. The structure is again ternary, and there is a resplendent coda in which the treble voices of 'choir 1' soar up to a radiant top 'A' on the word 'glories'.

Example 119

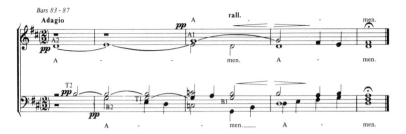

This masterly work has a vivid directness of expression and a fiery rhythmic impetus not common in Wood's church music.

Glory and honour and laud (D minor, 3/4, *Allegro ma no troppo*) is a setting of words by Theodulph of Orleans (9th-century), translated by J M Neale (1818-68), and demands a large choir capable of 8-part divisis. It was published in 1925 and received its first performance that same year at the Three Choirs Festival at Gloucester, conducted by Wood himself. It uses a free rondo form for its structural basis (A B A C A D A + coda) and is dominated by a striking unison statement in the Dorian mode:

Example 120

The second episode has a characteristic bell-like ostinato in the tenor part:

Example 121

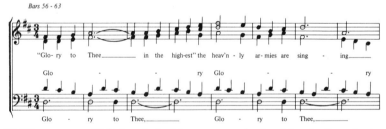

Dr Phillips wrote of it[9] that it 'achieves a convincing blend of ancient and modern which sums up the significance of Palm Sunday and can take a worthy place by the side of the two famous Tudor works written for the same occasion', and Sir Jack Westrup observed[10] of its 'robust vigour' that 'Wood's unerring sense of what constitutes effective choral writing and his capacity for combining brilliance of over-all effect with true economy of means were never more tellingly manifest'.

'Tis the day of Resurrection (F major, 3/4, *Allegro*), a companion Easter work, is a setting of the well-known Neale translation of St John Damascene's 8th-century original, 'The Golden Kanon for Easter', and was first performed at the Three Choirs Festival, at Hereford, in 1927[11]. Wood makes a ternary structure out of the 'Heirmos' and 'Troparia' of the original. The opening is a fine example of Wood's great control of the mathematics of music. A canon 4 in 2 in Choir 1 is answered by a triumphant paean when all eight voices coalesce. The use of interlocking 'trumpet figures' is unusual:

Example 122

In the contrasting middle section (F minor, 4/4, *Andante*), a Genevan psalm-tune[12] is introduced in Choir 2, with each successive line separated by a commenting interlude in Choir 1. The final section, beginning with the words 'Now let the heavens be joyful', recapitulates the opening music, and there is another of those exultant codas which are so distinctive a feature of the big double-choir works.

Father all holy (E flat major, 2/2, *Sostenuto*), a setting of some anonymous 9th- or 10th-century words translated by G R Woodward, is of a much simpler and more intimate nature, and has more of the character of a varied hymn-tune, as is shown by a brief look at the texture:

  v 1, SAB soloists, with SATB chorus providing introduction and interludes.
  v 2, — ditto —
  v 3, SATB (Choir 1) with SA (unison) TB (Choir 2).
  v 4, an extended last verse which begins TB, grows into SATB, and finally SSATB.

According to the original *Musical Times* review[13] and Harvey Grace's article on Wood in the 4th (1929) edition of *Grove*, this motet — to use its printed title — is based on a Genevan psalm-tune, but I have not been able to substantiate this assertion by identifying the particular tune used. I have come to suspect that the whole work, in its devotional simplicity, is pure Wood.

In *O King most high* (A flat major, 4/4, *Maestoso*), Wood set a translation from the Cluniac Breviary (1686) made by the Revd W J Blew (1808-1894), that had previously appeared in *Songs of Syon* (No 128 in the 4th edition). This is the most solid and contrapuntally intricate of all the large-scale anthems and is written throughout for double choir. It was first performed six years after Wood's death by the Norwich Philharmonic Society, in December 1932. There is massive choral antiphony in the opening and closing sections and some complex contrapuntal writing in the middle, with some wonderfully expressive canonic chromaticisms at the words 'O Christ, behold this orphan'd fold' (reminiscent of some of the *Psalm Tune Organ Preludes*). A choir capable of a good performance of this work would have much cause for self-congratulation.

The last of what may be called the multi-voiced unaccompanied anthems is *Once He came in blessing* (C minor, Phrygian mode, 4/4, *Poco adagio*) a setting of a 16th-century text by Johann Roh (d.1547) which was translated by Catherine Winkworth (1827-1878). The first section relies on a gentle apposition as between a tenor soloist and the four-part choir; the second (*Andante con moto*) has a more robust but similar antiphony between two four-part choirs. This is carried on into a third and more vigorously contrapuntal *Allegro moderato*. The choral writing has a glowing radiance that belies its surface austerity and apparent simplicity. Wood's technical mastery is here subsumed by his power of reaching out to the listener in a sort of spiritual communion, at least in the context of the liturgical situation: music and text are fused together into a complete experience.

To return to the chronological treatment of Wood's anthems, we find that his next, *True love's the gift*, a setting of a lyric by Sir Walter Scott, began its published life in 1914 as a part-song, but, presumably by reason of its suitability as a wedding adjunct, was transferred to the church music series. This is a short work, a setting for unaccompanied SATB in ternary form (D major, 4/4, *Adagio*) using Wood's personal 'chordal' style at its most appealing, presaging such works as *O Thou, the central orb* or *Expectans Expectavi*.

O Thou, the central orb, brought out in 1915, is one of Wood's best-known anthems. It is a setting of words by H R Bramley originally written to provide an English text for a Latin anthem composed by Orlando Gibbons, and has attracted the attention of more than one distinguished commentator. Dr Erik Routley wrote of its opening[14] that it 'is still one of the authentic "cathedral sounds" that remain in the memory of anybody who has attended evensong regularly', and Dr Phillips[15] talked of its 'glorious intricacies' and of Wood's delight 'in his beloved 7ths and 9ths'. Again Wood had chosen a text which permitted him a neat ternary structure. The opening (B flat major, 4/4, *Slow*) uses a high romantic idiom derived, at least spiritually, from *Die Meistersinger*:

Example 123

and is contrasted by a balancing middle section with an urgent bass solo (*see Example 124, overleaf*).

It is interesting to note that the top G flat climax in the treble part of the first section is matched by a top A flat in the treble of the recapitulation.

In 1919, in addition to *Hail, gladdening light* already discussed above, three other anthems were published. *Summer ended*, a harvest anthem

Example 124

Bars 23 - 26

Come, quick-ly come,_____ and let Thy glo - ry shine.

(words by Greville Phillimore, 1821-1884), had been composed by Wood to meet a somewhat out-of-the-way challenge, having been written in 1917 (first performance, October 14 of that year) for a boys' prep school choir (Heatherdown School, Ascot), containing six 1st trebles, six 2nd trebles, 1 tenor and 1 bass. To compensate for the relative simplicity of the vocal writing the organ part is correspondingly complex. The words are perhaps too exclusively eschatalogical to be universally acceptable, but the anthem as a whole (D major, 4/4, *Moderato*) is still one of the very few harvest anthems that a musician can take delight in for its musical virtues.

O Lord that seest from yon starry height (Longfellow) (F minor, 2/2, *Sostenuto*), for SATB and organ, begins with a long unison, first for the tenors and basses and then for the sopranos and altos. Unaccompanied choral passages alternate with unison octaves plus organ accompaniment. Though the 'personal' style is still employed, the fire of inspiration has burned lower.

The last of the 1919 anthems, *Expectans expectavi* (D flat major, 2/2, *Adagio*) has been recognised almost from its first appearance as having a quality something apart from all of Wood's other church music. Again the words set are non-scriptural. Their author, Charles Hamilton Sorley (1895-1915), son of a Cambridge professor who had been a personal friend of Wood's, had, like Wood's own elder son, been killed in the First World War, and Wood's setting was made not long after the posthumous publication of his *Marlborough, and other poems* (Cambridge University Press — 1919). *Expectans expectavi* is made up of the two last stanzas of a longer poem, and the parallel between its sentiment and that of Psalm 40 ('I waited patiently') has been duly acknowledged by more than one commentator. There can be little doubt that this anthem crystallised Wood's response to the tragedy of the First World War, both in its abstract and in its personal connotations. Professor Westrup has written[16] of its 'eloquent intimacy' and Dr Phillips comments[17] upon its being a 'deeply-felt miniature whose tenuous lines create a hushed beauty seldom achieved by

152

anyone in English church music' and that 'it exhales a strange suggestion of the New Testament and instinctively recalls the spirit of the first Christian martyrs'.

In 1920 a six-part Latin motet, *Haec Dies* (SSATBB), was brought out. This work (C major, 3/4, *Con spirito*) was one of the fruits of an association between RCM-trained composers and the Westminster Roman Catholic Cathedral that had grown up steadily since Sir Richard Terry (1865-1938) had been appointed director of music at the cathedral in 1901. It is possible that the catalyst was Wood's friend and fellow-student S P Waddington, who was a Roman Catholic. At all events, works by Howells, Wood, Buck, Holst, Vaughan Williams, Stanford and Waddington himself appeared on the cathedral service-lists, especially during the war and the immediate post-war years. Terry himself, writing in 1919, commented on Wood's *Haec Dies* — composed that same year — as being a particularly fine example of a piece of Catholic church music that reflected the very spirit and intent of Pope Pius the 10th's 'Moto Proprio' of 1903. The possibilities of antiphonal treatment inherent in an unaccompanied six-voiced work are exploited to the full. The idiom is that of the 16th century without being slavishly pastiche in its application, and Wood's inherent instinct for vocal sonorities is given full play[18].

In 1924 Wood published a version of Psalm CXIV (*In exitu Israel*) set to the 'tonus peregrinus' as pointed in Burgess's *Manual of Plainsong*. Written for unison voices — either boys or men or both — it makes use of what may be called a pre-J H Arnold style of plainsong accompaniment (a style made familiar to many through its employment in the 1904 edition of *Hymns Ancient and Modern* and the original edition of the *English Hymnal*). The organ part tends to be rather thickly written, though with considerable variety of texture as between verses.

The hymn tune *Cambridge* (F major, 3/4), which was commissioned for and appeared in the 1925 edition of the hymn-book *Songs of Praise*, is really a hymn-anthem with an independent organ part, constructed according to the simple formula v1 — SATB; v2 — unison; v3 — SATB; with an 'Amen' coda. What distinguishes it from other, and more mundane, settings is the subtlety and beauty of the folk-tune-like melody Wood evolved for Baxter's words (6 bars + 5 bars + 5 bars):

Example 125

153

The 'Amen' coda was omitted from the published version.

Wood's executors were active for some years after his death in publishing works that in his lifetime had remained in manuscript, and although the opinion has been expressed that in certain instances zeal outran discretion, among his church music at any rate a number of examples of his choicest inspirations were made available to the world. In few cases are there any surviving MSS and none of these are dated; this in itself suggests that the bulk of this material survives from the latter part of the composer's life.

In 1927 was brought out an unaccompanied SATB harmonisation of the 'proper' tune for *Jesu, the very thought is sweet* (original by St Bernard of Clairvaux, translated by J M Neale) as found in Woodward's edition of *Piae Cantiones* (No LXI, pp 126-130). Only two pages long, this little work (G minor, 4/4, *Adagio*) has an atmosphere of restrained yet intensive devotion. Wood's added parts are 'apt to the life of the words' and the nature of the melody, so that one could well conceive that all had evolved simultaneously from the same creative impulse.

Wood was almost alone among his contemporaries in using the metrical psalm-tunes of the 16th and 17th centuries as thematic bases for anthems and canticles[19]. As has been noted above, he began the practice during his student days, but it was not until after the period of his pre-occupation with the hymn-book *Songs of Syon* (early 1900s onwards) that he set out systematically to exploit their melodic richness in his own work.

God omnipotent reigneth (Dorian mode, 2/2, *Adagio*) is a setting for SATB and organ of a metrical paraphrase of Psalm XCIII made by G R Woodward. The 16th-century melody by Pierre D'Aques[20] appears twice. After an arresting organ opening the whole tune is heard in a stark harmonisation for unaccompanied voices. Then the organ opening is repeated and all forces join in a dramatically onomatopoeic, freely contrapuntal, setting (*see Example 126, opposite*).

God omnipotent reigneth is a resplendent and fiery work, very exhilarating to perform.

Two short introits (or prayers) were also brought out in 1927 (Year Book Press A51). *O most merciful* (G minor, 4/4, *Adagio*), for SATB with organ, is a setting of words by Bishop Heber (1783-1826), and *Oculi omnium* (E major, 4/4, *Adagio*), for unaccompanied SATB, of part of the Latin version of Psalm CIV, the same text he had already set for his 'prize' Grace (see p. 145)[21]. According to Harvey Grace the first is based on a melody from the Genevan Psalter, but which one has not yet been established. Both these settings are delicate and intimate miniatures, saying much in a few bars.

How dazzling fair (D major, 2/2, *Moderato*) for SATB and organ, which was published in 1929, is based on the melody of Psalm 1 of the French Psalter (Strasbourg, 1539)[22]. The words of Johann Scheffler (1624-1677) are paraphrased by G R Woodward, and the three verses are set as follows:

v 1 — SATB (melody in treble);
v 2 — SATB (melody in tenor) + free organ part;
v 3 — Unison with a further elaborated free organ part.

Wood is careful to preserve the rhythmical liveliness of the original melody.

Out of the deep (A minor, 4/2, *Andante*), words from Psalm CXXX, and *Bow down thine ear* (G minor, 4/2, *Moderato*), words from Psalm LXXXVI, appeared together in 1931. The first setting is based on the psalm tune *Du fond de ma pensée* (Strasbourg 1539), altered by L Bourgeois (1542), which Wood had already used in the anthem *'Tis the day of resurrection* (see p. 149). The second is based on the psalm tune *Mon Dieu, preste moy l'aureille* (Psalms 77 and 86) — a secular melody adapted by L Bourgeois (1542)[23]. Both works have a sombre dignity of style decidedly reminiscent of Orlando Gibbons.

Also in 1931 was brought out a further psalm-tune anthem for SATB and organ, *O thou sweetest source of gladness* (A flat major, 2/2, *Molto moderato*). This setting, based on Louis Bourgeois' melody for Psalm XLII in the Psalter of 1551, uses a translation by G R Woodward of words by Paul Gerhardt (1607-1706)[24]. It follows a similar structural pattern to *How dazzling fair*, namely:

v 1 — SATB (melody in treble);
v 2 — SATB (melody in tenor) with a more elaborate free organ part;
v 3 — largely unison with a yet more elaborate organ part.

Again the rhythmic freedom of the original melody is carefully preserved.

The last of Wood's anthems to achieve posthumous publication appeared

Example 126

in 1938, 12 years after his death. It is a setting for ATB and organ of Campion's *View me Lord* (C minor, 4/4, *Adagio*) and is founded on a melody which Woodward dated as 1457, set by Michael Weiss in the *Songbook of the Bohemian Brethren* (1531). The work is organised on the basis of:

v 1 — ATB (melody in alto) unaccompanied;

v 2 — basses only;

v 3 — ATB (melody in tenor), and

v 4 — unison.

As in similar anthems, the organ part becomes progressively more complex as the work proceeds. Altogether this anthem rounds off the tally of Wood's published anthems in a most satisfactory fashion. The appropriateness and liturgical propriety of its treatment, the reticence and control of the writing, and the underlying rock-like devotional commitment sum up Wood's church-music ethos in a most compelling way.

An undated setting of *Behold now praise the Lord* (F major, ₵), for unaccompanied SATB, uses Wood's more obviously strict-counterpoint-derived, pseudo-16th-century style. Four short antiphons or introits for SATB and organ, complete as to the vocal parts but wanting the organ part written out where, presumably, it merely doubles the vocal parts, also survive in undated MS form. The titles are as follows:

I am arisen and still with thee (A major, 3/4)

O Lord thou hast searched me out and known me (A major, 4/4)

This is the day which the Lord hath made (D major, 3/4)

The earth trembled and was still (B flat major, 3/4)

It is possible that these four short pieces may have been among Wood's last works and that the final editing of the MSS was left incomplete by reason of his fatal illness. This is a pity, for they are four gems — a miniature epitome of Wood's art and craft as a church composer, and having, for all their brevity, an almost mystical atmosphere in their faithfulness to the spirit of the words set.

Another eight works, otherwise unknown, survive in the form of complete short-score sketches from which it has been possible to re-construct performing versions. Included among them are two short introits for unaccompanied SATB both having the same title but different words:

O gladsome light (St Athenogenes, 3rd-century, translated Yattendon Hymnal) (E flat major, 4/2)

O gladsome light (Longfellow, from *The Golden Legend*) (D major, 4/2)

They are each deeply personal and as such would be worth publishing.

There is also a set of *Graces, before and after meat* (*Benedictus benedicat* and *Benedicto benedicatur*). Written polyphonically for ATB, they were presumably composed for use at Caius on formal occasions.

A strict-counterpoint setting for SATB of *Thy mercy, O Lord* (Psalm

XXXVI, v 5) (A major, 2/2), based on a semibreve *cantus firmus*, might just have been an exercise, but it is lively enough to merit performance.

A 'chorale motet' for unaccompanied SATB (F major, 2/2) which exists in MS sketch without words or other attribution, has been identified as being based on *Or soit loué l'Eternel*, a melody by Pierre D'Aques (1562)[25]. A similar setting (G minor, 2/4) of *Ye who the name of Jesus bear* (words from *Draft Scottish Translations and Paraphrases*, No 7 of the 1745 edition) is based on an as yet unidentified psalm-tune. Both settings are inventive and lively in their contrapuntal flow and would also be worth performing.

An examination of Wood's anthems as a whole leads one to some pertinent generalisations. One notes, for example, that the division between what has been called Wood's 'personal' style and his more austere pseudo-16th-century style is maintained throughout; that there is a predominance of non-scriptural texts in the words set; that there is a predominance of unaccompanied, as opposed to accompanied, settings; and finally that as many works appeared posthumously as in the composer's lifetime.

Wood's choral writing is rarely difficult. As Dr Routley observes[26]: '(Wood) had, like Parry, a good eye for a suggestive text — Biblical or extra-Biblical — and a great sense of dignity. He was not a rhythmic experimenter, even to the extent that Walford Davies was, but his gift of melody and sonorous harmony, of sensing what would sound well in an English cathedral, and of underlaying these with an unerring traditional craftsmanship, ensured that he would find a warm welcome wherever a music was looked for that would say the familiar things with decorum and cogency.'

Wood's organ writing sometimes tends to the massive, with fistfuls of notes — a natural consequence of the adoption of tubular-pneumatic action — but it is always effective.

The composing of 'services' was for Wood a constantly recurring activity throughout his adult life; indeed one feels with him, as with Telemann, that he could 'write a setting of the Magnificat as quickly as other people write a letter'. As with his anthems, a considerable number of his services were published posthumously, and there is a similar stylistic diversity in the works themselves.

We do not know when Wood wrote his first service. There is an interesting letter from Grove having a bearing on the matter, from which it appears that Grove had encouraged him to try his hand at service-writing with the idea of getting his name before a wider public:

My dear Wood,
 I have been talking to Dr Bridge about you and suggested that you should write a full morning and evening service for Novello's 8vo series. It would

157

make your name widely known, and, if done as I anticipate, would become popular. It should contain Te Deum, Jubilate, Benedictus (not Benedicite) — Communion Service, Kyrie, Gloria, Creed. Evening — Magnificat and Nunc Dimittis.

It should be short and not elaborate (*that* wastes time) (Sullivan's is too long). Bridge says that Garrett's services are useful models, as far as form goes, and I have told Novellos to send you a copy or two.

Forgive this interference. It is only because I think it will do you good and that you will do it well.

Yours ever and ever,

G Grove.

But it was not until Wood migrated to Cambridge that he began the systematic composing of service music, following, initially, in Stanford's footsteps.

Stanford had revolutionised the matter of setting the canticles to music in that for the old line-by-line method he had substituted what has sometimes been called 'symphonic technique', achieving musical unity through the use of short pregnant motifs in the vocal parts and accompaniment — this use of motifs being associated with a much more considered approach to tonality through the employment of structural modulations. As Sir Edward Bairstow put it[27]: 'For some time after Purcell our composers did not write in extended instrumental forms; there were few British sonatas or symphonies or chamber music; our music was in penny numbers, so to speak. Even Samuel Sebastian Wesley's great anthems and services are all in short movements, for though he had splendid musical ideas he never developed them. It was Stanford, with his experience and constant practice of sonata form, who first brought development into Church music. The result was that instead of the listener having to pick up the threads of interest with every short movement the attention was held throughout. This affected the Anthem to some extent, but it affected the Service far more. An Anthem is generally short, but the Te Deum, the Credo and the Magnificat are very great hymns and require . . . to set them one who has the technique of composition at his fingers' ends . . . English Church music has suffered because it has been largely composed by men who were Church musicians and organists first, and composers second. Stanford understood the requirements as well as they did, but had greater gifts. It is the most difficult thing to set the canticles to music. It has been done so often before. The limits of a church choir and organ must not be over-stepped. Each number must be short and concise.'

Wood's first published evening service (SATB and organ) appeared in 1891. The Magnificat (E flat major, C, *Allegro*) is vivid and sonorous, alternating massive unisons with four-part vocal writing, very much in the

Stanford fashion. The Nunc Dimittis (E flat major, 3/4, *Andante sostenuto*) is more lyrical. Both canticles share a resplendently dramatic Gloria.

A second evening service for SATB and organ, published in 1898, has some original features. The Magnificat (D major, 4/4, *Allegro*) makes use of the juxtaposition of unaccompanied and accompanied sections, and there are some telling and unexpected modulations. In the Nunc Dimittis (D major, 3/4, *Adagio*) the kernel of the work is given to the basses, with the upper parts murmuring the opening words above them as a commentary. Again, both canticles share the same Gloria.

The third service for SATB and organ, brought out in 1900, is still more original in that much of its thematic material is apparently derived from the characteristic melodic shapes of Irish folk-song. In the Magnificat (C minor, 4/2, *Allegro moderato*) the vocal parts come together in great unison/octave blocks of sound (see Example 1, p 30, above), and the opening of the Nunc Dimittis (C minor, 4/2, *Adagio*), with its gently moving quasi-ostinato bass, is an example of forward-looking writing:

Example 127

This evening service in C minor stands out as an early peak of achievement, and it would be a matter of enormous regret if the whirligig of liturgical change banished it to the museum.

Wood's next evening service (SATB and organ), which was published in 1908, is on the surface a much more conventional production, but a closer examination reveals a number of unobtrusive contrapuntal ingenuities. The opening of the Magnificat (F major, 3/2, *Allegro moderato*), for example, though apparently commonplace, is distinguished by the fact that although all four parts start together, the tenor part (after its first few notes) is in strict canon at the 9th below the treble as far as the words 'and Holy is His name'. In the next section (as far as 'all generations') the treble is similarly in canon at the 4th above the alto. At 'He hath shewed strength' it is the bass and treble that are in canon. The section beginning 'He hath put down' is a canon 4 in 2; at 'He, remembering His mercy' the canonic writing is between the tenor and bass at the 5th below, and the Gloria is wholly canonic 4 in 1. The Nunc Dimittis (D major, 4/2, *Adagio*) uses the device of augmentation in the first section, as far as 'thy word', and the tenor part throughout is a strict augmentation of the treble:

Example 128

The process is then reversed as far as the words 'all people', and reversed again for 'to be a light, etc'. These contrapuntal subtleties are not paraded as such — indeed the Nunc Dimittis is more remarkable for its expressive gentleness than its evident intellectual content. Wood's mind naturally thought in these terms.

In contrast to the subtle complexity of the Service in F, Wood's next set of evening canticles, brought out in 1911, exhibits an austere simplicity, being based on two plainsong tones — the Magnificat on Tone VI and the Nunc Dimittis on Tone V. The writing (SATB and organ) is antiphonal, alternating between unison and simple four-part harmony, and the organ part shows a considerable inventiveness within the limits of a deliberately restricted harmonic vocabulary:

Example 129

This is one of the earliest pieces of church music deriving specifically from Wood's interest in plainsong, and from now on plainsong was to have an increasingly important impact on his church music in general (see p. 143).

Wood's next two services, however, derive from and reflect an alternative pre-occupation. These are the Magnificat and Nunc Dimittis in G for unaccompanied male voices (ATB), which appeared in 1911, and the evening service for double choir (ATB), published in 1913. Whilst not slavishly imitative of the 16th century, they show an increasing awareness of 16th-century textures and word-setting techniques, and the latter service in particular achieves an impressive sonority as in the Amen to the Gloria of its Nunc Dimittis:

Example 130

Of the Cambridge colleges that boasted a full choir, the reputation of that of King's College stood perhaps highest[28], and in 1915 Wood produced an evening service for double choir and organ especially 'Written for the Choir of King's College and first performed in King's College Chapel'. This *Magnificat and Nunc Dimittis (Collegium Regale)* was published in 1920. The writing is not strictly in eight parts throughout, and there is considerable antiphony between the two choirs; indeed, Wood achieves a surprising number of vocal permutations of texture. Harmonically there is a certain austerity, reminiscent of 16/17th-century psalm-tune harmonisations, but the overpowering impression in the Magnificat (F major, 4/2, *Allegro moderato*) is of a soaring magnificence worthy of the building and the choir. In the Nunc Dimittis (F major, 4/2, *Adagio*) the melodic line of the 1st tenor and 2nd bass parts is taken — so a footnote informs us — from the French Psalter of 1549[29]. E H Fellowes suggested that Wood was here following the example set by T A Walmisley (1814-1856), who used a bass from an Agnus Dei by the French composer Dumont in the Gloria of his Magnificat in D minor[30]; but, as Fellowes goes on to observe, Wood carried the idea much further and in a new and original fashion. A second, similar setting in G major for unaccompanied double choir (MS dated August 15, 1915) had to wait until 1932 for publication, when it made a great impression on the *Musical Times* reviewer, who commented enthusiastically on the varieties of vocal combination used to serve the composer's expressive purpose.

Also in 1915 Wood brought out an evening service in A flat for men's and boys' voices in unison, or unison antiphony with organ accompaniment. As with the 1908 setting, it appears on the surface to be a comparatively straightforward work; but, again, a more detailed consideration discloses that the bass of the organ part is in strict canon with the vocal line throughout, sometimes at the 12th below, and sometimes at the 8ve or double 8ve, and in the Gloria of the Magnificat (A flat major, 4/2, *Allegro moderato*) by inversion at the 7th below. Again there is no blatant parading of these ingenuities: they are there simply because Wood could express himself fluently and naturally in canonic terms.

Two settings of the Latin text of the Nunc Dimittis were made expressly for Westminster Cathedral. The first, for unaccompanied SSATBB (B flat major, 4/4, *Adagio*), dated March 25, 1916, was performed at Saturday Compline in the cathedral on September 7, 1916, and the second — also for unaccompanied SSATBB — (A minor, erroneously given as C in the Faith Press edition, 4/2, *Adagio*), dated October 16, 1916, was first heard at Sunday evening Compline on March 3, 1917. Both settings were published posthumously in 1927, each with an English as well as the original Latin text. The former, presumably added for publication, is a somewhat clumsy fit[31]. These two settings use a solid diatonic style, somewhat Parryesque, and rely on antiphony between the upper and lower voices for textural contrast.

In 1918 Wood was once again stimulated by the choral magnificence of King's, to another experiment — one unique both in Wood's output and, indeed, in the whole body of Anglican liturgical music. Wood took the metrical version of the Magnificat and Nunc Dimittis from Sternhold and Hopkins (the 'Old Version') and set them for unaccompanied SATB, using as his thematic material metrical psalm-tunes (the Magnificat was included in its 1919 King's Carol Service); in the Magnificat (E flat major, 3/4, *Andante*), the proper psalm tunes for Psalm LXXVII which first appeared in the Anglo-Genevan Psalter of 1556 (see Frost, pp 103-4), and Psalm XLIV, which was first published in the English Psalter of 1562 (see Frost, pp 127-8), were used. The psalm tune used in the Nunc Dimittis is that set to Psalm XIX in the Anglo-Genevan Psalter of 1556 (see Frost, p 83). The vocal texture that Wood evolved is thoroughly in keeping with the basic material — compare, for instance, the opening of the psalm tune

Example 131

with the opening of the Magnificat evolved from it:

Example 132

The whole setting is so striking that one can only regret that a loyal sense of liturgical propriety must forbid its regular performance. It was published in 1920.

In 1923, having published a second Magnificat and Nunc Dimittis for SATB and organ based on plainsong themes (Tones IV and I), Wood at last interrupted the sequence of evening services with some setting appropriate to other occasions in the liturgical day. The first of these was a setting of the Te Deum and Benedictus for SATB and organ — the Te Deum (D minor, 2/2, *Allegro moderato*) being evolved from the settings by J H Schein and J S Bach of the proper Ambrosian chant for the canticle in its German metrical form (see *Songs of Syon*, nos 377 a and b), and the Benedictus (D major, 2/2, *Allegro moderato*) from the melody *Quando Christus ascenderat* to be found at pp 132-3 of Woodward's edition of *Piae cantiones*. The Te Deum is a notoriously difficult canticle to set, even adequately. Wood's version, mainly one note, one syllable, following Cranmerian precept, is brisk and direct, the thematic material being used with an eye on structural unity. The more gracious Benedictus makes an excellent foil to it.

The final 1923 publication, the *Short Communion Service in the polyphonic style, written for unaccompanied singing, chiefly in the Phrygian Mode*, familiarly known to two generations of church musicians as 'Wood in the fridge', is perhaps his best-known service and may well be regarded as his masterpiece. There is no settled number of component settings in a Communion service and Wood was never consistent in what he included or left out. The *Phrygian service* includes:

A three-fold Kyrie (adaptable by repetition for use as a nine-fold Kyrie)

Responses to the Commandments

The Credo, left unaccompanied to a '6th-century trad. melody'
The complete setting of the Nicene Creed for unaccompanied SATB was published separately and posthumously in 1927.

Responses before the Collect and before the Gospel of the day

Responses before the Preface

163

Sanctus
Benedictus
Agnus Dei
Pater Noster
Gloria

Wood evidently consulted Woodward, and fragments of a letter survive from the latter commenting in discerning fashion on the work[32]:

> . . . taking up the Kyrie one after another, but all ending at a full close, at the termination of the 3rd Kyrie of each group. I think (that) is how Vittoria, Palestrina, Croce and the like often treated the Kyries.
>
> But I do not wish to seem to dictate to you of all people, but only to suggest
>
> (1v) You see the Credo is in the Hypo-Phrygian Mode. So is your Lord have mercy; so is your Gloria in excelsis, Sanctus and Benedictus, if I remember right. So I thought there should be a contrast certainly in the Agnus Dei and this you have done.
>
> If you write the Nine-fold Kyrie, Christe eleison, I venture to think it would be advisable to write it in some other Mode, in either the 1st, 5th or 6th, or 7th Modes.
>
> For the rest, I am greatly pleased with all that you have done. I have noticed many of your clever and charming inventions, and most melodious pages; and certainly . . .

Wood's music alternates between the note-for-note harmonic simplicity of the homophonic passages and the relative complexities of intricately contrapuntal sections in which the individual melodic lines show an awareness of the characteristic melodic shapes of plainsong. Wood dispenses with accentual bar-lines, which again contributes to the rhythmic freedom and subtlety of the writing. The whole has about it an atmosphere of tender austerity (yet again these epithets spring to mind!) that reminds one of Byrd. Take, for example, the 'Hosanna in the highest' from the Benedictus:

Example 133

Wood published no more services in his lifetime, but his literary executors found a plenitude of unpublished material, much of which achieved print over the next few years.

The first of these services appeared in 1926 and consisted of a Magnificat (G major, 4/4, *Allegro*) and Nunc Dimittis (G major, 3/4, *Andante*), the first of which was 'founded on an old Scotch chant' — so far unidentified. Both canticles are set for SATB and organ, and follow the usual pattern of thematic usage found in Wood's psalm-tune services. Both share the same Gloria.

Of the four evening services for SATB and organ brought out in 1927, two are original, one in C major and one in E flat. Neither calls for extended comment. From a constructional point of view it may be noted that both make occasional use of the SA-TB two-part technique — an uncommon device in Wood's armoury, and both have that effectiveness in performance that sprang from his intimate practical knowledge of choirs and the art of writing appositely for them.

The other two settings are founded on older material. The Magnificat in E minor (Phrygian mode, 4/4, *Un poco maestoso*) is based on the melody of Psalm CIV in the Anglo-Genevan Psalter of 1561 (see Frost, pp 150-2), and its associated Nunc Dimittis (Phrygian mode, 4/4, *Andante*) on Psalm CXXXII in the same Psalter (see Frost, pp 100-1). The Magnificat of the other derived Evening service is founded (Phrygian mode, 4/2, *Allegro moderato*) on the melody *Bene quondam dociles*, to be found in *Piae Cantiones* (Woodward edition, pp 136-7), and its Nunc Dimittis (Phrygian mode, 4/2, *Andante*) on *Quando Christus ascenderat*, also from *Piae Cantiones* (Woodward edition, p 132). Both of these services are remarkable for their rather stark homophonic texture. Again the writing conforms largely to the Cranmerian doctrine of 'one note, one syllable'. One feels that Wood was largely influenced by such 16-century originals as Tallis's short service in the Dorian mode — as is shown by the opening of the Nunc Dimittis of the *Piae Cantiones* service:

Example 134

In addition to the setting of the Nicene Creed to which reference has already been made above, Wood's executors brought out no less than four complete Communion Services in 1927. The *Missa Portæ Honoris*, for SATB and organ, is an Anglican version of Wood's *Mass in F*, the adaptation of the original setting to the words of the Communion Service being made, and the title added, after Wood's death. It will be considered later, in its original form.

The Communion Service in C minor for SATB unaccompanied consists of:

> Three-fold Kyrie
> Responses to the Commandments
> Credo
> Sanctus
> Benedictus
> Agnus Dei
> Gloria

In style it is very reminiscent of the service in the Phrygian mode, but the writing is less smooth and perhaps more intellectually calculated, as, for example, in the ending of the opening Kyrie:

Example 135

A work that doubtless owed its inception to Wood's friendship with G R Woodward[33] was the 'Complete Communion Service that is to say Kyrie Creed Sanctus Benedictus Agnus Dei, and Gloria in Excelsis selected out of The Plainsong and Medieval Musick Society's Ordinary of the Mass and Harmonised for four voices by Charles Wood with organ or pianoforte accompaniment'. For some obscure reason the Kyrie is in actual fact a setting of the 'Responses to the Commandments' which open with the same words. Complete sketches for the true Kyrie exist, so why it was not included in this posthumous publication is something of a mystery.

The plainsong is set for voices (doubled in the accompaniment), and a detailed rubric gives suggestions as to modes of performance: 'The service may be sung in unison with Organ accompaniment, and in four parts with or without Organ accompaniment. The plainsong melody appears in the

166

treble part throughout except on page 15 where the Altos sing it, and on page 6 (except last bar) and top line of page 7, where the Tenor sings it.' The plainsong is harmonised on a strict note-for-note basis, with some occasional rhythmic independence in the lower parts — as at the opening of the Benedictus:

Example 136

But in general the voices move in strict homophony — in short, a pre-J H Arnold approach to the problem of plainsong accompaniment.

The Communion Service in F (Ionian mode), for SATB unaccompanied, otherwise known as the *Missa Sancti Patriccii* (MS dated August 9, 1922) is the most complete of the posthumous settings. It consists of the following movements:

Kyrie
Responses to the Commandments
Responses before the Collect and Gospel of the day
Sanctus
Benedictus
Agnus Dei
Pater Noster
Gloria

There is no Credo in the published version, but an MS setting of the Creed in Wood's fair copy has survived that may well have been originally intended for it. By reason of its major tonality the Communion Service in F has a more genial and serene atmosphere than have its companion services

Example 137

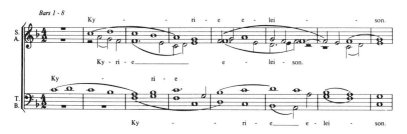

and the homophonic part-writing is more gentle in its chordal progress.

These published Communion Services of Wood's stand somewhat apart from his other service settings. For all their austerity of harmonic language and the circumscribed nature of their contrapuntal sections, they are highly personal works, having something of the authority of spiritual documents. One feels that this music was very close to Wood's heart, having its roots in the very core of his inner life.

In 1929 what was described as an anthem for SATB and organ, being a setting of the words *O be joyful in the Lord, all ye lands*, was published. It was, of course, a setting of the Jubilate, and was obviously founded on the psalm-tune *The Old Hundredth* — though this fact was not mentioned on the title page. The psalm-tune is heard complete three times — the first as far as the words 'sheep of his pasture', the second (melody in the tenor) as far as 'generation to generation' and the third for the Gloria. There is much unison writing, and the whole has an unsubtle directness that has endeared it to choirs since it first appeared:

Example 138

In 1933 were published a Te Deum in C minor, a Benedictus in A flat major and an Evening Service in A flat (all for SATB and organ). The *Musical Times* said of them[34] that they were 'examples of strong, soundly written work, straightforward in style, within the powers of the average choir.' The whole (including the Jubilate) form a complete day's services, though it is not certain whether this was Wood's original intention.

A Magnificat and Nunc Dimittis in E minor for unaccompanied SATB, which appeared in 1938, was the last of Wood's services to achieve posthumous publication, and in a sense it epitomises his service music. This unassuming, unpretentious work — so finely adapted to its purpose — represents a lifetime devoted to the adornment of the Anglican liturgy. Fashions in church music change, but as long as the tradition of sung Evensong is maintained, there will surely be a place for Wood's music as an aid to devotion and a symbol of the corporate aspect of worship.

As with Wood's anthems, there is a considerable number of unpublished services surviving in the form of complete fair copy MSS, and there is little to indicate why they should have been passed over, at least in terms of their quality. There are, in addition, a few unfinished fair-copy MSS that could be completed according to Wood's intentions, and a corpus of rough short-score MSS (apparently complete) from which performing versions can be reconstructed. None of these MSS are dated — but, as was the case with the anthems, their handwriting suggests that they come mostly from the latter part of Wood's life.

The completed MSS comprise a fine Magnificat and Nunc Dimittis in D minor for unison voices and organ, a Magnificat and Nunc Dimittis in C for SATB and organ that might be a companion to the late published service in E flat, and a Magnificat and Nunc Dimittis in F also, for SATB and organ, that is apparently founded on two metrical psalm-tunes — as yet unidentified. An interesting MS is that of a Magnificat and Nunc Dimittis for unaccompanied SATB, 'Founded on the melodies for these canticles in the Psalter of Sternhold and Hopkins'. The Magnificat (G minor, 2/2, *Rather fast*) is based on the tune for *The song of the Blessed Mary* in the English Psalter of 1560 (see Frost, p 57) and the Nunc Dimittis (G major, 3/2, *Slow*) on the tune for Psalm XIX in the Anglo-Genevan Psalter of 1556 (see Frost, p 57). Of all the surviving MS evening services, I would judge this the finest and most worthy of publication.

A simple 'plainsong' Magnificat (tone V) and Nunc Dimittis (tone VI) for SATB and organ is similar in texture to the published examples, as also is a Benedictus for SATB and organ (tone VII).

The complete Communion Service in C for SATB and organ is the most extensive service to remain in MS. It consists of:

      Responses to the Commandments
      Creed
      Sursam Corda
      Sanctus
      Benedictus
      Agnus Dei
      Pater Noster
      Gloria

In style it is far less austere than the published settings.

The unfinished Evening Service in A flat major for SATB and organ has a Magnificat that is complete as to the vocal parts but the organ part is largely missing from the words 'and the rich He hath sent . . .' to the ending of the Gloria. The Nunc Dimittis is complete as far as 'and to be the glory . . .' but its organ part only appears to be written out in full when it does not just double the voice parts. A rough sketch for the Gloria of the Nunc Dimittis survives and a reconstruction of the whole work should be perfectly feasible.

A Magnificat in the 8th tone for SATB and organ has the plainsong melody and the word underlay (both in the treble) in the hand of G R Woodward and the lower parts and accompaniment in Wood's hand. There is no harmonisation of the Gloria, and a letter is extant from Woodward on the subject[35]: 'I have a Magnificat in the 8th Mode, to show you: it was

169

harmonised by C W and is complete, all excepting the Gloria, which I hoped he would elaborate. Now I suppose we must supply it from Orlando di Lasso, Palestrina, or Scheidt.' An MS harmonisation by Scheidt of the Gloria (in Woodward's handwriting) is deposited with the MS in Caius library.

The miscellaneous sketches produce some interesting fragments, including two Kyries for SATB in C (Myxolydian mode) very much in the style of the Phrygian Communion Service; three Agnus Dei 'plainsong' arrangements for unison voices and organ; an original Agnus Dei (D minor, 4/4) for unaccompanied SATB; two 'plainsong' settings of the Lord's Prayer for unaccompanied SATB — one with the plainsong in the treble, the other in the tenor; an original Lord's Prayer for unaccompanied SATB (G major, 4/2); a simple but effective setting of the Benedictus (Communion Service) for SATB and organ, short enough to be quoted in full (*see Example 139, opposite*).

four sets of Responses to the Commandments for unaccompanied SATB; and a setting of the 'General Confession' for unaccompanied SATB (E flat major).

Likewise there are a number of separate settings of the canticles. The most important are a Te Deum (G major, 4/2) and Jubilate (G major, 3/2), both for unaccompanied men's voices ATB. These are in the same style as the Evening Service published in 1911 and may have been written at the same time as companion pieces. The other canticles, all for unaccompanied SATB, are: two settings of the Benedictus (C major, 2/2, and D major, 2/2); a Magnificat in C major; a Magnificat and Nunc Dimittis in G minor; a Nunc Dimittis in F and a Magnificat and Nunc Dimittis founded on metrical psalm-tunes — the Magnificat on a melody for Psalm CIV (see Frost, p 150) and the Nunc Dimittis on a tune as yet not identified. All these settings use a largely 16th-century harmonic vocabulary, are largely homophonic in texture, and, again, adhere consistently to the one-note-one-syllable principle.

The unfinished sketches provide a field for much fruitless speculation and induce in the researcher feelings both of regret and exasperation; regret that so much work was left unfinished and exasperation that Wood left so much of it nearly finished. There is a setting of the Benedictus for unaccompanied ATB (G major, 2/1) which wants only four-and-a-half bars in the middle and which was obviously a companion to the Te Deum and Jubilate discussed above. There are no less than four unfinished settings of the Te Deum for unaccompanied SATB; a Magnificat and Nunc Dimittis in E for SATB and organ; a Magnificat in E flat for unaccompanied SATB; a Benedictus and Jubilate in A flat for unison voices and organ; and a Magnificat and Nunc Dimittis in F for unaccompanied SATB complete except for the Gloria to the Nunc Dimittis.

170

Example 139

In the Easter vacation of 1920, Dr Eric Milner-White, the Dean of King's College, wrote to Wood from the Cambridge Nursing Home where he was recovering from an appendicitis operation[36]:

Dear Dr Wood,

We wanted badly this year during Holy Week to do some Passion Music at King's. Mann and I went through everything that exists . . . and could find nothing. The Bach Passions are far too vast for an ordinary choir, however good. The Bach Cantatas are unsuitable, not in length but in words and idea; further, Mann holds v. strongly that the Cantatas are impossible of satisfactory accompaniment on the organ.

So the College asked me to invent a Passion Cantata or a Passion Chorale. Not only the College, but several Public Schools have written to me for something of the sort within their scope. For the Public Schools now nearly always live in over Easter and are at their wits end what to do during Holy Week.

Also, it is about time that the bigger parish churches superseded Stainer's Crucifixion — or at least had an alternative.

But no satisfactory ideas came to me last term. Since getting to the Nursing Hostel (appendicitis) however, there has been time to think and I lay the sketch of a possible scheme before you in case you care to co-operate and do the really important part!!

My idea, then, is perhaps the simplest and most direct possible, that we do an actual Passion Gospel, say St Mark's, involving, with some easy and obvious omissions, the story of the Passion acc. to the A.V. text, from the Last Supper to the death.

The end — the actual crucifixion — might be supplemented by adding the Words from the Cross which S.Mk. omits, done according to the usual Sarum ending — the priest monotoning and inflecting the narration and the various speeches, 'voces turborum', comments, words, etc, by the various individuals in the Choir. At the Death, all would kneel, everything would come to an abrupt end and the whole congregation repeat a general confession and go out, perhaps in silence (but see scheme 3).

The Gospel falls obviously into five parts:—

1. The Last Supper — The Upper Room
2. Gethsemane and Betrayal — The Garden
3. The Jewish Trial — Jewish Council Chamber
4. The Roman Trial — The 'Pavement'
5. The Crucifixion — Calvary.

Between each of these, there is a *movement* from one place to the other. That in my scheme would be represented by a *musical movement* to contrast with or to sum up, the previous Gospel.

Now, *three* different suggestions have occurred to me for four or five movements

1) That the intervals shd. be filled by the Prayers which our Lord is known to have been repeating during His Passion, ie certain Psalms or bits of Psalms, eg parts of 55, 22, 28, etc.

The objection to this is that the Psalms freely treated give no popular relief. I fear that the result would simply mean some lovely anthems in the middle of solemn anthems.

2) That, instead of taking the P.B. version of the Psalms, we should employ the metrical version of George Wither (far the best I think). Then they could be treated in the bolder simpler style of hymns, perhaps with one or two good eg Genevan tunes running right through, binding the whole together.

3) Dropping all idea of the Psalms — to intersperse the scenes (and indeed begin the whole Passion) with stanzas of the splendid hymn "Sing

172

my tongue, the glorious battle" and stanzas of the sacramental "Of the glorious body telling".

We would not get short of verses, because it is traditional to use the stanza 'Faithful Cross, above all other' as often as we like. Thus, throughout the whole Passion, that one cd. keep recurring, perhaps to the well-known Mechlin* form of the melody for the whole Congregation to sing.

This last idea seems to me to be the best and strongest, as well as the simplest. Perhaps indeed the theme of 'Sing my tongue' might be the motif theme on which the whole singing of the free prose of the Gospel were subtly based. The tune is so well known and popular that I am sure it would help in winning popular favour for such a 'Passion'.

Probably I have quite failed to express my idea, and indeed it wd. require a good talk before I cd. do so wholly. But if you think there is anything in it and care to undertake the vital role of composer, may I come and talk in May when I return after convalescing? For its a *big* thing.

(Or until Friday next, I am always to be found sitting up in bed or in an armchair at the Nursing Hostel, Thompson's Lane!!).

But I do feel that in this matter, I speak for a tremendous and growing need of the Church.

Forgive my troubling you . . . (illegible)

Very sincerely yours,

E. Milner-White.

*When I say the *Mechlin* form of the melody, I only mean for the few verses here and there where all the congregation joins in. Whenever the choir sings it alone, it cd. be the Sarum; and now and then, it cd. be more drastically varied and a sub-theme, a second motif, introduced by passing to quite a different melody, eg Palestrina's Tantum Ergo (E.H. 326) or Ad perennis vitae fontem (S. Sion 90) or any of the others to 8.7.8.7.8.7. metre in Songs of Syon.

Perhaps you won't touch the Mechlin version at any price!!

Wood went to see Milner-White, and doubtless discussed the libretto which the latter had prepared while still a bed-patient[37]. The result of their discussions were some minor changes, chiefly in the choice of the interpolated hymns. Wood completed the composition of the music in nine days (MS dated August 9, 1920) and the work was first performed in King's Chapel on Good Friday, 1921.

The St Mark Passion is perhaps Wood's crowning achievement in the field of church music. It was conceived in terms of liturgical use as an act of devotion, and its mood is wholly appropriate to this purpose. In a sense Wood and Milner-White had reverted to an older, pre-Bachian tradition of Passion writing, for the St Mark Passion differs from other Bachian and post-Bachian settings in that there are no arias. The Gospel narrative is divided into five 'lessons' in which soloists and chorus present the unadorned biblical text to fitting music. Some of the choruses, only a few bars long, have a rare and expressive beauty:

Example 140

Each 'lesson' is rounded off by a congregational hymn, the whole work, as Milner-White suggested in his original letter, being introduced and concluded by extended settings of the plainsong *Pange lingua*. (It is characteristic of Wood that the other hymn melodies, *Chester* and Tallis's *1st mode melody*, are metrical psalm-tunes. There is, however, no ambiguity — the whole work is truly ecumenical). Sometimes the chorus takes over the function of narration, almost in the very accents of the pre-Bachian Passions:

Example 141

and the vocal line of the Evangelist, though sensitive, is, similarly, emotionally reticent.

In the final 'lesson', 'and when the sixth hour was come', the organ accompaniment ceases and the Evangelist and choir, unaccompanied,

174

gently and undemonstratively underline the climax of the story. As Dr Routley observed[38]: 'when seen in its historical context it is a work beyond all praise'.

In 1922, at the suggestion of S P Waddington — himself a Roman Catholic — Wood composed a Mass in F for SATB and organ (MS dated April 9, 1922), which was intended for liturgical use. As has been noted above, it was published posthumously in 1927 as the *Missa Portae Honoris*, adapted — a little uneasily — to the words of the Anglican Communion Service. In 1971 it was published in its original form and according to Wood's original intention.

It consists of the usual Kyrie, Gloria, Credo, Sanctus, Benedictus and Agnus Dei, and stands somewhat apart from Wood's other choral music by reason of its gentle sweetness (one is reminded in places of Fauré). Practical considerations probably dictated the amount of doubling between voice and organ — indeed Wood seems to have gone out of his way to produce a fool-proof edition. There is little of his more recondite contrapuntal style except in the Benedictus for three voices — where the soprano and tenor are in strict canon at the octave, with the alto providing a free inner part (*see Example 142, overleaf*).

The recent liturgical upheaval in the Roman Catholic Church reduces the chances of this Mass being widely used — but it could yet prove a significant contribution to the Roman liturgy.

In his valuable study *The Music of the Christian Hymnody* (London, Independent Press, 1957), Dr Erik Routley observed (p 137) that it would be to the regret of any historian of the subject that he (Wood) wrote only a handful of hymn-tunes. If one substitutes the word 'published' for 'wrote' this statement is true; for there is a considerable corpus of MS tunes which has remained unknown since Wood's death.

Wood had been actively concerned with the preparation of three hymn-books and was the original editor of a book of 'Children's Praise'published posthumously. We learn from the preface to the *Yattendon Hymnal* (1899) and from surviving letters to Wood from Robert Bridges, that he was helpful to the extent of 'two settings and occasional reading of music proofs'. From the time of his first meeting with G R Woodward in 1892/3, Wood was closely associated with him in his various musical publications. In his preface to the first edition of *Songs of Syon* (date October 15, 1904), Woodward concluded that he could not 'express gratitude enough to Dr Charles Wood . . . for his able and willing co-operation throughout this work.' The extent of Wood's participation was not made explicit until the third edition (August 4, 1910), the preface of which credits him with 'revising much of the harmony' and for making 'many new settings of his own, including two original tunes which now make their first appearance in

Example 142

print', and in the fourth edition (July 15, 1923), Woodward observed that 'at the advice, and under the care, of Dr Charles Wood, a few musical errors have been corrected. In two or three cases, only, finer melodies, or better harmonies, have been substituted'. In this fourth edition Wood had an acknowledged hand in 31 settings[39] and contributed two original tunes.

Wood was also a member of the music committee of the 1904 edition of *Hymns Ancient and Modern*[40] and contributed three original hymn-tunes to that book. He may well have had something to do with the plainsong harmonisations (two similar harmonisations were found among his posthumous papers) and he was certainly responsible for at least one setting.

He contributed two new original tunes and a setting to the *(Irish) Church Hymnal* (1919), and one new original tune to the *Public School Hymnal*

176

(also 1919). The hymn/anthem especially written for the 1925 edition of *Songs of Praise* has already been discussed on p. 153). Finally to Canon T Grigg-Smith's book of 'Children's Praise', *Hosanna* (London, SPCK, 1930) Wood contributed, at the instigation of Can & Guss Limited, eight original tunes, one melody, and ten special settings.

Of the published original hymn-tunes only *Rangoon* (1904, A and M) and *Cambridge* (1925, S of P) are at all well-known, so the number of published tunes — 18 — may come as something of a surprise to the generality of church musicians. It may well come as an even greater surprise to learn that Wood's published tunes and settings represent only the tip of the iceberg in comparison with the total number of his tunes and settings. Among his miscellaneous sketches preserved at Caius was found a great mass of material which, on being sorted and transcribed, yielded the following apparently complete items:

2	plainsong harmonisations
11	double chants
8	settings of hymn melodies by earlier composers
15	settings of melodies taken from Zahn
46	harmonisations of metrical psalm-tunes
23	original canonic hymn-tunes
72	original hymn-tunes.

Some of Wood's original tunes can be identified with specific words. Thus, for example, there is a set of 13 settings of poems by Campion which are examples, as Leonard Blake has observed[41], of 'Wood's sensitiveness to their intimate piety and chaste imagery, and his ingenuity in dealing with unusual metres . . . Campion's thought and style are matched by the graceful economy and serenity of the music in an idiom redolent of Orlando Gibbons.'

Example 143

Opening of tune for "Out of my soul's depth".

Wood was often experimenting with unusual metres and textures — sometimes, it would appear, for fun or to keep his contrapuntal tools sharp. The canonic tunes are ingenious but little more ('some men do the *Times* crossword, other write canons'). There are tunes and chants so craftily written that they can be read backwards as well as forwards. Some are obviously intended for possible inclusion in the 1904 A and M hymn-book or in later editions of *Songs of Syon*. 'There is an adventurous triple-time setting of "For all the Saints", with a change from F major to D minor and a different melody for verses 5 and 6. One can only speculate as to whether the 1904 committee . . . had both this and (Stanford's) *Engelberg* before them as possible alternatives to Barnby's hurdy-gurdy tune. Elsewhere . . . is a virile sequential tune which must assuredly have been intended for "Who would true valour see?", though no indication of words is given. It might have proved a better A and M competitor for *Monk's Gate* when Bunyan's verses were introduced into the 2nd supplement of 1916, than either of the tunes there has done.'[42]

Some of Wood's tunes are too specialised and subtle for congregational use. This certainly applies to a number of the Campion settings and, in quite a different vein, his music to Tennyson's *Crossing the bar* is an obvious choir piece. One is tempted to speculate here as to whether it was once in competition with Parry's *Freshwater* for inclusion in the 1904 A and M. Wood is, if anything, even more romantic than Parry in his harmony and key-changes, and spins out his rhythms more freely. A beautiful miniature, if hardly a Christian hymn!

'It is a pity that all this material of Wood's has remained untapped for so long. Changes in the patterns of public worship, revolutionary attitudes towards the church music of the past, and the urge to be one step ahead in the race for popular appeal, are already making the compilation of hymn-books a hazardous operation. Such classically grounded, undemonstrative and yet deeply sincere work as we find in Wood at his best seems likely to have less chance of achieving currency'[43].

As to Wood's harmonisations of pre-existing melodies — whether published in *Songs of Syon*, *Hymns A and M*, the *Irish Church Hymnal*, or remaining in MS — all that need be said is that his felicitous choice of progressions, firm and inevitable basses, and beautifully organised inner-parts make his settings models of their kind, grateful both to sing and to listen to.

There are also, both published and in MS, a number of fine free-organ accompaniments to various hymn-tunes, and some extended motet-like verses for choir only of certain of the *Songs of Syon* hymns, also a few *Songs of Syon* tunes arranged for four-part male-voice choir, presumably written for Wood's Caius singers.

Through his friendship with G R Woodward, Wood became an important figure in the late Victorian/Edwardian carol revival. In 1892, Woodward, then Rector of Chelmondistone, Ipswich, had brought out a slim volume of *Carols for Christmastide (Series One)*, which included — No 11 — Wood's harmonisation for SATB of *Sweet was the sounge the Vergin sange* (as spelt in that edition — the words taken from William Batten's Lute Book) — a version that was little different from the setting included later in the *Cowley Carol Book*. Wood apparently met Woodward for the first time soon after its publication, as Woodward later recollected[44] (see p. 32).

To a second series of carols, published in 1893, Wood contributed a harmonisation for SATB of *Blessed be that Mayde Mary*, set to a secular melody also from William Batten's Lute Book. A volume of *Carols for Easter and Ascensiontide*, which followed in 1899, contained two Wood settings, though the first appearance of *This Joyful Eastertide* contained therein, was harmonised by the Revd (later Bishop) W H Frere. A further volume of *Harmonies of Hymns and Carols for Christmastide*, which followed in 1897, contained none of Wood's work, but a copy in his possession had the grammatic solecisms in other people's settings all carefully marked in his own hand.

Out of these early volumes grew the *Cowley Carol Books*, brought out in two books, in 1901 (enlarged 1902) and 1919 respectively. Wood had been largely concerned with both volumes. In the preface to the first Woodward had written: 'It is the Editor's duty and pleasure to thank . . . Dr Charles Wood for much valuable help and good taste in harmonising . . . melodies. The fact that Dr Charles Wood has revised and passed the proof-sheets of the music is a guarantee of its correctness.' In the 1919 volume Wood's name appeared alongside Woodward's as co-editor.

Wood contributed six settings to the first collection, four of which had appeared in the earlier volumes. In the second collection Wood was responsible for 21 settings, five of which had appeared previously in *Songs of Syon*. The *Cambridge Carol Book*, edited jointly by Wood and Woodward and published in 1924, contained 53 carols, 30 of which were of Wood's setting.

These collections have their melodic sources largely in the corpus of 16th- and 17th-century liturgical melodies, but the second volume of the Cowley and the Cambridge book especially contain large numbers of 'synthetic carols' — traditional or composed melodies from various sources for which Woodward had written carol words. The best of Wood's harmonisations — *Blessed be that Maid Marie, Sweet was the song the Virgin sang, This joyful Eastertide, A Virgin most pure, King Jesus hath a garden, Shepherds, in the fields abiding, Ding Dong! merrily on high* and *Past three o'clock* — are classics of their kind.

An *Italian Carol Book* which had been published in 1920 consists of 37 carols mainly of the synthetic sort. The melodies, drawn largely from a tradition of popular sacred music of the 16th and 17th centuries, are set usually for four voices SATB, and of the 37 settings Wood contributed 33. G R Woodward was responsible for the words, and herein lies the rub. His

179

penchant for the pseudo-archaic is so pronounced as to be, in certain instances, positively ludicrous:

'Pontius Pilate, ere the break of day,
Sat on his doom-stool (Weyla wayaway).'

One of Wood's settings, *Hail blessed Virgin Mary*, has been widely sung, and two other settings, *Gaudate qui vobis* and *Ah, Gabriel*, are so melodically distinguished as to be worth revival as they stand. If the *Italian Carol Book* could be issued with new words it might become enormously popular.

Wood published a number of separate carols. In 1918, for instance, he brought out two for unison voices and piano, in which 15th-century texts are wedded to Irish traditional melodies. *Make we merry* (E minor, 4/4, *Allegro moderato*) is comparatively undistinguished — though enterprising enough in its variety of accompanimental textures. *Mater Ora Filium* (E flat major, 4/4, *Moderato*), on the other hand, has a melody of heart-easing loveliness, with an accompaniment the economy and effectiveness of which make a perfect foil to the vocal line:

Example 144

Two Christmas songs, *Christmas bells* (Longfellow) (C major, 3/4, *Andante con moto*), based on an Irish folk-melody, and *The Yule Log* (Longfellow)

180

(D minor, 2/4, *Allegro*), set to an original tune, are unremarkable. They were published in 1921 and 1924 respectively. In 1925, however, Wood brought out a setting of *The Virgin's Cradle Hymn* (the medieval Latin 'Dormi Jesu' in Coleridge's translation) (F major, 3/4, *Andante*) in which an exquisite melody by Corner (1625) is matched by a serenely rocking piano accompaniment. Brahms wrote nothing more tender:

Example 145

Also in 1925 Wood brought out an *Easter Carol* (J M Neale), for unaccompanied SATB (Dorian mode, 4/4, *Allegro*), a virile setting much in the style of his *Cowley Carol Book* harmonisations'

There were two unaccompanied posthumous carol publications. The first, a simple strophic setting for unaccompanied SATB of *The Burning Babe*, by Robert Southwell (1560-1593) (G major, 4/4) has an MS date December 20, 1920, and appeared in 1926, whilst the second, *Deck the hall* was brought out in 1927 and is much better known. This vigorous and straightforward arrangement for SATB of a Welsh Christmas melody (words Talhaiarn, translated Thomas Oliphant) (F major, 4/4, *Allegro con spirito*) has held its place in the repertory since it first appeared.

As with Wood's other church music, there is a body of carol material surviving — either in fair copy MS or complete short-score rough sketches. Under this heading may be noted a 'motet' setting of *All my heart this night rejoices* (Paul Gherhardt, translated Catherine Winkworth) which also exists in a plain SATB harmonisation (*see Example 146, overleaf*).

An SATB setting of *Adeste Fideles* which has some original touches should also be noted, together with a harmonisation of *Angelus ad virginem* (7th mode) for SATB, and settings of two 'Diocesan' French melodies which, though without words, have a carol-like lilt.

Wood's sketches include no less than 14 complete carol tunes, 12 of which are associated with specific words. An arrangement of *Gaudate, gaudate, Christus est natus* from *Piae Cantiones* (Woodward's edition, p 20)

181

Example 146

is a gem, and short enough to be quoted in full:

Example 147

Other completely sketched settings include:
> *Here is holly that is so gent* (trad)
> *Christmas day* (Christina Rosetti)
> *A Christmas Carol* (James Russell Lowell)
> *Hark how all the welkin rings* (Charles Wesley)
> *New prince, new pomp* (Robert Southwell)
> *See the dawn* (Thomas Moore), and
> *An Ode on the Birth of our Saviour* (Robert Herrick)

All these have character and would be worth performing.

In our age of feverish liturgical experiment, the considerable rejection of the immediate past — as far as church music is concerned — seems inevitable. The struggle to keep the cathedral/choral tradition in being seems more and more futile, and yet there is in this music that which feeds the spirit. Wood's own contribution may well be recognised one day for what it is — a body of work that represents the great Anglican 'Via Media' in an incomparable musical expression.

NOTES

1. In an unpublished article on Stainer, Peter Warlock drew attention to stylistic parallels between aspects of the *Crucifixion* and Sullivan's 'Savoy Opera' manner.
2. Hadow, Sir W H, *Church Music*, The Liverpool Diocesan Board of Divinity Publications (London, Longmans, 1926), p 15.
3. There is a parallel here with Bruckner, whose choral style similarly derived from his contrapuntal studies in the Fux tradition.
4. Phillips, Dr C B, *The Singing Church* (London, Faber, 1945 — 2nd edition edited by Professor Arthur Hutchins, 1968), p 227.
5. Routley, Dr Erik, *Twentieth Century Church Music* (London, Herbert Jenkins, 1964), pp 105-6.
6. Stanford's setting is dated 'Easter Day, 1913'.
7. Wood had a very personal love for Campion's work, as the number of extant settings demonstrate. A different setting of *Never weather beaten sail* was lost by a publisher posthumously.
8. Letter to the author dated September 16, 1968.
9. Phillips/Hutchins. *Op cit*, p 227.
10. Westrup's edition of Fellowes's *English Cathedral Music* (London, Methuen, 1969), p 258.
11. Wood was to have conducted this first performance.
12. *Du fond de ma pensée*, Ps CXXX, Strasbourg 1539: altered by L Bourgeois (1542). See *Songs of Syon*, No 236a.
13. *Musical Times*, October 1929 (Vol 71, No 1040), p 902.
14. Routley, *Op cit*, p 34.
15. Phillips/Hutchins, *Op cit*, p 241.
16. Fellowes/Westrup, *Op cit*, p 258.
17. Phillips/Hutchins, *Op cit*, p 241.
18. Andrews, Hilda, *Westminster Retrospect — a Memoir of Sir Richard Terry* (London, OUP, 1948, pp 132-4.
19. Stanford's *O for a closer walk with God*, brought out in 1910, is an early example.
20. Tune *Donnez au Seigneur Gloire* (Ps CVII). See Frost, p 153, and Zahn, No 5261.
21. A version of *Oculi omnium* for ATB exists in MS form.
22. See *Songs of Syon*, No 330a.
23. Ibid, 383a.
24. Ibid, 125b. See also Frost, pp 92-3. Wood seems to have followed the version in Zahn 6543.
25. Ibid, 308a.
26. Routley, *Op cit*, p 33.
27. Greene, Plunket, *Charles Villiers Stanford* (London, Arnold, 1935), pp 218-21.
28. See Andrews, *Op cit*, pp 8-12.
29. As yet unidentified.
30. Fellowes/Westrup, *Op cit*, p 257.
31. Wood's original MS gives the Latin words only.
32. Preserved with the Wood MSS at Caius.
33. Letter to Wood written from 48, West Hill, Highgate Village, N6, dated August 17, 1923: 'I am very glad you are harmonising some of the ordinary of the Mass; I am sure you know how to phrase it perfectly well. The Sanctus that you have chosen is a great favourite of mine, now for exactly 50 years since I first heard it'.

34. *Musical Times*, November 1933 (Vol 74, No 1089), p 997.
35. Letter to J M Tatton, written Highgate, and dated Saturday, October 23 (1926).
36. Letter preserved with Wood's MSS at Caius.
37. Libretto preserved with Wood's MSS at Caius.
38. Routley, *Op cit*, p 35.
39. Plus five carol harmonisations which were later reprinted in the 1919 *Cowley Carol Book*, and one setting that had already appeared in the *Yattendon Hymnal*.
40. Under the chairmanship of Bishop Frere, the committee met for the first time in 1896. The other musical members were Parratt, Luard Selby, Stanford, Steggall, and H E Wooldridge. See Lowther-Clarke, W K, *A Hundred years of Hymns Ancient and Modern* (London, W Clowes, 1960), p 72.
41. Blake, Leonard, article in *The Bulletin of the Hymn Society*, Vol 7, No 124, April 1972, p 194.
42. Ibid, p 195.
43. Ibid, p 197.
44. Letter to Wood written from Highgate and dated July 23, 1923 (see p 35, note 10).

Epilogue

The musical world in which Charles Wood lived and worked is as remote from our own age as is the age of the horse cab from that of the intercontinental jet, and for musicians who have entered the profession since the Second World War the large-scale music of Edwardian England (outside of Elgar, some Delius, and a few works by Stanford and Parry) is almost a closed book. Their immediate predecessors, the generation of musicians who had been brought up under the direct influence of the founding fathers of the English musical renaissance, had, naturally enough, reacted against their music. To a composer like Warlock, for instance, the Parry style was something to be dismissed with a sneer, and to some extent this attitude has clouded contemporary evaluations of the music of the Parry/Stanford generation. Inherited attitudes and opinions are accepted at their own face value: after all, the music itself is mostly unperformed and long out of print, and there is little incentive to question the conclusion that it is deservedly dead and not worth resuscitation.

This rejection — unheard — of the music of the immediate and fairly immediate past is very characteristic of the British attitude generally towards its own artists. On the Continent, and more especially in the Slav countries, the cherishing of all periods of a nation's musical past is accepted as a duty. I do not doubt that, had Wood been born in Ruritania, a complete edition of his works, supported by a fully documented biography and analytical discussion, would by this time have been issued almost as a matter of course by the state publishing house. In this study, I have, at least, attempted to deal with the latter lacuna, and the reader must judge to what extent I have succeeded.

When one has lived for four years in intimate contact with a composer's work, it is difficult to separate the general from the particular in assessing its worth. What, indeed, can one say about Wood's music when it is considered as a whole? What overall impression does he leave? What in common have the services and anthems, the solo songs, the chamber works, the operas, cantatas and folk-song settings?

Speaking personally, I am left with a sense of Wood's total artistic and technical integrity. In all his works I have not found one scamped bar, or the slightest hint that he was anywhere writing below his true form. As a friend put it to me 'he never lets you down', by which is meant that Wood's music never promises more than it can perform.

Wood was a prolific composer (the obituary notice that spoke of his exiguous output betrayed a pitiful knowledge of the facts), and it is obvious that there were few periods during his adult life when he did not have something or other on hand. Equally obviously his works must differ in value, and time has robbed some of them of their original virtues. There are works whose *raison d'être* seems to reside solely in the exercise of a superb composing technique. There are some works which said much to their own time but which say little to us unless we can exercise considerable historical imagination. But there are works, few in number perhaps, which may yet prove to be among the glories of their time.

Most of Wood's life was lived quietly under the shadow of other men, and when, in his last two years, the Cambridge Professorship might have set him in his rightful place in the musical heirarchy of the country, ill-health, and finally death, snatched him away from the honoured regard that was his due. But there have always been a devoted few who have cherished his music, and because good work never dies, more and more people will join them in the recognition that Wood was a fine composer with something to say far beyond any temporal or local relevance.

Appendix One: Wood's pupils

From 1880, when he joined the teaching staff at the RCM, until his death, in 1926, Wood had a hand in the training of over two generations of musicians. At the RCM, where, until the latter part of his life, he taught, principally harmony and counterpoint, a number of musicians who later distinguished themselves as composers were his pupils. It was a matter of regret to him that he had to pass them on subsequently to others — Stanford especially. At Cambridge, on the other hand, a very large number of undergraduates came to him to be helped over the Mus Bac hurdle. The list of his pupils given below is far from exhaustive, but does give some idea of the extent of his influence as a teacher:

Hugo Anson (C)
Sir Thomas Beecham (private)
W Denis Browne (C)
Coleridge Taylor (RCM)
Prof E J Dent (C)
Nicholas Gatty (C)
Armstrong Gibbs (C)
Prof Herbert Howells (RCM)
Prof C H Kitson (C)
Harold Rutland (C) (RCM)
Heathcote Statham (C)
Sir Michael Tippett (RCM)
R Vaughan Williams (C)
Eric Warr (C)

Appendix Two: Bibliography

For details of *Musical Times* and other reviews, also extracts from *The Times* newspaper, the reader is referred to the footnotes appended to each individual chapter.

Andrews, Hilda: *Westminster Retrospect — a memoir of Sir Richard Terry* (London, OUP, 1948).

Beecham, Sir Thomas: *A Mingled Chime* (London, Hutchinson, 1944).

Blake, Leonard: 'New light on Charles Wood', *The Hymn Society of Great Britain and Ireland Bulletin*, Vol 7, No 10, April 1972.

Blom, Eric: *Music in England* (London, Penguin Books, 1942).

Butcher, A V: 'Walt Whitman and the English Composer', *Music and Letters*, Vol 28, No 2, April 1947.

(Caian, The): Unsigned obituary in *The Caian*, Vol 34, No 3, Michaelmas term 1926.

Copley, I A: 'Charles Wood, 1866-1926', *The Musical Times*, Vol 107, No 1480, June 1966.
'An unusual glimpse of Sir George Grove', *RCM Magazine*, Vol 65, No 2, Summer term 1969.
'Charles Wood — and the Hymn-Book that never was', *The Hymn Society of Great Britain and Ireland Bulletin*, Vol 7, No 10, April 1972.

Coward, Sir Henry: *Reminiscences of Henry Coward* (London, Curwen, 1919).

Dent, Prof E J: Introduction to *Eight String Quartets by Charles Wood* (London, OUP, 1929).

Dunhill, Thomas F: Article in *Cobbett's Cyclopedic Survey of Chamber Music*, ed W Cobbett (London, OUP, 1922).

Fellowes, Dr E H (ed Westrup): *English Cathedral Music* (London, Methuen, 1969).

Foss, Hubert: *Vaughan Williams* (London, Harrap, 1950).

Frost, Dr Maurice: *English and Scottish Psalm and Hymn Tunes* (London, SPCK and OUP, 1953).

Greene, Harry Plunket: *Charles Villiers Stanford* (London, Edward Arnold, 1935).

Grace, Dr Harvey: Obituary in *The Musical Times*, Vol 67, No 1002, August 1926.

Graves, C L: *The Life and Letters of Sir George Grove*, CB (London, Macmillan, 1903).

(Grove): *Grove's Dictionary of Music and Musicians*, 5th Edn, ed E Blom (London, Macmillan, 1954).

Hadow, Sir W H: *Church Music* (London, Longmans, 1926).

Horton, John: Chapter 8 (The Choral Works), *Schumann, a Symposium*, ed Abraham (London, OUP, 1952).

Howells, Prof Herbert: Essay in *English Church Music* (RSCM, 1966).

Howes, Frank: *Folk music of Britain and beyond* (London, Methuen, 1969). *The English Musical Renaissance* (London, Secker and Warburg, 1966).

Hull, Robin: 'Charles Wood — Quartet in D', *The Listener*, Vol 17, No 418, January 13, 1937.

Joyce, Dr P W: *Old Irish folk music and song* (London, Longmans, & Dublin, Figgis, 1909).

Kennedy, Michael: *The works of Ralph Vaughan Williams* (London, OUP, 1964).

Long, Kenneth: *The Music of the English Church* (London, Hodder and Stoughton, 1971).

Lowther-Clark, W K: *A Hundred Years of Hymns Ancient and Modern* (London, W Clowes, 1960).

Lumsden, Dr David: Note on Wood in *The Treasury of English Church Music*, Vol 5, 1900-1965, ed Dr Gerald Knight and Dr William L Reed (London, Blandford Press, 1965).

Moore, Dr Gerald: *Singer and accompanist* (London, Methuen, 1953).

Nosek, Margaret Hayes: 'Wood: a personal memoir', article in *The Musical Times*, Vol 107, No 1480, June 1966.

Phillips, Dr C B (ed Hutchins): *The Singing Church* (London, Faber, 1968).

(RCM): Obituary, unsigned, in the *RCM Magazine*, Vol 22, No 3, Midsummer term, 1926.

Routley, Dr Erik: *20th Century Church Music* (London, Herbert Jenkins, 1964).

Scott, Marion: 'The Chamber Music of Charles Wood', article in Chamber Music Supplement to *The Music Student*, No 18, January 1916.

Scholes, Percy: *The Oxford Companion to Music*, 7th edn (London, OUP, 1947). *The Mirror of Music 1844-1944* (London, Novello and OUP, 1947).

Seaver, George: *John Allen Fitzgerald — Archbishop* (London, Faith Press, and Dublin, Figgis, 1963).

Stanford, Sir Charles V: *Pages from an unwritten diary* (London, Arnold, 1914). *Musical Composition — a short treatise for students* (London, Macmillan and Stainer & Bell, 1911).

Tovey, Sir Donald F: *Essays in Musical Analysis*, Vol 2 (London, OUP, 1935).

(Ulster Gazette): *Ulster Gazette and Armagh Standard*, issue of June 3, 1947.

Vaughan Williams, Ursula: *RVW* (London, OUP, 1964).

Waddington, Sidney P: article in *Dictionary of National Biography*, 1922-30 (London, OUP, 1937).

Walker, Dr Ernest: 'Charles Wood's String Quartets' in *Monthly Musical Record*, Vol 59, No 708, December 1929.

Wood, Dr Thomas: *True Thomas* (London, Jonathan Cape, 1936).

Young, Dr Percy M: *A History of British Music* (London, Benn, 1967).

Zahn, Johannes: *Die Melodien der deutschen evangelischen Kircheslieder* (Güterslow, 1889-1893).

Appendix Three:
Catalogue of works

In this catalogue the title of a work is given first, the works themselves being listed in categories according to the previous chapters of the book. Then follow:
(w) the authorship of the words, if any;
(c) the year of composition, where known;
(pu) the year of publication and the name of the present publishers (the name of the original publishers being added in parenthesis where appropriate);
(d) the dedicatee, if any;
and under (MS), the whereabouts is indicated of the manuscript, where known, under the symbols P (private ownership), G (the Library of Gonville and Caius College, Cambridge), BM (The British Museum Library), RCM (the Library of the Royal College of Music) and CU (the Cambridge University Library).

CANTATAS

The Lord is my shepherd (SATB and small orch) (c) 188-? (MS) G (full-score).

Spring's summons (ten, bar, and sop soli, mixed chorus and orch) (w) A P Graves (c) 1885 (MS) G (full-score).

Song of welcome (SATB, violin solo, harp & organ) (w) Sir Francis Cook, Bart (c) 1886/7 (pu) 1887 RCM/ Spottiswoode.

Psalm 104 (Praise the Lord, O my soul) (solo quartet, bar, solo, mixed chorus, organ and orch) (c) 1886/7 (MS) G (full-score).

Unto Thee will I cry (sop solo, mixed chorus, organ and strings) (c) 1889 B Mus exercise (MS) CU (full-score).

Ode to the West Wind (Op 3) (ten solo, mixed chorus and orch) (w) P B Shelley (c) 1889 ? (pu) 1890 Novello (MS) BM (full-score).

Music — an ode (sop solo, mixed chorus and orch) (w) A C Swinburne (c) 1892/3 (pu) 1893 Stainer & Bell (Augener) (MS) G (full-score).

The white island (SATB soli, double chorus and orch) (w) R Herrick (c) 1894 D Mus exercise (MS) CU (full-score).

On Time (mixed chorus and orch) (w) J Milton (c) 1897/8 (pu) 1898 Boosey & Hawkes (MS) G (piano score).

Dirge for two veterans (bass solo, mixed chorus and orch) (w) Walt Whitman (c) 1900/1 (pu) 1901 Boosey & Hawkes (MS) G (piano score).

The Song of the Tempest (sop solo, mixed chorus and orch) (w) Sir Walter Scott (c) 1902 (pu) 1903 Keith Prowse (MS) G (full-score).

A ballad of Dundee (bass solo, mixed chorus and orch) (w) W E Aytoun (c) 1904 ? (pu) 1904 Breitkopf and Härtel (MS) G (piano score).

Eden spirits (female voices and piano) (w) E B Browning (c) 1915 ? (pu) 1915 Chappell (Year Book Press) (MS) G.

FRAGMENTARY CANTATA SKETCHES

By the North Sea (mixed chorus and orch) (MS) G. Cantata for women's voices and piano (E maj) (w) apparently metaphysical poem (MS) G.
Songs in a cornfield (women's voices and piano) (w) Christina Rossetti (MS) G.

LOST CANTATAS

The ballad of Agincourt (male voices and piano duet) (w) M Drayton (c) 1924 ?
A cantata entitled *Once more the Heavenly power* was performed at the RCM during Wood's student days. The words, copied out by Grove, are bound up in the score of *Spring's summons*.

CHAMBER MUSIC

STRING QUARTETS

Andante-Allegro con brio in A minor (c) 1883 (MS) G.
Allegro in A minor (c) 1883 (MS) RCM.
Andante in D major (MS) G.
Scherzo (Allegro molto) in A minor (MS) G.
Allegro in A major (MS) G.
Quartet in D minor (*Allegro, Molto adagio, Presto, Allegro vivace*) (c) 1885 (pu) 1929 O.U.P. (MS) G.
Quodlibet in C major (with an extra part) (c) 1888 (MS) P.
Quartet in E flat major (Highgate) (*Allegro con moto, Molto moderato, Adagio ma non troppo, Molto animato*) (c) 1892/3 (pu) 1929 OUP (MS) G.
Quartet in A minor (*Allegro un poco maestoso, Presto, Adagio cantabile, Allegro molto*) (c) 1911/12 ? (pu) 1929 OUP (MS) G.
Quartet in E flat major (Harrogate) (*Allegro con moto, Prestissimo, Adagio, Allegro molto (Reel)*) (c) 1912 (pu) 1929 OUP (MS) G.
Quartet in F major (*Poco adagio, Allegretto, Allegro un poco vivace*) (c) 1914/5 ? (pu) 1929 OUP (MS) G.
Quartet in D major (*Allegro con moto, Allegro vivace, Adagio, Allegro molto*) (c) 1915/6 ? (pu) 1929 OUP (MS) G.
Variations on an Irish Folk Song (c) 1917 ? (pu) 1929 OUP (MS) G.
Quartet movement in G minor (c) 1916/7 ? (pu) 1929 OUP (MS) G.

Ibid (2nd version) (c) 1916/7 (MS) G.
Unfinished quartet movement in G minor (c) 1916/7 (MS) G.
Unfinished set of variations for quartet in A minor (MS) G.

Short-score sketches for string quartet

An *Irish Dance* in D major (unfinished) based on Joyce nos 132, 520 & 521 (MS) G.
2 *Irish Dances* arr string quartet founded on Joyce nos 686 & 494 (MS) G.
An *Irish Dance* in G major (MS) G.
An *Irish Dance* for string quartet founded on Joyce nos 737, 782 & 347 (MS) G.
33 folk-melodies taken from Joyce, Petrie, Feis Coil, etc. arr string quartet (MS) G.
Quodlibet arr string quartet (MS) G.
Theme and variations for string quartet (?) based on Joyce 708 (MS) G.

MIXED ENSEMBLES

Septet in C minor for cl (B flat), bassoon, horn, violin, viola, 'cello and double bass (*Allegro moderato, Andante, Presto (Scherzo), With vigour*) (c) 1889 (MS) G.
Quintet in F major for fl, ob, cl, (B flat), horn and bassoon (*Allegro con moto, Molto vivace, Andante grazioso, Allegro moderato*) (c) 1891 (pu) 1933 (parts only) Boosey & Hawkes.

TRIOS

Allegro in D minor for piano trio (c) 188-? (MS) G.
Andante quasi Adagio in A minor for piano trio (c) 188-? (MS) G.
Presto in D minor for piano trio (c) 188-? (MS) G.
Allegro moderato in D major for piano trio (c) 188-? (MS) G.
String trio in C major in one movement (*Allegro*) (1st violin part only survives) (MS) G.

Short-score sketches for string trio

Quodlibet (MS) G.

DUO SONATAS

Sonata in D minor for violin and piano in 2 movements (*Andante, Allegro vivace*) (c) 1882 (MS) G.
Sonata movement in G minor for violin and piano (*Adagio-Allegro*) (c) 188-? (MS) G.

Unfinished sonata in G major for 'cello and piano (*Allegro moderato, Andante*) (c) 1884 (MS) G.

Sonata in G major for violin and piano (*Allegro, Adagio, Presto*) (c) 1886 (MS) G.

Sonata in A major for violin and piano (*Andante, Adagio, Allegro ma non troppo*) (c) 189-? (pu) Chappell (Year Book Press) (MS) G.

DUO PIECES

Variations on 'The meeting of the waters' for violin and piano (c) 1882 (MS) G.

Two Pieces for violin and piano *'Jig* (founded on Joyce 829 & 831) *and Planxty'* (Joyce 586 & 287) (c) 192-? (pu) 1923 Stainer & Bell (MS) G (sketches only).

Two Irish Dances for violin and piano (*Moderato* — founded on Joyce 595 & 762) (*Allegro moderato* — Joyce 231) (c) 192-? (pu) 1927 Chappell (Year Book Press) (MS) G (sketches only).

Irish Dance (E minor) for violin and piano (inc Joyce 27 & 39) (c) 192-? (MS) G.

Irish Dance (G major) for violin and piano (inc Joyce 447 and Hoffman/Petrie 81) (c) 192-? (MS) G (sketches only).

Irish Dance (D major) for violin and piano (inc Hoffman/Petrie 16 and 126) (c) 192-? (MS) G (sketches only).

Irish Air for violin and piano (inc Joyce 708) (c) 192-? (MS) G (sketches only).

The Tullock Reel arr cello and piano (Feis Coil Collection no 15) (c) 192-? (MS) G (sketches only).

Two interlinked Irish Airs for violin and piano (Petrie nos 38 & 103) (c) 192-? (MS) G (sketches only).

Unfinished *Rondel* for violin and piano (MS) G.

Adagio for violin and piano in G major (MS) G.

SOLO INSTRUMENTS

PIANO

Piano sonata in G major (*Allegro con brio, Adagio cantabile, Scherzo (Allegro molto), Rondo (Allegretto)*) (c) 1882 (MS) G.

Fugue in A major (c) 1882 (MS) G.

Variations and fugue on a theme of Beethoven (c) 1884 (MS) G.

4 characteristic pieces in canon (Op 6) (*Allegretto, Andante espressivo, Tempo di valse, Allegro molto*) (c) 1892/3 (pu) 1893 Stainer & Bell (Augener) (MS) BM.

ORGAN

Variations and fugue on 'Winchester Old' (c) 1907/8 (pu) 1908 Stainer & Bell (MS) G.

3 preludes founded on melodies from the Genevan Psalter (Psalm XII, Song of Symeon, Psalm CXXIV) (c) 1907/8 (pu) 1908 Stainer & Bell (MS) G.

16 preludes founded on melodies from the English and Scottish Psalters. Bk 1 (St. Mary's, Old 77th Psalm, Martyrs' Tune, York Tune, Cheshire Tune, Newtoun Tune, Southwell Tune, Old 113th Psalm) Bk II (Old 136th Psalm, Lincoln Tune, Old 137th Psalm, Psalm 23 (H Carey), Old 104th Psalm, Old 25th Psalm, Nunc Dimittis, Old 132nd Psalm) (c) 1911/12 (pu) 1912 Stainer & Bell (MS) G (a few sketches only).

Suite in the Ancient Style (*Allemande, Courante, Sarabande, Bourée I and II, Gigue*) (c) 1915 ? (pu) 1st three movements, 1928, last two 1915 Chappell (Year Book Press) (MS) G (last two movements only).

Andante in D major contributed to *A Little Organ Book in memory of Hubert Parry* (pu) 1924 Chappell (Year Book Press).

Prelude and fugue in G minor (pu) 1933 Chappell (Year Book Press).

Fugue on 'Song of Symeon' (or Laisses Createur) in A major (MS) G.

Fugue in D minor (MS) G.

Psalm-tune prelude on Psalm 26 (c) 1911/12? (MS) G (sketches).

Unfinished psalm-tune prelude in A major (c) 1911/12? (MS) G (sketches).

2nd unfinished psalm-tune prelude in A major (c) 1911/12? (MS) G (sketch).

Unfinished set of variations on an original theme in D major (MS) RCM and G (sketches).

Unfinished set of variations on a psalm tune in B minor (MS) G (sketches).

Unfinished set of variations in E flat major (MS) G (sketches).

ORCHESTRAL WORKS

Piano concerto in F major (*Allegro molto ma tranquillo, Adagio, Allegro ma non troppo*) (c) 1885/6 (MS) G.

Concert overture *Much Ado About Nothing* (c) 1889 (MS) P.

Iphigenia in Tauris orchestral suite based on the incidental music (MS) Stainer and Bell have parts.

Patrick Sarsfield symphonic variations on an Irish air (c) 1899 (MS) RCM.

Unfinished symphonic fragment in F major (MS) G.

Unfinished symphonic fragment in C minor (*Allegro ma non troppo*) (MS) G.

Unfinished symphonic fragment in D major (MS) G.

Set of Schubert Valses scored for small orchestra (MS) G.

Arrangement for string orchestra of *The Dear Irish Boy* (Feis Coil no 59) (MS) G (short score).

Lost orchestral compositions

Concert overture in D minor written while at the RCM.

Concerto in one movement (F major) for organ and strings (c) 1899 (MS) G has string parts, but solo part and full score are missing.

MILITARY BAND

Quick march for the Cambridge University Volunteer Rifles (c) 1886 (MS) G.

Regimental march of the Royal Signals (C) 1926 (pu) 1927 Boosey & Hawkes (parts only) (MS) G (sketches, full score not in Wood's writing).

MUSIC FOR THE THEATRE

Incidental music for the *Ion* of Euripides Op 4 (c) 1890 (pu) 1890 MacMillan and Bowes & Bowes (vocal score) (MS) G (full score).

Incidental music for the *Iphigenia in Tauris* of Euripides (c) 1894 (pu) 1894 MacMillan and Bowes & Bowes (vocal score) (MS) G (vocal score only, full score has been lost) — see 'Orchestral works' above.

A scene from Pickwick chamber opera in one act (c) 1921 (MS) P (full score) RCM (vocal score).

The Family Party chamber opera in one act (c) 1923 (MS) G (full score).

Unfinished opera *Pat in Fairyland* (unfinished overture, prologue in two scenes and part of Act 1 in full score — sketches for much of the remainder (w) Dr John Todhunter (c) 190-? (MS) G.

SOLO SONGS

ORIGINAL

Oh, skylark, for thy wing (w) Mrs Hemans (c) 1884 (MS) G.

Had I a cave (version also with orch. accmpt) (w) R Burns (c) 1884 (MS) G.

As o'er her loom (w) T Moore (c) 1884 (MS) G.

Song of Thekla (w) Schiller tr S T Coleridge (c) 1885 (MS) G.

The splendour falls (w) Lord Alfred Tennyson (c) 1886 (pu) 1927 in 'Five songs for high voice' Boosey & Hawkes (MS) G.

Up-hill (version also with orch accmpt) (w) Christina Rossetti (c) 1886 (MS) G.

At the mid hour of night (w) T Moore (c) 1886 (pu) 1927 in 'Five songs for High Voice' Boosey & Hawkes (MS) G.

Goldthred's song (w) Sir Walter Scott (c) 1886 (pu) 1927 in 'Ten songs for low voice' Boosey & Hawkes (MS) G.

Bright are the skies above me (w) Lord Beaconsfield (c) 1886 (MS) G.

Ask me no more (w) Lord Alfred Tennyson (c) 1886 (pu) 1927 in 'Five songs for high voice' Boosey & Hawkes (MS) G.

Echo (w) Christina Rossetti (c) 1886 (pu) 1927 in 'Five songs for high voice' Boosey & Hawkes (MS) G.

Fortune and her wheel (w) Lord Alfred Tennyson (c) 1886? (pu) 1927 in 'Five songs for high voice' Boosey & Hawkes (MS) G.

Youth and age (w) S T Coleridge (c) 1887 (MS) G.

Shall I forget (w) Christina Rossetti (c) 1887 (pu) 1927 in 'Ten songs for low voice' Boosey & Hawkes (MS) G.

A Summer's wish (w) Christina Rossetti (c) 1887 (MS) G.

Alas so long (w) D G Rossetti (c) 1887 (MS) G.

The Hour and the Ghost (w) Christina Rossetti (c) 1887 (MS) G.

Through the twilight (w) Alexander Grant (c) 1887 (MS) G (incomplete).

The Maid of Neidpath (w) Sir Walter Scott (c) 1888 (MS) G.

They are all gone into the world of light (w) Henry Vaughan (c) 1888 (MS) G.

The death of Clanronald (w) Mrs Hemans (c) 1890? (MS) G.

Lament of an Irish mother (w) Mrs Hemans (c) 1890 (MS) G.

The rover (w) Sir Walter Scott (c) 1890 (pu) 1927 in 'Ten songs for low voice' Boosey & Hawkes.

The Windflower (w) Sir H Boulton (c) 1890 (pu) 1891 in 'Twelve new songs by some of the best and best-known British composers' Leadenhall Press (MS) G.

Darest thou now, O soul (w) Walt Whitman (c) 1891 (pu) 1927 in 'Ten songs for low voice' Boosey & Hawkes.

Four songs with pianoforte accmp't (pu) 1892 Stainer & Bell (Augener):
  An ancient love song (w) anon (c) 1891?
  Why so pale and wan (w) Suckling (c) 1891 (MS) G.
  How can the tree (w) Lord Vaux (c) 1891 (MS) G.
  Ah! Robin, Jolly Robin (w) Wyatt (c) 1891 (MS) G.

By the bivouac's fitful flame (w) Walt Whitman (c) 1897 (MS) RCM.

I was wishful he'd stay (w) A P Graves (1897) (pu) 1901 Novello (MS) and sketches G.

O Captain! my Captain (w) Walt Whitman (c) 1898 (pu) 1899 Boosey & Hawkes (MS) and sketches G.

Ethiopia saluting the colours (also version with orchestral accompaniment) (w) Walt Whitman (c) 1898 (pu) 1898 Boosey & Hawkes (MS) Fitzwilliam museum, Cambridge.

The outlaw of Loch Lene (w) tr J J Callanan (c) 1898 (pu) 1900 Boosey & Hawkes (MS) G.

One morning in May (w) A P Graves (c) 1898? (pu) 1899 Boosey & Hawkes (MS) G (unfinished).

The Potato Song (w) A P Graves (c) 1908/9? (pu) 1909 Boosey & Hawkes (MS) G.

Fineen the rover (w) R D Joyce (pu) 1912 Stainer & Bell.

Home to Glentees (w) Patrick Macgill (pu) 1912 Chappell (Year Book Press).

Tim, an Irish terrier (w) W M Letts (pu) 1913 Stainer & Bell.

Roll up the map of Europe (w) W L Hutchinson (c) 1914? (MS) G.

The Munsters at Mons (w) A P Graves (c) 1915 (MS) G.

On the Camp Hill, Hastings (w) Thomas Campbell (MS) G.

Holy Thursday (w) W Blake (pu) 1931 Boosey & Hawkes.

Resignation (w) A Proctor (MS) and sketches G.

Boys (w) W M Letts (MS) G.

Song of the Cyclops (w) T Dekker (pu) 1927 in 'Ten songs for low voice' Boosey & Hawkes.

The dead at Clonmacnois (w) tr T W Rolleston (pu) 1927 in 'Ten songs for low voice' Boosey & Hawkes (MS) G (sketches only).

At sea (w) Moira O'Neill (pu) 1927 in 'Ten songs for low voice' Boosey & Hawkes.

Birds (w) Moira O'Neill (pu) 1927 in 'Ten songs for low voice' Boosey & Hawkes.

The sailorman (w) Moira O'Neill (pu) 1927 in 'Ten songs for low voice' Boosey & Hawkes.

Denny's daughter (w) Moira O'Neill (pu) 1927 in 'Ten songs for low voice' Boosey & Hawkes.

Unfinished settings
The new Guy Fawkes (w) anon (MS) G.
Roseen Dhu (w) tr Thomas Furlong (MS) G.
(sketches of at least six other songs survive in fragments).

Lost setting
The King of Thule (w) Goethe tr? (accompt for string quintet).

FOLK-SONG ARRANGEMENTS
Irish Folk Songs (w) A P Graves (pu) 1897 Boosey & Hawkes (d) Charles Villiers Stanford. Contents: *The cuckoo madrigal* (*The cobbler of Castleberry*) (c) 1895?; *The merchant's daughter* (c) 1895?; *The Kerry cow* (*The spotted cow*) (c) 1895? (MS) G; *Love at my heart* (*Daniel the Worthy*) (c) 1895? (MS) G; (2 MSS, one in F major, one in E flat

major), *Beside the River Loune* (c) 1895? (MS) G; *When we were boy and girl* (*Nancy Vernon*) (c) 1895? (MS) G; *Darby Kelly* (c) 1895 (MS) G; *The blackberry blossom* (c) 1895? (MS) G; *The song of Naimh of the Golden Tresses* (*The wicked Kerryman*) (c) 1895? (MS) G; *The sentry box* (c) 1895? (MS) G; *The lost child* (*name unknown*) (c) 1895? (MS) G; *Come sit down beside me* (*Connemara air*) (c) 1895? (MS) G; *I'm the boy for bewitching them* (c) 1895? (MS) G; *They know not my heart* (*Coolun Das*) (c) 1895? (MS) G; *Over here* (*over there*) (c) 1895? (MS) G; *The magic mist* (c) 1895? (MS) G; *I'd roam the world over with you* (*I'd roam the world*) (c) 1895? (MS) G; *For I had a spirit above my degree* (c) 1895? (MS) G; *Credhe's lament for Cail* (*A little hour before day*) (c) 1895? (MS) G; *Hey ho, the morning dew* (c) 1895?; *O love, 'tis a calm starry night* (c) 1895? (MS) G; *The jug of punch* (*The robber*) (c) 1895 (MS) G; *The brave Irish lad* (c) 1895? (MS) G; *The blackbird and the thrush* (c) 1895?; *The song of the woods* (c) 1895?

Nell Flaherty's drake (w) A P Graves (pu) 1895 Boosey & Hawkes.
I mayn't or I may (w) A P Graves (pu) 1901 Novello (MS) G.

Irish County Songs, Volume 1, 'Written, edited and arranged by Alfred Percival Graves & Charles Wood' (pu) 1914 Stainer & Bell (d) Harry Plunket Greene: *The sea singer* (*The mermaid*) (w) A P Graves (MS) G (sketch); *My Wicklow mountains* (w) A P Graves; *The enchanted valley* (w) A P Graves; *The high-caul cap* (w) P J McCall (MS) G (sketch); *The winding banks of Erne* (*The River Roe*) (w) William Allingham; *Kate of Garnavilla* (*Roy's wife of Aldvalloch*) (w) Edward Lysaght (MS) G (brief sketch).

Irish County Songs, Volume II, 'Written, edited and arranged by Alfred Percival Graves & Charles Wood' (pu) 1927 Stainer & Bell: *The invention of wine* (*Kerry for me*) (w) A P Graves; *My own Lake of Lakes* (w) A P Graves; *Lament for King Laery* (*Limerick's lamentation*) (w) A P Graves; *The doom of Deirdre* (w) A P Graves; *I bridled my nag* (w) A P Graves; *Andy* (*The stooped old man*) (w) A P Graves.

Irish County Songs, Volume III, 'Words by P J McCall, music arr by Charles Wood' (pu) 1928 Stainer and Bell; *Down by the sally gardens* (w) P J McCall; *The bonny blue handkerchief* (*In mantle so green*) (w) P J McCall (MS) G (sketch); *Herself and myself* (*Young Jenny the pride of our town* and *Reel and song air — Joyce 293*) (w) P J McCall (MS) G (sketch); *Hush a by baby* (w) P J McCall; *Minding Mary* (*The scalded poor man*) (w) P J McCall (MS) G (sketch); *Molly my own love* (w) P J McCall; *The bracken lane* (w) P J MCall.

Anglo-Irish Folk Songs, Volume I, 'Written, edited and arranged by Padraic Gregory & Charles Wood' (pu) 1931 Stainer & Bell: *Molly Asthoreen* (w) P Gregory (MS) G (sketch); *Your milkin' days are over* (*The rambling reaper*) (w) P Gregory; *A Braid Valley love-song* (*The jacket blue*) (w) P Gregory (MS) G (sketch); *It's nae the could wind* (*The croppy boy*) (w) P Gregory (MS) G (sketch); *Newcastle Fair* (*The winnowing sheet*) (w) P Gregory (MS) G (sketch); *The funny wee man* (trad Antrim air) (w) P Gregory (MS) G (sketch).

The Crucifixion (w) A P Graves (MS) G (+ version with accompaniment for string quartet and piano).

The following arrangements exist in the form of sketches from which full versions can be reconstructed. It is known that many MSS were lost by a publisher who had accepted them:
Curly locks (Hoffman/Petrie no 36) (w) P J McCall (MS) G (sketches); *Oliver's advice* (*Captain Thompson*) (w) William Blacker (MS) G (sketches); *The battle eve of the Brigade* (*Contented I am*) (w) Thomas Davis (MS) G (sketches); *His own and his own country* (*All alive*) (w) Emily H Hickey (MS) G (sketches); *The forester's complaint* (unknown) (w) Sir Samuel Ferguson (MS) G (sketches); *Kathleen O'More* (w) George Nugent Reynolds (MS) G (sketch); *The wild geese* (w) Dr Drennan (MS) G (sketch); *My Connor* (*The dear Irish boy*) (w) anon (MS) G (sketch); *Oh, the marriage* (*The swaggering jig*) (w) Thomas Davis (MS) G (sketch); *The Lake of Coolfin* (w) Old ballad adapted by Patrick Weston Joyce (MS) G (sketch); *The*

Drinanan Dhun (*The brown thorn*) (w) Robert Dwyer Joyce (MS) G (sketch); *My love wrote me a letter* (MS) G (sketch); *The boatman of Kinsole* (*The angler*) (w) Thomas Davis (MS) G (sketch); *The red-haired man's wife* (w) Kathleen Hinkson adapted A P Graves (MS) G (sketch); *Draheren O Machree* (*Little brother of my heart*) (w) Michael Hogan (MS) G (sketch); *Song of an island fisherman* (*Lamentation air*) (w) Kathleen Hinkson (MS) G (sketch); *Sho ho* (or *lullaby*) (w) A P Graves (MS) G (sketch); *Among the heather* (w) William Allingham (MS) G (sketch); *St Stephen's Night* (*The Wren*) (w) William Allingham (MS) G (sketch); *Irish Molly-o* (w) ?(MS) G (sketch).

Sketches of 11 folk-song arrangements survive of which the words have not been identified.

Sketches of 6 presumed folk-song arrangements survive of which neither words nor tunes have been positively identified.

Lost folk-song arrangements (some of which may be represented above): *The blossom of the lime* (soprano song) (w) A P Graves; *The banks of Ahasnagh* (Soprano song) (w) A P Graves; *The County Limerick buck hunt* (contralto song) (w) Pierce Creagh; *Drimmin Dhu Dheelish* (soprano song) (w) A P Graves; *Dublin Bay* (soprano song) (w) Lady Dufferin; *Eileen Dheelish of Athenry* (soprano song) (w) Joyce McCall; *My heart is in Innisbower* (w) A P Graves; *Galway Bay* (soprano song) (w) A P Graves; *Grasmere (?) spinning song* (w) A P Graves; *Grasmere (?) lullaby* (w) A P Graves; *Im bo* (*milking song*) (contralto song) (w) A P Graves; *The Kilruddery Hunt* (contralto song) (w) Thomas Moore; *Life like ours* (soprano song) (w) A P Graves; *Love is a boundless bliss* (soprano song) (w) A P Graves; *Limerick road* (soprano song) (w) Joyce McCall; *The minstrel lover* (soprano song) (w) A P Graves; *The nobleman's wedding* (soprano song) (w) adapted by Allingham; *One morning, by the streamlet* (soprano song) (w) Grace O'Brien; *Pasteen Fione*; *Proud Maurya* (soprano song) (w) A P Graves; *Rose of the desert* (soprano song) (w) adapted from Thomas Moore; *Sea song*; *The snowy-breasted pearl* (contralto song) (w) tr from the Irish by G Petrie; *Song of the corncrake* (soprano song) (w) Joyce McCall; *There once was a jolly blade* (w) A P Graves; *The welcome* (soprano song) (w) Thomas Davis.

SMALLER SECULAR VOCAL WORKS

MADRIGALS FOR MIXED VOICES
If love be dead (SSATB) (w) S T Coleridge (c) 1886? (pu) 1886 Novello.
Slow, slow fresh fount (SSATB) (w) Ben Jonson (c) 1888 (pu) 1889 Stanley Lucas, Weber & Co (d) Charles Morley Esq (MS) G.
Love farewell (SATB) (w) Robert, Earl of Essex, 1599 (c) 1888 (MS) G.
Whence comes my love (SSATB) (w) Sir John Harrington c 1550 (c) 1891 (MS) G.
The complaint of a deserted lover (SATB) (w) Sir Thomas Wyatt (c) 1891 (MS) G.
Come, you servants of proud love (SSATB) (w) Beaumont and Fletcher (MS) G.
The bag of the bee (SSATB) (w) R Herrick (c) 1895-1925? (pu) 1929 OUP.

Lost madrigal
The alienated mistress.

GLEES FOR MIXED VOICES
Song for a dance (SATB) (w) Francis Beaumont (pu) 1927 Chappell (Year Book Press) (MS) G (sketch).

PART-SONGS FOR MIXED VOICES
How sweet the moonlight sleeps (SATBB) (w) Shakespeare (c) 1887/8? (pu) 1888 Novello.
Blow, blow, thou winter wind (SATB) (w) Shakespeare (c) 1888? (pu) 1890 Novello.
The Hemlock Tree (SATB) (w) German tr H W Longfellow (c) 1890/1? (pu) 1891 Novello.
Full fathom five (SATB) (w) Shakespeare (c) 1890/1? (pu) 1891 Novello.
Hero and Leander (SATB) (w) Thomas Moore (c) 1892 (MS) G.
It was a lover (SATB) (w) Shakespeare (c) 1892/3? (pu) 1893 Novello.
Wanderer's night song (SATB) (w) Goethe tr Longfellow (c) 1892/3 (pu) 1893 Novello.
The widow bird (SATB) (w) P B Shelley (c) 1895/6? (pu) 1896 Novello.
A land dirge (SATB) (w) J Webster (c) 1898? (pu) 1898 Novello.

The countryman (SATB) (w) anon (1588) (c) 1898? (pu) 1898 Novello (MS) G (sketch).

A century's penultimate (in 'Choral songs by various writers and composers in honour of Her Majesty Queen Victoria') (SSATBB) (w) A C James (c) 1899 (pu) 1899 Macmillan (MS) G.

Nights of music (SATB) (w) Thomas Moore (c) 1899? (pu) 1900 Novello (MS) G (sketch).

As the moon's soft splendour (SATB) (w) P B Shelley (c) 1905? (pu) 1905 Novello.

The whispering waves (SATB) (w) P B Shelley (c) 1905? (pu) 1905 Novello (MS) G (incomplete).

I call and I call (SATBB) (w) R Herrick (c) 1906 (pu) 1908 Stainer & Bell (MS) G.

How sweet the tuneful bells (SATB) (w) W L Bowles (c) 1906 (pu) 1908 Stainer & Bell (MS) G.

Come sleep (SATB) (w) Beaumont and Fletcher (c) 1908? (pu) 1908 Stainer & Bell (MS) G (sketch).

When whispering strains (SSATB) (w) William Strode (c) 1908? (pu) 1908 Stainer & Bell (MS) G.

Fain would I change (SATB) (w) anon (1605) (c) 1908? (pu) 1908 Stainer & Bell (MS) G.

Music, when soft voices die (SATB) (w) P B Shelley (c) 1908? (pu) 1908 Stainer & Bell (MS) G.

Haymakers, rakers (SATB) (w) T Dekker (c) 1908? (pu) 1908 Stainer & Bell (MS) G.

Time (SATB) (w) Sir Walter Scott (c) 1914 (pu) 1914 Chappell (Year Book Press).

Awake, awake (SATB) (w) T Campion (c) 1914? (pu) 1914 Chappell (Year Book Press).

Sea children (SATB) (w) anon (c) 1914 (MS) G.

To the troubler of the world (SATB) (w) anon (c) 1914 (MS) G.

Love, what wilt thou (SATB) (w) French tr H W Longfellow (c) 1921? (pu) 1921 Chappell (Year Book Press) (MS) G.

Follow, follow (SATB) (w) T Campion (c) 1922? (pu) 1922 Chappell (Year Book Press) (MS) G (sketch).

Shepherd's Sunday song (SATB) (w) Uhland tr G R Woodward (c) 1923? (pu) 1923 Stainer & Bell.

Autumn (SATB) (w) P B Shelley (c) 1924? (pu) 1924 Stainer & Bell.

Wassail (SATB) (w) John Bale (c) 1925? (pu) 1925 Chappell (Year Book Press).

Spring song (SATB) (w) German tr G R Woodward (c) 1923? (pu) 1926 Stainer & Bell.

Lullaby (SATB) (w) T Dekker (pu) 1927 Chappell (Year Book Press) (MS) G (sketch).

The Lamb (SATB) (w) W Blake (pu) 1927 Chappell (Year Book Press).

Down in yon summer vale (SATB) (w) Thomas Moore (pu) 1927 Novello (originally for male voices).

Hence away, begone (SATB) (w) French tr H W Longfellow (pu) 1929 Chappell (Year Book Press).

The solitary reaper (SATB) (w) W Wordsworth (pu) 1930 Novello (Arnold) (MS) G (sketch).

Rose-cheeked Laura (SATB) (w) T Campion (pu) 1931 Stainer & Bell (MS) G (sketch).

When to her lute (SATB) (w) T Campion (pu) 1933 Chappell (Year Book Press) (MS) G (sketch).

Spring time (SATB) (w) French tr H W Longfellow (pu) 1937 Chappell (Year Book Press).

To music bent (SATB) (w) T Campion (MS) G (sketch — full MS in the handwritting of S P Waddington).

Oh! thou alone (SATB) (w) Mrs Hemans (MS) G (sketch — full MS in the handwriting of S P Waddington).

A song of olden time (SATB) (w) Thomas Moore (MS) G (in the handwriting of S P Waddington) and sketch.

A farewell to arms (SATB) (w) G Peele (MS) G and sketch.

Counsel to girls (SATB) (w) R Herrick (MS) G.

Hymn to Pan (SATB) (w) Beaumont & Fletcher (MS) G (sketch).

If I hope to fear (SATB?) (w) T Campion (MS) G (sketch).

See the dawn (SATB) (w) T Moore (MS) G (sketch).

Were my heart as some men's are (SATB) (w) T Campion (MS) G (sketch).

Follow thy fair sun (SATB) (w) T Campion (MS) G (sketch).

Thy sky is beauty rack'd (SATB) (w) ? (MS) G (sketch).

Unfinished mixed-voice part-songs
This time of year (SATB) (w) ? (MS) G.
Take, O take (SATB) (w) Shakespeare (MS) G.
To his sweet lute (SATB) (w) T Campion (MS) G (sketch).
How soft the music of the village bells (SATB) (w) W Cowper (MS) G (sketch).
Midnight (SATB) (w) Harold Boulton (MS) G (sketch).
O hush thee my baby (SATB) (w) Sir Walter Scott (MS) G (sketch).
The summer's call (SATB) (w) Mrs Hemans (MS) G (sketch).
Simon and Laura, a pastoral for SATB soloists and piano (orchestra?) (MS) G (sketch).
Night and death (SATB) (w) Joseph Blanco White (MS) G (sketch).
There are sketches of 2 part-songs the words of which cannot be identified (MS) G.

Lost mixed voice part-songs
Proud Maisie (w) Sir Walter Scott.
The golden mean (w) Gilbert Murray.
The sultan's daughter.
The Wanderer.
Early Morning.
The Reaper.

PART-SONGS FOR MALE VOICES (TBB)
Neptune's empire (TBB) (w) T Campion (pu) 1927 Chappell (Year Book Press) (MS) G (sketch).
Robin Hood (TBB) (w) Robert Jones (pu) 1927 Chappell (Year Book Press) (MS) G (sketch).
Robin Hood (TBB) (w) T Campion (pu) 1927 Chappell (Year Book Press) (MS) G (sketch).
The peaceful western wind (TBB) (w) T Campion (MS) G (sketch).
In Sherwood lived stout Robin Hood (TBB) (w) T Campion (MS) G (sketch).
Love me or not (TBB) (w) T Campion (MS) G (sketch).
Follow your saint (TBB) (w) T Campion (MS) G (sketch).
Triolet (TBB) (w) Robert Bridges (MS) G.

EXTENDED SONGS FOR TBB AND PIANO
The sailors' song (TBB and piano) (w) S Dobell (MS) G (vocal part and sketch of piano part).

PART-SONGS FOR ATBB & ATTB (unaccompanied)
It was a lover (ATTB) (w) Shakespeare (c) 1892/3? (pu) 1893 Novello (see also part-songs SATB).
There comes a new moon (ATTB) (w) Charles Dickens (c) 1907/8? (pu) Stainer & Bell (MS) G.
When winds that move not (ATTB) (w) P B Shelley (c) 1912/13? (pu) 1913 (Stainer & Bell) (d) To the Gentlemen of St George's Choir, Windsor.
There be none of beauty's daughters (ATTB) (w) Lord Byron (c) 1926 (pu) 1927 Chappell (Year Book Press) (MS) G (unfinished fair copy MS and sketch) (d) The King's College, Cambridge, Quartet.
Invocation (ATTB) (w) Mrs Hemans (pu) 1930 OUP.
Shows and nightly revels (ATTB) (w) T Campion (MS) G.
If thou art sleeping, maiden (ATBB) (w) H W Longfellow (c) 1888 (MS) G.

Unfinished male-voice part-song
I have a horse (ATTB) (MS) G (sketch).

PART-SONGS FOR TTBB
O mistress mine (TTBB) (w) Shakespeare (c) 1889 (MS) G.
Still like dew in silence falling (TTBB) (w) T Moore (c) 1890 (MS) P.
It was an English ladye bright (baritone solo and TTBB) (w) Sir Walter Scott (c) 1899 (pu) 1909 Novello (MS) G.
Down in yon summer vale (TTBB) (w) T Moore (c) 1901? (pu) 1902 Novello (see also part-songs SATB).
The Russian lover (TTBB) (w) T Moore (c) 1921/2? (pu) 1922 Chappell (Year Book Press) (MS) G.
A clear midnight (TTBB) (w) Walt Whitman (pu) 1926 Stainer & Bell (MS) G (sketch).
When thou art nigh (TTBB) (w) T Moore (pu) 1927 Chappell (Year Book Press) (MS) G.
Paty O'Toole (TTBB) (w) anon (c) 1922 (pu) 1933 Chappell (Year Book Press) (MS) G (sketch).
What is a day (TTBB) (w) T Campion (MS) G.

PART-SONGS FOR TTBB WITH PIANO ACCOMPANIMENT

Fight, brothers, fight (TTBB and piano) (c) 1888 (MS) G (piano intro missing).
A message to Phyllis (TTBB and piano) (w) Thomas Heywood (MS) G.

UNISON MALE VOICES AND PIANO

Carmen Caianum (c) 1891/2? (pu) 1892 Cambridge University Press.

GLEE FOR TTBB

A woman's love (TTBB) (w) Shakespeare (c) 1893? (MS) G.

Lost part-songs for male voices

Chorus from Gilbert Murray's translation of the Hyppolytus.
The Vagabond.

PART-SONGS FOR FEMALE VOICES SSAA OR SSSS (unaccompanied)

The nymph's faun (SSAA) (w) Andrew Marvell (c) 1908? (pu) 1908 Stainer & Bell (MS) G.
Golden slumbers (SSSS) (w) T Dekker (c) 1919/20? (pu) 1920 Novello (Arnold).

PART-SONGS FOR SSAA/SSSS WITH PIANO ACCOMPANIMENT

Cowslips for her covering (Canon VI) SSAA & accompaniment) (w) R Herrick (c) 1912/13? (pu) 1913 Chappell (Year Book Press).
Sunlight all golden (SSSS and accompaniment) (w) Paul Gerhardt tr G R Woodward (c) 1918 (pu) 1919 Chappell (Year Book Press) (MS) G.

PART-SONGS FOR SSA (unaccompanied)

The starlings (SSA) (w) Charles Kingsley (c) 1918/9? (pu) 1919 Novello (Arnold).
Lilies (SSA) (w) Leigh Hunt (c) 1918/9? (pu) 1919 Novello (Arnold).
To welcome in the year (SSA) (w) W Blake (c) 1923/4? (pu) 1924 Chappell (Year Book Press).
The blossom (SSA) (w) W Blake (pu) 1926 Chappell (Year Book Press) (MS) G.

PART-SONGS FOR SSA WITH PIANO ACCOMPANIMENT

Echo (SSA and Piano) (w) W E Henley (c) 1908/9? (pu) 1909 Chappell (Year Book Press) (MS) G.
Good precepts (Canon VII) (SSA and piano) (w) R Herrick (c) 1912/3? (pu) 1913 Chappell (Year Book Press).
Music when soft voices die (SSA and piano) (w) P B Shelley (c) 1914/5? (pu) 1915 Chappell (Year Book Press) (orchestral accompaniment available).
To music bent (SSA and piano — accompaniment for 2 violins as alternative) (w) T Campion (c) 1920/1? (pu) 1921 Chappell (Year Book Press) (MS) G.
What is a day (SSA and piano) (w) T Campion (pu) 1927 Chappell (Year Book Press) (MS) G.

UNISON SONGS WITH PIANO ACCOMPANIMENT

She will not drink the blood-red wine (unison and piano) (w) anon (c) 1908/9? (pu) 1909 Chappell (Year Book Press) (MS) G.
The onset (unison and piano) (w) Barry Cornwall (c) 1914/5? (pu) 1915 Chappell (Year Book Press) (MS) G.
Jack and Joan (unison and piano) (w) T Campion (c) 1916/7? (pu) 1917 Chappell (Year Book Press) (MS) G (sketch).
In *Kookoorookoo* and other songs (ed Martin Ackermann) (unison and piano): *Boats sail on the rivers, What is pink?, Mix a pancake* (w) Christina Rossetti (c) 1916 (pu) 1916 Chappell (Year Book Press).
The knight's tomb (unison and piano) (w) S T Coleridge (c) 1917/18 (pu) 1918 Novello (Arnold).
As they did, you know when-a! (unison and piano) (w) anon (16th c) (c) 1917/18? (pu) 1918 Chappell (Year Book Press).
The dream of home (unison and piano) (w) T Moore (c) 1920/21? (pu) 1921 Chappell (Year Book Press) (MS) G.
In *Kikirikee* and other songs, (ed Martin Ackermann) (unison and piano): *All the bells were ringing, An emerald is as green as grass, Lie abed, sleepy head, Angels at the foot* (w) Christina Rossetti (c) 1924/5 (pu) 1925 Chappell (Year Book Press).
I have a clock (unison and piano) (w) Mabel Trustram (c) 1924/5? (pu) 1925 Chappell (Year Book Press) (MS) G.
Trees (unison and piano) (w) Mabel Trustram

(pu) 1926 Chappell (Year Book Press) (MS) G.

A song of the sea (unison and piano) (w) anon (pu) 1926 Chappell (Year Book Press) (MS) G.

The seas of England (unison and piano) (w) de la Mare (pu) 1928 Chappell (Year Book Press).

The trees in England (unison and piano) (w) de la Mare (pu) 1929 Chappell (Year Book Press).

Sleep my baby (unison and piano) (w) Mabel Trustram (pu) 1929 Chappell (Year Book Press).

Where do all the fairies play? (unison and piano) (w) Mary Trustram (pu) 1930 Chappell (Year Book Press).

In mother's garden (unison and piano) (w) Mary Trustram (pu) 1931 Chappell (Year Book Press).

Butterflies gay (unison and piano) (w) Mary Trustram (pu) 1933 Chappell (Year Book Press).

Maid Marion's song (unison and piano) (w) George Darley (MS) G (sketch).

Quoth John to Joan (w) trad (MS) G (sketch). Fragmentary sketches exist of a setting (apparently for unison voices with a piano) of *Little Billie* (Thackeray).

2-PART SONGS WITH PIANO ACCOMPANIMENT

6 two-part songs: *Now the bright morning star* (w) J Milton (c) 1888; *To daffodils* (w) R Herrick (c) 1888; *La fileuse* (w) Julian Fane (c) 1888; *Evening* (w) J Fletcher (c) 1888; *Young and old* (w) Sir Walter Scott (c) 1888.

Under the greenwood tree (w) Shakespeare (c) 1888; (pu) 1892 Novello (MS) G (d) Professor C V Stanford.

When young leaves are springing (w) M J (c) 1908/9? (pu) 1909 Chappell (Year Book Press).

Who is Sylvia? (w) Shakespeare (c) 1891 (pu) 1909 Chappell (Year Book Press) (MS) G.

A visit from the Sea (w) R L Stevenson (c) 1910/11 (pu) 1911 Chappell (Year Book Press) (MS) G.

The sword (w) Michael Joseph Barry (c) 1910/11? (pu) 1911 Chappell (Year Book Press) (MS) RCM.

Osme's song from 'Sylvia' (w) G Darley (c) 1911/12? (pu) 1912 Chappell (Year Book Press).

Lucy Ashton's song (Canon 1) (w) Sir Walter Scott (c) 1912/13? (pu) 1913 Chappell (Year Book Press).

The best of rooms (Canon 2) (w) R Herrick (c) 1912/3? (pu) 1913 Chappell (Year Book Press) (orchestral version of accompaniment available).

To music (Canon 3) (w) R Herrick (c) 1912/13? (pu) 1913 Chappell (Year Book Press).

The primrose (Canon 4) (w) R Herrick (c) 1912/13 (pu) 1913 Chappell (Year Book Press).

The ride of the witch (*The hag*) (Canon 5) (w) R Herrick (c) 1912/13 (pu) 1913 Chappell (Year Book Press) (orchestral version of accompaniment, made by Gordon Jacob, available).

A spirit song (Canon 8) (w) W Wordsworth (c) 1912/13? (pu) 1913 Chappell (Year Book Press).

What the birds say (Canon 9) (w) S T Coleridge (c) 1912/13? (pu) 1913 Chappell (Year Book Press).

Gypsy song (w) Ben Jonson (c) 1914/15? (pu) 1915 Chappell (Year Book Press) (MS) G.

Gypsy benediction (w) Ben Jonson (c) 1914/15? (pu) 1915 Chappell (Year Book Press) (MS) G.

I have twelve oxen (w) anon (15th cent) (c) 1915/16 (pu) 1916 Chappell (Year Book Press) (MS) G.

The peaceful western wind (w) T Campion (c) 1917/18? (pu) 1918 Chappell (Year Book Press) (MS) G (+ sketch).

To blossoms (w) R Herrick (c) 1917/18? (pu) 1918 Novello (Arnold).

The summer winds (w) G Darley (c) 1918/19? (pu) Chappell (Year Book Press) (MS) G.

No surrender (optional piano accompaniment) (w) Martin Tupper (c) 1918/19? (pu) 1919 Chappell (Year Book Press) (MS) G.

Together (optional piano accompaniment) (w) Martin Tupper (c) 1918/19? (pu) 1919 Chappell (Year Book Press).

Courage (optional piano accompaniment) (w) Martin Tupper (c) 1918/19? (pu) 1919 Chappell (Year Book Press) (MS) G.

Orpheus with his lute (w) Shakespeare (c) 1918/19? (pu) 1919 Novello (Arnold).

The Milkmaid (w) Thomas Nabbes (17th cent) (c) 1918/19 (pu) 1922 Novello (Arnold).
A barcarolle (w) Mrs Hemans (c) 1921/22? (pu) 1922 Novello (Arnold).
The isle (w) P B Shelley (c) 1922/23? (pu) 1923 Novello (Arnold).
My dove (w) J Keats (c) 1922/23? (pu) 1923 Chappell (Year Book Press).
O'er the valley (w) G Darley (pu) 1927 Chappell (Year Book Press) (MS) G (sketch).
When a daffodil I see (w) R Herrick (pu) 1931 Boosey & Hawkes.
O sweet content (w) T Dekker (pu) 1931 Boosey & Hawkes.

Lost two-part songs
The coral grove.
The first summer bee

FOLK-SONG ARRANGEMENTS (MIXED VOICES — UNACCOMPANIED)

Lochinvar choral variations on an 'old Scotch air' (SATB) (w) Sir Walter Scott (c) 1912/13? (pu) 1913 Chappell (Year Book Press).
Come, lasses and lads, choral variations on an 'English folk tune' (SATB) (c) 1913 (pu) 1925 Chappell (Year Book Press) (MS) G.
Life and its follies (air — 'David of the white rock') (SATB) (w) Talhaiarn tr T Oliphant (pu) 1927 Chappell (Year Book Press) (MS) G.
The flower of beauty (Irish air — 'Miss Hamilton') (SATB) (w) G Darley (pu) 1934 Stainer & Bell (MS) G.
Hark! Hark! The soft bugle (Irish air — 'The Banks of Dunmore') (SATB) (w) Gerald Griffin (pu) 1934 Stainer & Bell (MS) G.
A chieftain to the Highlands bound (Irish air — 'The charming fair Eily') (SATB) (w) Campbell (MS) G (sketch).
The sack of Baltimore (Irish air — 'The chiefs of old times') set as a set of choral variations (unfinished) (SATB) (w) Thomas Davis (MS) G (sketch).

Folk-tunes arranged for SATB without words
Petrie 125 1039 1180; Joyce 105 106 324 335 641; Graves 16 (MS) G (short-score sketches).

Lost arrangement
O well do I remember (Welsh air).

FOLK TUNES ARRANGED FOR MIXED VOICES WITH PIANO ACCOMPANIMENT
The song of the heather (founded on 'Brian Boru's March') (tenor solo + SATB) (w) A P Graves (c) 1925/26 (pu) 1926 Boosey & Hawkes (MS) G.

FOLK-SONG ARRANGEMENTS FOR MALE-VOICES (TTBB UNACCOMPANIED)
The British Grenadiers (variations on an 18th cent air for TTBB) (w) anon (c) 1911/12? (pu) 1912 Stainer & Bell.
Oh! Breathe not his name (Irish air arr TTBB) (w) T Moore (c) 1913/4? (pu) 1914 Stainer & Bell.
Song of Innisfail (Irish air arr TTBB) (w) T Moore (c) 1913/14? (pu) 1914 Stainer & Bell.
I've a secret to tell thee (Irish air arr TTBB) (w) T Moore (c) 1913/14? (pu) 1914 Stainer & Bell.
Night closed around (Irish air arr TTBB) (w) T Moore (c) 1920/21? (pu) 1921 Stainer & Bell.
Hob a derry danno (Welsh folk-song arr TTBB) (w) Talhaiarn tr T Oliphant (c) 1922/23? (pu) 1923 Stainer & Bell (MS) G (sketch).
In merry mood (Welsh folk-tune 'The Dove' arr TTBB) (w) Talhaiarn tr Thomas Oliphant (c) 1922/23? (pu) 1923 Chappell (Year Book Press) (MS) G (sketch).
Echo (Irish air arr TTBB) (w) T Moore (c) 1923/24? (pu) 1924 Stainer & Bell.
The girl I left behind me (choral variations for male voices on the air 'Brighton Camp') (w) anon (c) 1924/25? (pu) 1925 Chappell (Year Book Press).
How dear to me (Irish air arr TTBB) (w) T Moore (c) 1925/26? (pu) 1926 Stainer & Bell.
O'Rourke's noble fare (Irish air arr TTBB) (w) tr J Swift (pu) 1927 Chappell (Year Book Press) (MS) G.
Three Scots airs *Hey, the dusty miller, There's none to sooth, O Spring's a pleasant time* (arr TTBB) (w) trad (pu) 1928 Chappell (Year Book Press) (MS) G.
And must we part? (Irish air 'Ni meallfar mé arts') (w) J J Callanan (pu) 1931 Stainer & Bell (MS) G (sketch).
I hear the trumpet sounding (Welsh air 'The

Camp' arr TTBB) (w) Talhaiarn tr Thomas Oliphant (MS) G (sketch).

Raise on high a royal lay (Welsh air 'The King's delight' arr TTBB) (w) Talhaiarn tr Thomas Oliphant (MS) G (sketch).

O where's the slave so lowly (Irish air 'Down beside me' arr TTBB) (w) T Moore (MS) G (sketch).

Send round the cup (Welsh air 'Black Sir Harry' arr TTBB) (w) Talhaiarn tr Thomas Oliphant (MS) G (sketch).

While gazing at the moon's light (Irish air 'Oonagh' arr TTBB) (w) T Moore (MS) G (sketch).

At the mid hour of night (Irish air 'Molly my dear' arr TTBB) (w) T Moore (MS) G (sketch).

I tell thee, Dick, where I have been (Old English air arr TTBB) (w) Sir John Suckling (MS) G (sketch).

O lov'd maid of Broka (Irish air 'I would rather than Ireland' arr TTBB) (w) tr Macneill (MS) G (sketch).

Lost settings

Arise from thy slumbers (air 'The old Traigha') (w) tr Miss Balfour.

The Rose.

FOLK-SONG ARRANGEMENTS FOR MALE VOICES (TBB UNACCOMPANIED)

O spring's a pleasant time (Scots air arr TBB) (w) anon (MS) G (sketch).

O the sighs that come fro' my heart (old English air arr TBB) (w) anon (MS) G (sketch).

A-hunting we will go (old English air arr TBB) (w) John Fielding (MS) G (sketch).

FOLK-SONG ARRANGEMENTS FOR FEMALE VOICES (UNACCOMPANIED)

The willow tree (choral variations on an 'Old English tune' for SSAA) (w) anon (c) 1913/14? (pu) 1914 Chappell (Year Book Press).

Unidentified *Lullaby* arr SSAA (MS) G (sketch).

UNISON FOLK-SONG ARRANGEMENTS WITH PIANO ACCOMPANIMENT

The holly and ivy girl (Irish air *O fair John my love*) (w) John Keegan (c) 1915/16? (pu) 1916 Chappell (Year Book Press) (MS) G.

The Fairy Queen of the May (Irish air) (w) G Darley (c) 1923/24? (pu) 1924 Chappell (Year Book Press) (MS) G (sketch).

FOLK-SONG ARRANGEMENTS FOR TWO VOICES WITH PIANO ACCOMPANIMENT

That voice (Irish air) (w) T Moore (c) 1911/12? (pu) 1912 Chappell (Year Book Press).

CHURCH MUSIC
ANTHEMS ETC.

Be thou exalted, Lord (SATB and organ) (c) 1882 (MS) G.

O Lord, rebuke me not (SSAATTBB) (c) 1885 (MS) G.

Praise God from whom all blessings flow (canonic doxology for double choir unaccompanied) (c) 1886 (MS) G.

O God of hosts, the mighty Lord (metrical version of 84th Psalm based on 'Bedford', SSAATTBB unaccompanied) (c) 1886 (MS) G.

Through the day thy love has spared us (SATB unaccompanied) (w) T Kelly (c) 1886 (MS) G.

The eyes of the Lord are over the righteous (ATTB unaccompanied) (c) 188-? (MS) G.

O Rex gloriae (grace anthem for Ascension Day, SATB unaccompanied) (c) 1889 (MS) G.

Try me O God (SATB and organ) (c) 1890? (pu) 1890 Novello.

Precamini Felicitatem (grace anthem, SATB and organ) (c) 1890 (pu) 1892 Novello (MS) G.

I will arise (SATB and organ) (c) 1893/94? (pu) 1894 Novello.

Heaven (SATB and organ) (w) Jeremy Taylor (c) 1898 (pu) 1898 Novello (MS) G (+ sketch).

Oculi omnium (canonic grace, SATB unaccompanied) (c) 1905 (pu) 1932 Cramer (MS) G.

I will call upon God (canon, ATB unaccompanied) (c) 1905 (pu) 1912 Chappell (Year Book Press) (MS) RCM.

Glorious and powerful God (SATB and organ) (c) 1910 (pu) 1910 Novello (MS) G.

Never weather-beaten sail (SATB and organ) (w) T Campion (c) 1910 (pu) 1935 Chappell (Year Book Press) (MS) P.

Ascension hymn (When Christ the Lord to heaven upraised) (SATB and organ) (w) A P

Graves. Altered to *Who through the desert vale* (w) E Tatton (pu) 1927 Stainer & Bell (MS) P.

Great Lord of Lords (double choir ATB unaccompanied) (w) H R Bramley (c) 1912? (pu) 1913 Chappell (Year Book Press) (MS) G.

True love's the gift (SATB unaccompanied) (w) Sir Walter Scott (wedding anthem later re-issued as a part-song) (c) 1912? (pu) 1914 Chappell (Year Book Press).

O Thou, the central orb (SATB and organ) (w) H R Bramley (c) 1914/15? (pu) 1915 Chappell (Year Book Press) (MS) G.

Hail gladdening light (double choir unaccompanied) (w) John Keble (c) 1912? (pu) 1919 Chappell (Year Book Press) (MS) G.

Summer ended (Harvest anthem SATB and organ) (w) Greville Phillimore (c) 1917 (pu) 1919 Chappell (Year Book Press) (MS) G.

O Lord that seest from yon starry height (SATB and organ) (w) Spanish tr H W Longfellow (c) 1918/19? (pu) 1919 Chappell (Year Book Press) (MS) G (sketch).

Expectans expectavi (SATB and organ — also orchestral accompaniment) (w) C H Sorley (c) 1919 (pu) 1919 Chappell (Year Book Press).

Haec dies (motet SSATBB unaccompanied) (c) 1919 (pu) 1920 Chappell (Year Book Press) (MS) G.

In exitu Israel (Psalm CXIV) (based on 'Tonus Peregrinus', unison antiphony and organ) (c) 1923/24? (pu) 1924 Chappell (Year Book Press).

Glory and honour and laud (SSAATTBB unaccompanied) (w) Theodulph of Orleans tr J M Neale (c) 1912? (pu) 1925 Chappell (Year Book Press).

Christ who knows all his sheep ('Cambridge' SATB and organ) (w) Richard Baxter (c) 1925 In 'Songs of Praise' (OUP) (MS) G.

'Tis the day of Resurrection (double choir unaccompanied) (w) St John Damascene tr J M Neale (c) 1912? (pu) 1927 Chappell (Year Book Press) (MS) G.

Jesu, the very thought is sweet (founded on 'Piae Cantones LXI', SATB unaccompanied) (w) St Bernard of Clairvaux tr J M Neale (pu) 1927 Faith Press (MS) G (sketch).

God omnipotent reigneth (founded on a psalm tune by Pierre D'Aques, SATB and organ) (w) Ps. 93 paraphrased by G R Woodward (pu) 1927 Chappell (Year Book Press) (MS) G (part MS).

Two introits — *O most merciful* (w) Bishop Heber and *Oculi omnium* (both SATB unaccompanied) (there is also an MS version of *Oculi omnium* for ATB (unaccompanied)) (pu) 1927 Chappell (Year Book Press) (MS) (ATB version) G (short score).

How dazzling fair (founded on a melody of Psalm 1 Genevan Psalter) (SATB and organ) (w) G R Woodward after J Scheffler (pu) 1929 Chappell (Year Book Press).

Father all holy (double choir unaccompanied) (w) Latin tr G R Woodward (c) 1912? (pu) 1929 Chappell (Year Book Press).

O thou sweetest source (founded on a melody by Bourgeois, SATB and organ) (w) German tr G R Woodward (pu) 1931 Chappell (Year Book Press).

2 short anthems (based on Genevan psalmtunes): *Out of the deep* and *Bow down thine ear* (SATB unaccompanied) (pu) 1931 Chappell (Year Book Press) (MS) G (sketch).

O King most high (double choir unaccompanied) (w) Cluniac Breviary tr H J Blew (c) 1912? (pu) 1932 Chappell (Year Book Press).

Once He came in blessing (double choir unaccompanied) (w) Johann Roh (16th cent) tr Catherine Winkworth (c) 1912? (pu) 1935 Chappell (Year Book Press).

View me Lord (founded on a 15th cent Bohemian melody, ATB and organ) (w) T Campion (pu) 1938 Chappell (Year Book Press) (MS) G (sketch).

Behold now praise the Lord (SATB unaccompanied) (MS) G.

4 antiphons: *I am risen, O Lord, thou has searched me out, This is the day that the Lord hath made, The earth trembled and was still*; (SATB and organ — accompaniment not written out in full) (MS) G.

O gladsome light (SATB unaccompanied) (w) St Athenogorus tr Yattendon Hymnal (MS) G (sketch).

O gladsome light (SATB unaccompanied) (w) H W Longfellow (MS) G (sketch).

Graces before and after meat (ATB unaccompanied) (MS) G (sketch).

Thy mercy, O Lord (SATB unaccompanied) (MS) G (sketch).

Motet on a Psalm tune (or *Soit loue*

L'Eternelle) (SATB unaccompanied) no words (MS) G (sketch).
You who the name of Jesus bear (SATB unaccompanied) (w) anon (MS) G (sketch).

Unfinished anthems
I will lay me down in peace (canon 4 in 1, SATB unaccompanied) (MS) G (sketch).
Short anthem having a canon at the 9th between S and T (SATB unaccompanied) no words (MS) G (sketch).
When shall I come to hear the angel song (SATB) (MS) G (sketch).

Lost anthems
Let us now praise famous men (commemoration anthem) (TTBB and organ).
O Saviour of the world (SATB and strings) (MS) G (string parts only).
Lord come away (SATB and organ) (w) Jeremy Taylor.

LARGE-SCALE LITURGICAL WORKS
The Passion of our Lord according to St Mark (treble, tenor, baritone and bass soli, SATB and organ) (c) 1920 (pu) 1921 Faith Press (MS) G.
Mass in F (SATB and organ) (c) 1922 (pu) 1971 St Martin's Publications (originally published as an Anglican Communion Service *Missa Portae Honoris* Faith Press 1927) (MS) G.

SERVICES
Magnificat and Nunc Dimittis in E flat major (SATB and organ) (c) 1890/1? (pu) 1891 Novello.
Magnificat and Nunc Dimittis in D major (SATB and organ) (c) 1897/98? (pu) 1898 Novello.
Magnificat and Nunc Dimittis in C minor (SATB and organ) (c) 1899/1900? (pu) 1900 Novello.
Magnificat and Nunc Dimittis in F major (SATB and organ) (c) 1907/8? (pu) 1908 Stainer & Bell (MS) G.
Magnificat (Tone VI) & Nunc (Tone V) (SATB and organ) (c) 1910/11? (pu) 1911 Chappell (Year Book Press) (MS) G.
Magnificat and Nunc Dimittis in G major (ATB unaccompanied) (c) 1910/11 (pu) 1911 Chappell (Year Book Press).

Magnificat and Nunc Dimittis in E major (ATB double choir, unaccompanied) (c) 1912/13? (pu) 1913 Chappell (Year Book Press).
Magnificat and Nunc Dimittis in A flat major (unison voices and organ) (c) 1914/15? (pu) 1915 Chappell (Year Book Press) (MS) G.
Magnificat and Nunc Dimittis (Collegium Regale) in F major (double choir and organ) (c) 1915 (pu) 1920 Chappell (Year Book Press) (MS) G.
Magnificat and Nunc Dimittis in E flat major (Sternhold and Hopkins metrical version of words) (SATB and organ) (c) 1918 (pu) 1920 Chappell (Year Book Press) (MS) G.
Magnificat and Nunc Dimittis (Tones IV & I) (SATB and organ) (c) 1922/23? (pu) 1923 Chappell (Year Book Press) (MS) G.
Te Deum (based on settings by J S Bach and J H Schein of the Genevan metrical form of the Ambrosian chant) and Benedictus (based on melody 'Quando Christus ascenderat' in Piae Cantiones). (SATB and organ) (c) 1922/23? (pu) 1923 Faith Press (MS) G (Te Deum sketches).
Short Communion Service in the Phrygian mode (SATB unaccompanied) (c) 1922/23? (pu) 1923 Faith Press (MS) G (sketches).
Magnificat (founded 'on an old Scotch chant') and Nunc Dimittis in G major (SATB and organ) (pu) 1926 Stainer & Bell.
The Nicene Creed (Phrygian mode) (SATB unaccompanied) (c) 1922/23 (pu) Faith Press (MS) G (sketches).
Magnificat and Nunc Dimittis founded on melodies 'Bene quondam dociles' and 'Quando Christus' (Piae Cantiones) (SATB and organ) (pu) 1927 Faith Press (MS) G.
Magnificat and Nunc Dimittis founded on melodies of Psalm CIV and CXXXLV (Genevan Psalter) (SATB and organ) (pu) 1927 Faith Press (MS) G.
Communion Service in C minor (SATB unaccompanied) (pu) 1927 OUP (MS) G.
Communion Service based on Plainsong and Medieval Music Society's edition of the ordinary of the Mass (SATB and organ) (c) 1922/23 (pu) 1927 OUP (MS) G (sketch).
Communion Service in F major (Ionian mode) (Missa Sancta Patricii) (SATB and organ) (c) 1922 (pu) 1927 Faith Press (MS) G.
Magnificat and Nunc Dimittis in C major (SATB and organ) (pu) 1927 Stainer & Bell.

205

Magnificat and Nunc Dimittis in E flat major (SATB and organ) (pu) 1927 Chappell (Year Book Press).

Nunc Dimittis in B flat major (SSATBB unaccompanied) (Latin and English) (c) 1916 (pu) 1927 Faith Press (MS) G.

Nunc Dimittis in A minor (SSATTB unaccompanied) (Latin and English) (c) 1916 (pu) 1929 Chappell (Year Book Press) (MS) G.

Magnificat and Nunc Dimittis in G major (double choir unaccompanied) (c) 1915 (pu) 1922 Chappell (Year Book Press) (MS) G (+ sketches).

O be joyful in the Lord (Jubilate) based on 'Old 100th' (SATB and organ) (pu) 1929 Chappell (Year Book Press).

Te Deum in C minor (SATB and organ) (pu) 1933 Chappell (Year Book Press).

Benedictus in A flat major (based on 'Old 100th'?) SATB and organ) (pu) 1933 Chappell (Year Book Press) (MS) G (sketch).

Magnificat and Nunc Dimittis in A flat major (SATB and organ) (pu) 1933 Chappell (Year Book Press).

Magnificat and Nunc Dimittis in E minor (SATB and organ (ad lib)) (pu) 1937 (MS) G (+ sketch).

Magnificat and Nunc Dimittis in D minor (unison and organ) (MS) G.

Magnificat and Nunc Dimittis in C major (SATB and organ) (MS) G.

Magnificat and Nunc Dimittis in F major (chant setting) (SATB and organ) (MS) G.

Magnificat and Nunc Dimittis in G minor founded on melodies for the canticles in the psalter of Sternhold and Hopkins (SATB unaccompanied) (MS) G.

Magnificat (Tone V) and Nunc Dimittis (Tone VI) (SATB and organ) (MS) G.

Benedictus in the 7th tone (SATB and organ) (MS) G.

Communion Service in C minor (SATB and organ (ad lib?)) (MS) G.

2 Kyries (SATB unaccompanied) (MS) G (sketch).

3 harmonisations of the plainsong Agnus Dei (unison and organ) (MS) G (sketch).

Agnus Dei in D minor (English words SATB unaccompanied) (MS) G (sketch).

Harmonisation of Lord's Prayer (plainsong — Dorian mode) (SATB unaccompanied) (MS) G (sketch).

Lord's Prayer in G major (SATB unaccompanied) (MS) G (sketch).

Benedictus (Communion Service) in E flat major (SATB and organ) (MS) G (sketch).

Responses to the commandments in D minor (SATB unaccompanied) (MS) G (sketch).

Responses to the commandments in F major and D minor (SATB unaccompanied) (MS) G (sketch).

General confession in E flat major (SATB unaccompanied) (MS) G (sketch).

Te Deum and Jubilate in G major (ATB unaccompanied) (MS) G (sketch).

Magnificat based on 'Cevit lygurs' in C major (SATB unaccompanied) (MS) G (sketch).

Benedictus in D major (SATB unaccompanied) (MS) G (sketch).

Benedictus in C major (SATB unaccompanied) (MS) G (sketch).

Magnificat and Nunc Dimittis in G minor (SATB unaccompanied) (MS) G (sketch).

Nunc Dimittis in F major (SATB unaccompanied) (MS) G (sketch).

Jubilate in A flat major (unison voices and organ) (MS) G (sketch).

Unfinished settings

Magnificat in the 8th Tone (SATB and organ) (MS) G.

Magnificat and Nunc Dimittis in A flat (SATB and organ) (MS) G.

Magnificat and Nunc Dimittis founded on metrical psalm tunes (MS) G (sketch).

Benedictus in G major (ATB unaccompanied) (MS) G (sketch).

Te Deum in E flat major (SATB and organ) (MS) G (sketch).

Te Deum in G minor (SATB and organ) (MS) G (sketch).

Te Deum in Dorian mode (SATB and organ) (MS) G (sketch).

Te Deum in G minor (SATB and organ) (MS) G (sketch).

Magnificat and Nunc Dimittis in E major (SATB and organ) (MS) G (sketch).

Nunc Dimittis in E major (SATB and organ) (MS) G (sketch).

Magnificat in E flat major (SATB and organ?) (MS) G (sketch).

Benedictus in A flat major (unison and organ) (MS) G (sketch).

Magnificat and Nunc Dimittis in F major (SATB and organ?) (MS) G (sketch).

Lost services etc.
Litany (SATB).
Morning services for ATB.
Magnificat and Nunc Dimittis in D major.
Magnificat and Nunc Dimittis in C major.

CAROLS AND OTHER SEASONAL MUSIC

The following arrangements contributed to 'Carols for Christmastide' (Series 1) compiled and arranged by the Revd G R Woodward MA (pu) 1892 Pickering & Chatto:
Sweet was the sounge the Virgin sange (words and melody from 'William Ballet's Lute Book' c 1600) arr SATB (c) 1891/92? (MS) G.
Ibid (Series 2): (pu) 1893 Pickering & Chatto:
Blessed be that Mayde Mary (words from B M Sloane MS 2593 early 15th cent arr (c) 1892/93? melody: from 'William Ballet's Lute Book' arr SATB).
In 'Carols for Easter and Ascension-tide' (pu) 1894 Pickering & Chatto:
Hail, Easter bright, in glory dight (words tr G R Woodward from the Latin, melody 'In peascod time') arr SATB (c) 1893/94.
Jesus Christ is risen (*Christus ist erstanden*) (words Trier Gesangbuch tr G R Woodward, melody: 'Trier Gesangbuch' arr SATB) (c) 1893/94?

In 'The Cowley Carol Book' (first series) compiled and arranged by G R Woodward (pu) 1901. Revised and enlarged edn 1902 Mowbray.
Blessed be that Maid Marie (as in 'Carols for Christmastide' series 2 above).
Sweet was the song the the Virgin sung (slightly revised version of setting, as in 'Carols for Christmastide', series 1 above).
A day, a day of glory (words J M Neale, melody 'an old French air' arr SATB) (c) 1895/1901?
Jesus Christ is risen (as in 'Carols for Easter and Ascension-tide' above).
Hail Easter bright (as in 'Carols for Easter and Ascension-tide' above).
This joyful Eastertide (words G R Woodward, melody 'Hoe groot der vrugten zijn') arr SATB (c) 1895/1901?

In 'Songs of Syon' ed G R Woodward (3rd edition 1910):

Quem vidistis, Pastores (words 'Shepherds in the fields abiding,' ancient antiphon paraphrased G R Woodward, melody French arr SATB) (c) 1902-10?
Von himmel kompt, O Engel, kompt (words 'Descend from heav'n Ye Angels, come' (Mainz (1628)) tr G R Woodward, melody ibid arr SATB) (c) 1902-10?
Dum Virgo vagieatum (words 'I heard an infant weeping' (Daniel's 'Thesaurus Hymnologius') tr G R Woodward, melody 'Ein Kindlien in der weigen' from Corner's Nachtigall (1649) arr SATB) (c) 1902-10?
O Jesulien zart (words 'Wo, Jesu, is me' from Corner's Gesangbuch (1631) tr G R Woodward, melody Mainz (1661) arr SATB) (c) 1902-10?
Heer Jesus heeft een hofken (words 'King Jesus hath a garden' in Geestlijke Harmonie (Emmerich 1633) tr G R Woodward, melody Bruges (1609) arr SATB) (c) 1902-10?

Make we merry (words anon 15th cent, melody 'based on an Irish folk-song' arr unis voices and piano) (c) 1917/18? (pu) 1918 Novello (Arnold).
Mater ora filium (words anon 15th cent, melody 'based on an Irish folk-song' arr unison voices and piano) (c) 1917/18? (pu) 1918 Novello (Arnold).

In 'The Cowley Carol Book' (second series) compiled and arranged by G R Woodward and Charles Wood (pu) 1919 Mowbray:
A virgin most pure (words trad, melody from 'Some ancient Christmas Carols' by David Gilbert (1822-23) arr SATB) (c) 1902/19?
King Jesus hath a garden as in 'Songs of Syon' above.
Shepherds in the field abiding as in 'Songs of Syon' above.
Descend from heav'n ye angels, come as in 'Songs of Syon' above.
A star doth bedizen (words G R Woodward, melody 'Come o'er the bourne, Bessie' arr SATB) (c) 1902/1919?
Wo, Jesu, is me as in 'Songs of Syon' above.
Of these four letters sing would I (words G R Woodward, melody 'Johnny Faa' or 'Gypsy Laddie' arr SATB) (c) 1902/1919?
Through Gabriel his message mild (words G R Woodward, melody 'Grailtoune' or 'Sir John Malcolm' arr SATB) (c) 1902/1919?

Today Maiden Mary foretold by the seer (words from the Greek Horologion tr G R Woodward, melody Irish mixolydian air arr SATB) (c) 1902/1919?

In Bethlehem city, on Christmas-day morn (words based on excerpts from the Greek Menaeon by G R Woodward, melody Old English or Irish melody arr SATB) (c) 1902/19?

Welcome, Christmas, welcome here (words Miss Mary Ann Stodart (c 1840), melody 'Disciplinae filius' from Piae Cantiones arr SATB) (c) 1902/19?

Iure plaudant omnia (words text and melody from 'Paderborn Gesangbuch' (1608) arr SATB) (c) 1902/19?

Bethlehem — Judah 'twas there on a morn (words G R Woodward, melody 'Glenogie' (Scottish melody) arr SATB) (c) 1902/19?

Ever-Virgin undefiled (words from 'O Maria Jungfrau rien' versified G R Woodward, melody 'Jesu, zu rufen wir' (1712 or earlier) arr SATB) (c) 1902/19.

Joy! Joy! from every steeple (words G R Woodward, melody Andro and his cutty gun arr SATB) (c) 1902/19?

There Joseph on his Sleeping lay (words from 'Cursor mundi' (14th cent), melody 'Gude Wallace' arr SATB) (c) 1902/19?

I heard an Infant weeping as in 'Songs of Syon' above.

One yule-night, as abed I lay (words G R Woodward, melody 'Der wechter der bliesz an den tag' (Nürnberg 1542) arr SATB) (c) 1902/19?

Magdalen, cease from sobs and sighs (words 'Pone luctum, Magdalena' tr G R Woodward, melody 'Nicht ruhen Magdalena kundt' (Cöln, 1623) arr SATB) (c) 1902/19?

Sun, if thou think thy sphere (words G R Woodward, melody 'Tu crois, O beau soleil' (Chanson du Roi Louis 13th) arr SATB) (c) 1902/19?

On Easter-morn ere break of day (words from a Greek liturgy for Lauds on Easter day, tr G R Woodward, melody 'On a bank of flowers ae simmer day' arr SATB) (c) 1902/19?

Farewell, night with mist o'er shrouded (words G R Woodward after 'Ite noctes, ite nubis', melody Highland air arr SATB) (c) 1902/19?

The teams are waiting in the field (words J M Neale, melody 'Chevy Chase' arr SATB) (c) 1902/19?

In 'An Italian Carol Book' ed Charles Wood and George Ratcliffe Woodward (pu) 1920 Faith Press:

Once, as I remember (words G R Woodward, melody 'Antururu' (Corona di Sacre Canzoni 1689) arr SATB) (c) 1917/20?

Lassie and lad, array you (words G R Woodward, melody 'Bellissima Regina' (Ibid) arr SATB) (c) 1917/20?

While certain herdsmen (words G R Woodward, melody 'Bergamasca', or 'Lerulleru' (ibid arr SATB) (c) 1917/20?

Jesu, born to save the lost (words 'Mundi salus qui masceris' (Paris Breviary) tr G R Woodward, melody 'Caro liet' amato di' (Waldensian) arr SATB) (c) 1917/20?

Christen people, Christmas morn (words G R Woodward, melody 'Caro Leit' amato Di' (Waldesian) arr SATB) (c) 1917/20?

Gaudete, quia vobis (words G R Woodward, melody 'Ecco la Bella Lisa' or 'Chicchirichi' (Corona di Sacre Canzoni 1689) arr SATB) (c) 1917/20?

Ah! Gabriel, Ah! Gabriel (words G R Woodward, melody 'Girolamo Girolamo' (ibid) arr SATB) (c) 1917/20?

Make thee ready, as best thou art able (words Byzantine Greek tr G R Woodward, melody 'La speranza mi va consolando' (ibid) arr SATB) (c) 1917/20?

Ho! Merry headman (words G R Woodward, melody 'Lieti pastori, venite alla capanna' (ibid) arr SATB) (c) 1917/20?

When sin had set our world at six and seven (words G R Woodward, melody 'Lo rosignolo canta alla gaiola' (ibid) arr SATB) (c) 1917/20?

From fields beyond Euphrates (words G R Woodward, melody 'Madre non mi far monaca' (ibid) arr SATB) (c) 1917/20?

With sanctified festivity (words G R Woodward, melody 'Mira cuor mio durissimo' (ibid) arr SATB) (c) 1917/20?

Fa la Ninna, Fa la Nanna (words G R Woodward, melody 'Quant' è dolce il vagheggiare' (ibid) arr SATB) (c) 1917/20?

Lording and lady (words G R Woodward, melody 'Questo è quel loco, dov' ho il mio cuor perduto' (ibid) arr SATB) (c) 1917/20?

It was a young mother (words G R Woodward, melody 'Saione' (ibid) arr SATB) (c) 1917/20?

T'other day in mid-winter (words G R Woodward, melody 'Scappino' (ibid) arr SATB) (c) 1917/20?

Let us remember (words G R Woodward, melody 'Volgi iole i tuoi bei lumi' (ibid) arr SATB) (c) 1917/20?

Why, why be heavy hearted? (words 'Cedant, justi signa luctus (Adam of St Victor) tr G R Woodward, melody 'Felicissimo giorno' or 'Sison' (ibid) arr SATB) (c) 1917/20?

From Heav'n above thou camest hither-ward (words G R Woodward, melody 'O Clorida' (ibid) arr SATB) (c) 1917/20?

Joy for mid-winter day (words G R Woodward, melody 'Ogni cuor guibbili' (ibid) arr SATB) (c) 1917/20?

The ruddy dawn is breaking (words 'Aurora lucis rutilat' tr W J Blew, melody 'Questo nobil Bambino' set (STB) Alessandro Gardano, alto added C Wood) (c) 1917/20?

Of His own will on Good Friday (words G R Woodward, melody 'Ruggieri o Aria dell' ortolano' (Corona di sacre canzoni 1689) arr SATB) (c) 1917/20?

Tell it out among the heathen (words G R Woodward, melody 'Siamo quattro fantolini' (ibid) arr SATB) (c) 1917/20?

For the name of my Lady (words G R Woodward, melody 'Ghirumetta' (ibid) arr SATB) (c) 1917/20?

O virgo virginum (words Greater antiphon (O virgo virginum) tr G R Woodward, melody 'Gran borè' (ibid) arr SATB) (c) 1917/20?

Hail! Blessed Virgin Mary (words G R Woodward, melody 'Moda' (ibid) arr SATB) (c) 1917/20?

Presentation of our Lady (words G R Woodward, melody 'Veddi una pastorella' (ibid) arr SATB) (+ version with melody in tenor) (c) 1917/20?

Light ever gladsome (words St Athenogorus tr G R Woodward, melody 'Andiam, compagni, alla riviera' (old French (16th cent) Firenze (1685) arr SATB) (This setting had first appeared in Songs of Syon' no 186) (c) 1902/10?

Once, and at evenfall (words G R Woodward, melody 'Corrono' fuggono volano i di' (Corona di Sacre Canzoni 1689) arr SATB) (c) 1917/20?

Pontius Pilate, ere the dawn of day (words G R Woodward, melody 'Leggiadra donna, il vostro volto fu' (ibid) arr SATB) (c) 1917/20?

Thorns of iniquity (words tr G R Woodward, melody 'Mostri Terribili' (ibid) arr SATB) (+ setting with melody in bass) (c) 1917/20?

Why weep ye, broken hearted (words from the Greek Euchologion tr G R Woodward, melody 'Ninfa cinta le chiome' (ibid) arr SATB) (c) 1917/20?

If on this planet, oft a scene of gladness (words G R Woodward, melody 'Se questa valle' (ibid) arr SATB) (c) 1917/20?

Mine be Sion's habitation (words Hildebert, Bishop of Mons, afterwards Archbishop of Tours tr J M Neale, melody 'Verginella' (ibid) arr SATB) (c) 1917/20?

Christmas Bells (words H W Longfellow, melody based 'on an Irish Folk-song (Petrie 81)' arr unison voices and piano) (c) 1920/21? (pu) 1921 Novello (Arnold) (MS) G (sketch).

The Yule Log (words tr from the French by H W Longfellow, arr unison voices and piano) (c) 1923/24? (pu) 1924 Chappell (Year Book Press) (MS) G (sketch).

In 'The Cambridge Carol Book' ed Charles Wood and George Ratcliffe Woodward (pu) 1924 SPCK:

Although at Yule it bloweth cool (words G R Woodward, melody 'Der wind der wet, der han der kret (1554)' arr 2 voices) (c) 1919/24?

As I went to Bethlehem (words 'Quem vidistis pastores' freely tr G R Woodward, melody 'As I went to Walsingham' arr SATB) (c) 1919/24?

Beholde a sely tender babe or *New Prince, new pompe* (words Robert Southwell, melody 'We are poor frozen-out gardeners' arr SATB) (c) 1919/24?

Ding dong! Merrily on high (words G R Woodward, melody 'Branle de l'Official' Arbeau's 'Orchésographie' arr SATB) (c) 1919/24?

Get ivy and hull, woman, deck up (words Thomas Tusser (c 1523-1580), melody 'Bannocks — o' barley meal' arr SATB) (c) 1919/24?

Hail! Holy child, lain in an oxen manger (words G R Woodward, melody 'Quittez, pasteurs, vos brebis et houlette' (old Flemish) arr SATB) (c) 1919/24?

Heap on more wood! The wind is chill (words Sir Walter Scott, melody 'Corn rigs' arr SATB) (c) 1919/24?

Ho! Steward, bid my servants (words J M Neale, melody 'John Anderson, my jo' arr SATB) (c) 1919/24?

Hob and Colin, Yule is come (words founded on 'Guillo, pran ton tamborin (1720)', melody Proper tune arr SATB) (c) 1919/24?

In Bethlehem hear I today (words St John Damascene tr G R Woodward, melody tune from H v Loufenberg's 'Geistliche Lieder' 'Ich wollt dasz ich daheime wär' (c 1420) arr SATB (2 versions)) (c) 1919/24?

Let such (so fantastical) liking not this (words Thomas Tusser — melody Old English arr SATB) (c) 1919/24?

O the morn, the merry merry morn (words G R Woodward, melody 'O the broom, the bonny, bonny broom' (16th or 17th c) arr SATB) (c) 1919/24?

Our Lady sat within her bower (words G R Woodward, melody Phrygian mode tune from 'Hayn v Themar's Lieder, 1590' arr SATB) (c) 1919/24?

Past three o'clock (w) (G R Woodward trad refrain, melody 'London Waits' arr SATB) (c) 1919/24?

The mirrour of the Father's face (words G R Woodward, melody 'En Trinitatis speculum' arr SATB) (c) 1919/24?

To redeem a race forlorn (words G R Woodward, melody 'Anni novi novias' (from a Mosburg Gradual 1360) arr SATB) (c) 1919/24?

To us this morn a child is born (words G R Woodward, melody 'Jog on, jog on the footpath way' (Elizabethan melody) arr SATB) (c) 1919/24?

'Twas in a cave on Christmas morn (words G R Woodward, melody 'Dich grüssen wir, O Jesulein' (Constance 1623) arr SATB) (c) 1919 24?

Jesus is the sweetest name (words G R Woodward, melody 'Jesus ist ein süsser nam' (Munich 1586) arr SATB) (c) 1919/24?

There stood in Heaven a Linden Tree (words from v Loufenberg's 'Geistliche Lieder' c 1420 tr G R Woodward, melody ibid arr two voices) (c) 1919/24?

Weep not o'er me, o mother mine (words Byzantine tr G R Woodward, melody 'A the syghes that come fro my herte' (MS Reg App 58) arr SATB) (c) 1919/24?

Jewry, why with Bulrush mock him? (words G R. Woodward, melody 'Put the gown upon the Bishop' (old Scottish) arr SATB) (c) 1919/24?

O for a lay! For on this day (words G R Woodward, melody 'Mit Freuden zart zu dieser Fahrt' (Bohemian Brethren 1566) arr SATB) (c) 1919/24?

Moses, sing unto Christ thy King (words G R Woodward, melody 'Old King Cole' arr SATB) (c) 1919/24?

Thus on Easter-morrow (words G R Woodward, melody 'Branle des sabots (Orchésographie 1588' arr SATB) (c) 1919/24?

Nightingale, thy Lordly Lays (words tr G R Woodward from D G Corner 1625, melody ibid arr SATB) (c) 1919/24?

When the earth, with spring returning (words St Fulbert tr J M Neale, melody 'Mos florentis venustatis) (Mosburg Gradual 1360) arr SATB) (c) 1919/24?

I was, and am, and ay shall be sad-hearted (words G R Woodward, melody 'Ic seg adieu' (Dutch 1602) arr SATB) (c) 1919/24?

A song for the times (words J M Neale, melody 'Prince Rupert's March' (early 17th cent) arr SATB) (c) 1919/24?

The Virgin's Cradle Hymn (words tr S T Coleridge, melody Corner (1625) arr unison voices and piano (c) 1924/25 (pu) 1925 Chappell (Year Book Press).

An Easter Carol (words J M Neale set for SATB (unaccompanied)) (c) 1917 (pu) 1925 Chappell (Year Book Press) (MS) G.

The burning babe (words Robert Southwell set SATB (c) 1920 (pu) 1926 Chappell (Year Book Press) (MS) G.

Deck the Hall (words Talhaiarn tr T Oliphant, melody Welsh air arr SATB) (pu) 1927 Chappell (Year Book Press).

Ibid arr TTBB (MS) G (sketch).

In 'Hosanna', a book of praise for young children, ed T Grigg-Smith, Charles Wood and Hubert Middleton (pu) 1930 SPCK:

Away in a manger (words tr from Martin Luther, melody J D Meyer, Seelenfreud 1692 (tune 'Manger Throne') arr SATB).

210

How blessed are the Angels (words J Russell Derbyshire, melody Charles Wood, harmonised (SATB) by Hubert Middleton) (tune Michaelmas).

Kings on camels rode and rode (words Susan Moon Hayman (tune Camel Kings) set SATB).

All my heart this night rejoices (words Paul Gerhardt tr Catherine Winkworth, melody proper tune set SATB) (MS) G (sketch).

Adeste Fideles (melody J F Wade harmonised SATB) (MS) G.

Angelus ad virginem (words Latin (1250-1260)), melody VIIth mode arr unison voices and organ (?) (MS) G.

2 French Paroissiens harmonised SATB (one untitled (E minor), the other Rouen Church melody (Vide St Venantius E H 38)) (MS) G.

Gaudate, gaudate, Christus est natus (words and melody 'Piae cantiones no XIV' arr SATB) (MS) G.

While shepherds watched their flocks (words Nahum Tate, set for SATB) (MS) G.

Here comes Holly that is so gent (words 15th cent, set for SATB) (MS) G.

Christmas day (words Christina Rossetti, set for SATB) (MS) G.

A Christmas Carol (words James Russell Lowell, set for SATB) (MS) G.

Hark how all the welkin rings (words Charles Wesley, set for SATB) (MS) G.

New prince, new pompe (words Robert Southwell, set for SATB) (MS) G.

See the dawn (words Thomas Moore, set for SATB) (MS) G.

There is a flower (words ?, melody, Petrie 1565 arr SATB) (MS) G.

In numbers, and but few (words R Herrick, set SATB) (MS) G.

O lovely voices of the sky that hymn the Saviour's birth (words Mrs Hemans, set SATB) (MS) G.

Another setting of the same (MS) G.

Of lily white and rose of price (words ?, set for SATB) (MS) G.

Two carol (?) tunes without words: F major (10.10.10) and F major (4.4.8.4.4.4. 4.4.8.4.4.4. 4.8) (MS) G.

4 transcriptions of 15th century carols (MS) G.

Original canonic carol ? tune (SATB) (w) none given but name of Coleridge is attached (MS) G (sketch).

Unfinished carols

There is a flower (words ?, set in two parts (MS) G.

Earthly friends will change and falter (words J M Neale, melody Piae Cantiones 'Omnis mundus incuaditur', set SATB) (MS) G.

Original carol ? tune for SATB (w) from *Wind in the Willows* (animals all?) (MS) G (sketch).

Original carol ? tune in D major (w) none but there is an Alleluia refrain (MS) G (sketch).

Lost settings

Italian carol *Lewhèt amato dé.*

This joyful Eastertide set as a tenor solo in A major. 9-bar fragment exists (MS) G (sketch).

HYMN-TUNES

PUBLISHED (ORIGINAL)

Rangoon (irregular) in 'Hymns A & M' (1904) (c) 1903/4?

Gonville (10.11.11.11.12.12.10.11.) ibid (c) 1903/4? (MS) G.

Cranmer (6.6.8.D) ibid (c) 1903/4?

Finita iam sunt praelia (irregular) in 'Songs of Syon' 3rd edition (1910) (c) 1909/10? (MS) G (Trochaic, 8.8.6.6.3) ibid (c) 1909/10?

Armagh (6.6.6.6.D) in 'Irish Church Hymnal' (1918) (c) 1916?

Emain Macha (8.6.8.6.8.8.) ibid (c) 1916?

Recessional (8.8.8.8.8.8.) in 'Public School Hymnal' (c) 1918/19? (MS) G.

Cambridge in 'Songs of Praise' (1925), see under anthems above.

Alderley (8.8.7.) in 'Hosanna' (SPCK — 1930) (c) 1926?

Autumn (5.5.5.5.1.1.1.0) ibid (c) 1926?

Hans (LM) ibid (c) 1926?

Michaelmas (7.6.7.6.D) ibid (c) 1926? see under carols above.

Camel Kings (7.7.7.7.) ibid (c) 1926? ditto.

Agnus (6.6.7.7.7.7.7.7.6.6) ibid (c) 1926?

Harvest fields (5.6.6.5.9) ibid (c) 1926?

Morning (CM) ibid (c) 1926?

Confession (irregular) ibid (c) 1926?

PUBLISHED ARRANGEMENTS AND HARMONISATIONS OF HYMN-TUNES

In 'Yattendon Hymnal' (1899):
Old 100th (L Bourgeois) (LM) set with melody in tenor (c) 1898/99?
Nun Danket (J Crüger) (6.7.6.7.6.6.6.6) (c) 1898/99?

In 'Hymns Ancient and Modern' (1904 edition):
Hemsley (8.7.8.7.1.2.7) (18th century melody) (c) 1903/4? (MS) G.

In 'Songs of Syon' (3rd edition, 1910):
Gott wills machen dasz die sachen (trochaic — 4.4.7.4.4.7) (melody from Johann Ludwig Steiner) (1688-1761).
Psallat scholarum concio (iambic trochaic 8.6.8.6.7.7.8) (melody from Piae Cantiones) arr (v4) with melody in tenor.
Iam desinant suspiria (Old 25th Psalm) (iambic 6.6.8.6.D) (melody from Estes' Psalter
Gestiegen ist vom Himmels-thron (irregular) (melody from Trier Gesangbuch).
Maria ist Geboren (iambic 7.6.7.6) (melody Cöln (Brachel 1623)).
Auch Döhterlin min sel gemeit (iambic 8.7.8.7) (melody in or by Heinrich v Loufenberg (c 1415-1443)).
This tune and setting was also used for *That night in May*, words G Drosini tr G R Woodward (pu) 1919 Faith Press.
Seigneur, je n'ay point (p 131) (iambic 8.8.8.8) (melody in third mode Geneva, Crispin (1551)).
Da Jesus an dem kreutze stund (8.8.7.8.7) (melody from J Leisentrit (1567)).
Ad perennis vitae fontem (trochaic 8.7.8.7.8.7) (French melody?).
Erstanden ist der Heilig Christ (iambic 8.8.8.4.8) (melody Köln (1599)).
Agincourt (iambic 8.8.8.8.5) (melody c 1415).
Old 77th Psalm (iambic 8.6.8.6.D) (melody Thomas Este's Psalter (1592), (MS) G.
Donne secours, Seigneur, il en est heure (Psalm 12) (iambic 11.10.11.10) (melody by Louis Bourgeois (1551)).
Andiam, compagni, alla riviera (Dactylic 10.5.4.10.5.3), see Italian Carol Book above.
Thys endere nyght I saw a syght (iambic 4.4.6.4.4.6) (melody from BM, MS Royal, appendix 58 (early 16th century)).

Meine armuth macht mich schreyen (8.11.8.11) (melody by J A Freylinghausen (1706)). (Harmonization not attributed to Wood in 'Songs of Syon').
Keiner schöner schönheit hat die Welt (trochaic 7.7.7.7) (melody in Joseph's Seelenlust (1657)).
Hertzlich thut mich erfreuen (iambic 7.6.7.6.7.6.7.6) (melody — 16th century secular air).
In Pescod time (iambic 8.6.8.6) (melody — old English folk-song (16th century)).
Lobet den Herren aller Herren (dactylic-iambic 9.8.9.8.8.8.8.) (melody Salenharpf, Onolzbach (1664)).
See Songs of Syon, No 313 (trochaic-iambic 7.7.3.3.7.3.3.4) (melody — ancient Japanese).
Earth, with her ten thousand flowers (trochaic, 7.7.7.7.7.7) (melody — Cambrian tune).
Heirusalem, du hochgebaute Stadt (4.6.6.4.6.6.7.6.7.6) (melody by Melchior Franck? Erfurt, GB (1663)).
Was Gott thut das ist wolgethan (iambic 8.7.8.7.4.4.7.7) (melody and bass from 'Gesangbuch Nürnberg' (1690)).
Or sus, serviteurs du Seigneur (Psalm 134) (The Old 100th) (iambic 8.8.8.8.) see Yattendon Hymnal above.
Ach! dass nicht die letzte stunde (8.7.8.7.8.7) (melody and bass from Schemelli's GB (1736)) mean parts by CW with J A Langdon.
Herr, nun lass in Friede (trochiac 6.6.6.6.6.6) (melody by J S Bach) Bach's setting simplified by CW.
Glück zu kreuz von ganzen herzen (trochaic 8.7.8.7) (Proper melody).
Ich glaub' an Gott (iambic-dactylic 4.4.7.4.4.7.5.5.8) (melody from 'Eichsfelder Gesangbuch' (1724)).
Ach alles, was Himmel (Amphibrachic 12.12.12.12) melody from Darmstadt (1698).
Old 44th Psalm (8.6.8.6.D) (melody for the same).
Sie ist mir lieb, die werde Magd (iambic 8.7.8.7.4.4.4.7.8.7.6) (melody from Babst (1545)) setting Praetorius (1610) and CW.
Quem vidistis, pastores, see carols above.
Von himmel kompt, O Engel, Kompt (irregular 8.1.3.8.8.8), see carols above.
Ein Kindlien in der Weigen (iambic 7.6.7.6.6) see carols above.

O Jesulien zart (Amphibrachic — iambic 5.5.5.5.4.5.4.5), see carols above.
Heer Jesus Heeft een hofken (irregular), see carols above.

In 'Irish Church Hymnal', see above:
Munster (LM) (trad Irish melody) (c) 1916.

In 'Hosanna', see above:
House meadow (SM) (melody?) (c) 1925/26?
Manger Throne (11.11.11.11) (melody by J D Meyer in Seelenfreud (1692)) (c) 1925/26?
Cotgrave (CM) (trad English melody) (c) 1925/26?
Resurrexit Dominus (4.4. Ter.) (melody from Bohemian Brothers) (c) 1925/26?
Störl (CM) (melody from Störl 1710) (c) 1925/26?
Morning Hope (7777) melody: Bohemian Brothers Horn 1544 (c) 1925/26?
Heer Jesus heeft een hofken (irregular), see 'Songs of Syon' above.
Sichart (CM) (melody from MS Sichart (1755)) (c) 1925/26?
London Wait (4.6.4.6.5.5.5.5), see 'Cowley Carol Book' above.
Oblation (8.8.9.9) (melody from Strattner 1691) (c) 1925/26?
Scarborough (8787) — melody (abridged) by Revd W E Miller (c) 1925/26?

UNPUBLISHED HYMN-TUNES
In a projected hymn book for Caius College, Cambridge:
Tune for *A charge to keep I have* (Charles Wesley, 6.6.8.6.D major) (MS) G.
Tune for *For all thy saints O Lord* (Richard Mant, 6.6.8.6 A flat major) (MS) G.
Tune for *For the beauty of the earth* (F S Pearpoint, 7.7.7.7.7.7 D major) (MS) G.
Tune for *From all that dwell below the skies* (Isaac Watts, 8.8.8.8.LM F major) (MS) G.
Tune for *Happy are they* (C Coffin tr Yattendon Hymnal, 8.6.8.6 (CM) G major) (MS) G.
Tune for *Lead me, almighty father* (William Stubbs, 10.10.10.10.10.10. F major) (MS) G.
Tune for *Lord of mercy and of might* (R Heber, 7.7.7.6 A flat major) (MS) G.
Tune for *O Brightness of the Eternal Father's face* (tr John Keble, 10.6.10.6. D major) (MS) G.

Tune for *Once to every man and nation* (J Russell Lowell, 8.7.8.7.7.7.8.3 E flat major) (MS) G.
Tune for *Out of my soul's depth* (De Profundis tr T Campion 1.2.1.2.1.1. E minor) (MS) G.
Tune for *Strong son of God* (A Tennyson 8.8.8.8 (LM) E flat major) (MS) G.
Tune for *Sing a song of Joy* (T Campion 5.5.6.8.D, A major) (MS) G.
Tune for *Sunset and Evening Star* (A Tennyson irregular E flat major) (MS) G.
Tune for *The Saint who first found grace to pen* (L Housman LM B flat major) (MS) G.
Tune for *Ye servants of God* (Charles Wesley 5.5.5.5.6.5.6.5 G major) (MS) G.

OTHER ORIGINAL HYMN-TUNES
For all the saints (Walsham How, 10.10.10.4. F major) (MS) G.
2nd tune for *Sing a song of Joy* (T Campion, 5.5.6.8.D. E flat major) (MS) G.
2nd tune for *Out of my soul's depth* (De profundis tr T Campion, 12.12.12. G minor) (MS) G.
Tune for *Tune thy music to thy heart* (T Campion 7.10.7.10. E flat major) (MS) G.
Tune for *I praised the earth in beauty seen* (R Heber) or *The Lord my pasture shall prepare* (Addison, 8.8.8.8. D major) (MS) G.
Tune for *The Son of God goes forth to war* (R Heber 8.6.8.6 E minor) (MS) G.
Tune for *Lo, when back mine eye pilgrim like I cast* (T Campion 10.6.8 A major) (MS) G.
Tune for *The man of life upright* or *View me, Lord, a work of thine* (T Campion 7.7.7.7 E flat major) (MS) G.
Tune for *Come let us sing with melody the praises* (T Campion 11.11.11.5 G major) (MS) G.
Tune for *Seek the Lord and in his ways persevere* (T Campion 10.8.6.11 A major) (MS) G.
Tune for *Come to the Lord of peace* (Mrs Hemans 6.10.10.6 E flat major) (MS) G.
Tune for *Walk in the light so shalt thou know* (Bernard Barton 8.6.8.6 G major) (MS) G.
Tune for *Glory and honour and Laud* (Theodulph of Orleans tr J M Neale, 'Songs of Syon' no 69) (15.13.17.14. D minor) (MS) G.

Tune for *De Profundis* (tr T Campion 12.12. 11. F major) (MS) G.

Tune for *Never weather beaten sail(?)* (T Campion, 13.14.15.14. D major) (MS) G.

Tune for *Author of light, revive my dying spirit* (T Campion 10.12.8.14.10.16 F major) (MS) G.

Tune for *Ere God had built the mountains* (W Cowper 7.6.7.6.7.6.7.6) (MS) G.

Tune for *He who would valiant be* (J Bunyan 6.6.11.6.6.6.6 G major) (MS) G.

There are also 25 tunes not associated with particular words (some are palindromic in structure). There are also 9 unfinished hymn-tunes, 22 canonic hymn-tunes, and 6 unfinished canonic hymn-tunes. There are also 8 original double chants (some of which are palindromic). All the above MS are in G.

UNPUBLISHED ARRANGEMENTS AND HARMONISATIONS OF TUNES SET TO KNOWN WORDS

In 'Caius Hymnal' as above:

Herr, deisen zorn (5.6.5.6.5.6.5) melody J Crüger (Zahn 996) set to 'Come, let us sound with melody the praises' (author unknown) (MS) G.

Ps. LXXII (Christ Hospital tune (CM) Ravenscroft (Frost 233)) set to 'Eternal God we look to thee' (James Merrick) (MS) G.

Nun komm der Heiden Heiland (7.7.7.6) (88 in Layring 'Kirschengesangen' Zahn 1174) set to 'In the hour of my distress' (R Herrick) (MS) G.

Tune by Thos. Sella (1685) (In Zahn 6243) (6.5.6.5.6.5.6.5) set to 'In the hour of trial' (James Montgomery) (MS) G.

Melody by Richard Jensen (1838) (8.8.8.8.8.8) in Zahn 2626 set to 'O King of kings, before whose throne' (John Quarles & Thomas Darling) (MS) G.

Sternhold. 'The Lamentation of a Sinner' (14.14.14.16) (Frost 61) set to 'O Lord, turn not thy face away from them that lowly lie' (?) Pryce's Psalter 1621 (MS) G.

Tune from Zahn 5860 a (8.8.8.8.8.8.8.8) set to 'O Saviour is thy promise fled' (R Heber) (MS) G.

Melody from Gregor (1784) given in Zahn 6248 (6.5.6.5.D) set to 'Summer suns are glowing' (Walsham How) (MS) G.

Melody from Zahn 2614 (8.8.8.8.8.8) set to 'The Lord my Pasture shall prepare' (Addison) (MS) G.

Melody from Görlitz (1599) (8.6.8.6) given in Zahn 205 set to 'The Heaven of Heaven' (Drehnan) (MS) G.

Melody given in Zahn 1229 (7.7.7.7) set to 'View me, Lord, a work of thine' (T Campion) see also 'Hosanna' above (MS) G.

Other Zahn arrangements to which no words are attached: 413, 824, 936, 950, and 1310 (MS) G.

OTHER MISCELLANEOUS ARRANGEMENTS

Lower parts for *Dir, dir, Jehovah, will ich singen* Schemelli's Gesangbuch 1736 (MS) G.

Unknown Phrygian melody set with CF in tenor (MS) G.

Unknown melody set with CF in tenor, G minor (MS) G.

Melody 'Jesu Kreuz, Lieden in Pen' (Melchior Vulpius 1609) (7.6.7.6.7.6.7.6) (MS) G.

45 psalm-tunes harmonised for 4 voices (MS) G.

2 plainsong harmonisations (MS) G.

Special 'Songs of Syon' arrangements:

193a version for unison male voices, with free organ part for v 2 (MS) G.

201 'Motet' version of v 2 for SATB, also a version (unfinished) for double choir of v 8 or an alternative SATB 'motet' version of v 7.

203 alternative harmonisation (SATB) of tune, also unfinished 'motet' version with free organ part of v 2 (MS) G.

339 arr TTBB (unaccompanied) (MS) G.

345 arr TTBB (unaccompanied) (MS) G.

400 arr TBB (unaccompanied) (MS) G.

403 arr TTBB (unaccompanied) (MS) G.

407 arr TTBB (MS) G.

346 arr TBB (MS) G.

410b arr TBB (MS) G.

410b arr TTBB (unaccompanied) (MS) G.

FREE ORGAN ACCOMPANIMENTS

In 'Varied harmonies for organ accompaniment (and voices ad. lib) of certain tunes in 'Hymns Ancient & Modern' (pu) William Clowes & Sons 1912:

Lo, He comes with clouds descending (Helmsley) v 2 & last v (c 1911/12?).

Now my tongue the mystery telling (St Thomas) last v.
How sweet the name of Jesus sounds (St Peter) v 3).
Thou, judge of quick & dead (Southwell) v 2 and 4, v 6 and last v.
Oh, what their joy and their glory must be (O quanta qualia) v 4 and last v.
O God unseen yet ever near (St Flavian) last v.
Disposer supreme (Hanover) v 3 and v 4 and last v.

When I survey the wondrous Cross (18th cent tune harmonized by Sir Hubert Parry, v 3 and 4 (pu) 1926 Chappell (Year Book Press) (MS) G.

In 'English Hymnal Organ and Choir book of varied accompaniments and descants' ed by Revd J Lionel Bennett (pu) 1926 OUP:
169 *Blessed City, Heavenly Salem* or 170 *Christ is made the sure foundation* (Urbs Beata — plainsong Mode 1) v 3 of 169, v 5 of 170 (MS) G (sketch).
238 *Jesu, the very thought is sweet* (tune from Cöln Gesangbuch 1619, v 2 v 3 and v 5 (MS) G (sketch).
375 *City of God, how broad and far* 471 *Praise to the Holiest in the height* v 2 375 v 4, v 5 (MS) G (sketch).

LOST HYMN-TUNES
Settings of *Isaie dere profeten, There is joy in heaven, Glory to God.*

Melody by E M S Wood arr violin and piano and as a canon 8 in 1 (alternatively 16 in 1) (MS) P.
Come again sweet Love J Dowland arr TTBB (MS) G.
Bach *Two and three-part Inventions* arr 2 violins and organ pedal (MS) G.
Caius Chapel Chimes based on opening of *It was an English Ladye Bright* (c) 1910 (MS) G.
Missing tenor part of a Tallis Mass reconstructed at request of Sir R Terry.

MISCELLANEOUS
(7) Songs by Lord Tennyson set to music by Lady Tennyson arr for voice and piano and edited by Natalia Janotha (the accompaniments revised by CW) (c) 1892 (pu) N D Chappell.

ARRANGEMENTS
Symphony No 3 Op 28 by Sir C V Stanford, arr piano duet CW (pu) 1888 Novello.
Symphony No 4 Op 34 by Sir C V Stanford arr piano duet by CW (pu) 1888 Novello.
The Irish Dump arr piano solo (MS) G (sketch).
The Brook melody by P B S Wood arr violin and piano (MS) P.